United States Foreign Policy in the Middle East

The Historical Roots of Neo-Conservatism

Revised First Edition

By Farrokh Moshiri

California State University, Fullerton

cognella®
academic publishing

Title page image:
Shaking Hands: Iraqi President Saddam Hussein greets Donald
Rumsfeld, then special envoy of President Ronald Reagan, in
Baghdad on December 20, 1983.
Source: Iraqi State Television / Public Domain.

Bassim Hamadeh, CEO and Publisher
Michael Simpson, Vice President of Acquisitions
Jamie Giganti, Senior Managing Editor
Jess Busch, Senior Graphic Designer
Marissa Applegate, Senior Field Acquisitions Editor
Luiz Ferreira, Senior Licensing Specialist
Mandy Licata, Interior Designer

www.cognella.com   800-200-3908

Contents

Dedication

Manizheh Moshiri,
my hero
02/22/1924–02/12/2014

This book is dedicated to my mother Manizheh Moshiri, whose unconditional love, kindness, courage, and support has been the key source of my strength.

Preface

When I was about eleven years old, my uncle, Taghi Moshiri, gave me a gift that I have treasured for more than forty years: a three-volume history of ancient Iran (*Tarikh-e Iran e Basetan*) written by Hassan Pirnia (see the references for more information).

Pirnia's voluminous work covered the Achaemenid, often referred to as the Persian Empire (550–330 BC), and the Arsacids (the Parthians [247 BC–224 AD] or Ashkanian in Persian).

Achaemenid Iran was the first true world empire and at its height governed parts of India, Afghanistan, Pakistan, Central Asia, Iran, the Caucasus, Turkey, Iraq, Syria, Lebanon, Palestine, Egypt, and Northern Greece. Battles between Achaemenid Iran and the Greeks became the stuff of legend and gave birth to events such as the Marathon run in the Olympics and Hollywood's bizarre reproduction of the battle in the Thermopylae pass in the movie *300* and its sequel, *The Rise of an Empire*.

Much of Pirnia's writing on Achaemenids was based on the work of Greek historians, such as Herodotus, who often portrayed the Greeks in a heroic light and exaggerated Persian troop numbers and Persian character deficiencies alike.

Pirnia was apt to point out these exaggerations; for instance, Greek historians claimed that the Persian army that fought with the Spartans and their allies in Thermopylae and eventually captured and burned Athens numbered in the millions. Based on population figures of the empire, most historians now number the

Persian army at less than one hundred thousand, perhaps somewhere between sixty thousand and eighty thousand.[1] The other big lie, which has now become part of the popular culture, thanks to *300* and Hollywood, is the fact that only three hundred Spartans held the pass against this multi-million-man army. There were about seven thousand Greek troops who supported the three hundred for much of their confrontation with the Persians.

The Greek historians lied about the troop numbers to magnify the extent of Greek heroism and in a sense show and magnify Greek superiority to the Asiatic and the Persian. Part of this book, chapter one and chapter four, discusses these issues in much more detail and argues that the so-called "clash of civilization," the East-West conflict, Orientalism—the perceived moral, political, and cultural superiority of the West to the East and the systems of scholarship and thought that it generated, including the origins of neoconservatives' (neocons') thinking—all go back to the Greek–Persian rivalry and Greek attempts to define themselves in superior terms to those they called Barbarians.

This Greek world view was then reinforced and transmitted through their cultural successors, the Romans, who also, incidentally, fought for world hegemony with Iranian empires, the aforementioned Parthians and the even more powerful Sasanids,[2] who routinely defeated Roman legions and even killed and captured several Roman emperors. The Islamic conquest of Iran and the Middle East, the Crusades, and battles between Muslims and Rome's successor European states continued to exacerbate this Western misperception of the Middle Eastern people and their feelings of moral, political, cultural, and, indeed, racial superiority. In 1648, when the Treaty of Westphalia, which is used by historians and political scientists alike as the origin of our modern state system, was signed, the Middle East, much of it governed by the mighty but oriental and Muslim Ottoman Empire, was not considered "on par" with European states and was excluded from the state system.[3] In fact, it was only two centuries later when Western Europeans were concerned about the collapse of the Ottoman Empire that the Ottomans were assimilated in the Westphalian state system.[4]

---

1 See Lindsay Allen, *The Persian Empire* (Chicago: The University of Chicago Press, 2005), 54. Allen calls Herodotus's estimate of more than two million troops an exaggeration (quite an understatement to me) and believes the Persian troop numbers to have been well under one hundred thousand.

2 "Sasanids" is also spelled "Sassanids." You will see that many Persian and Muslim names have different spellings. "Mossadegh" is sometimes written as "Mosaddegh," "Shi'a" is spelled as "Shiite" or "Shiie," and so on.

3 This is a point that is made forcefully by Columbia historian Rashid Khalid in *Sowing Crisis: The Cold War and American Dominance in The Middle East* (Boston: Beacon Press, 2009), 74.

4 The exact time of assimilation of the Ottomans in the state system might be subject to debate. Professor Rogan, in "The Emergence of the Middle East into the Modern State System," cites the London Convention of 1840 as the time of Ottoman entry into the state system. Eugene Rogan, "The Emergence of the Middle East into the Modern State System," in *International Relations of the Middle East*, 3rd ed., ed. Louise Fawcett (Oxford: Oxford University Press, 2012).

This mentality then continued into the eighteenth and nineteenth centuries, where colonialism reinforced the thought system and developed it further into a complete system supported by governments and academics alike—a system of thought that Edward Said called Orientalism.

Connection to US Foreign Policy

So if you want to find the origins of Orientalism, you need to go back to the Persian Wars and 472 BC and the Greek play *Persae*, not eighteenth-century Europe. That is a point that I am making here, which is also discussed in detail in chapters one and four, but how does this connect to the United States' foreign policy toward the Middle East?

The answer is rather simple. America was a novice in the Middle East when in 1942 she started her involvement on a large scale. American diplomats relied for almost a decade on the advice of the British and the French diplomatic corps, who were completely Orientalist in their thought (see "Curzon's Persia" in chapter one), and the British and the French got their thoughts from this history of looking at the Middle Easterners as the inferior Other—a history that I argue goes back all the way to 472 BC, not the eighteenth century. This is all discussed in detail in chapters one and four.

Chapter one also explains why so much of the focus of the book is on Iran. Put simply, Iranian empires ruled the entirety of the Middle East either by themselves or in conjunction with Rome for more than one thousand years, from around 550 BC to around 630 AD and the fall of the Sasanids, so the history of the Middle East for this long time period is essentially the history of the Iranian empires and their conflict with Greece and Rome. In modern times, Iran is important again for the central challenge that it has presented to the United States' foreign policy and its influence and role in the Middle East.

Finally, a significant point made in chapter one is highlighting the *connection between foreign policy,* as measured by defense spending, *and the growth of income inequality and the laggardness of the United States in social progress* compared to her European peers.

Data is obtained from Michael Porter's 2014 Social Progress Index Report and correlated with data on defense expenditures. Data on defense spending is also correlated with the Gini coefficient of income equality for the United States. The results are striking and provide strong support for my argument that the current foreign policy of the United States not only has produced disastrous and costly results abroad; it has also contributed to the growth of income inequality in the United States and her laggardness in social progress.

In chapter two I expand on this point and discuss in detail how this framework of thought, which was flawed at its foundation, is partly responsible for leading America to make mistake after mistake in the Middle East, mistakes that have been enormously costly for the American people in terms of blood and treasure and that will haunt America and the region for years to come.

Furthermore, in chapter two, I point out that these costs consist of both immediate and legacy cost in both blood and treasure. In terms of immediate costs, we have lost about eight thousand American troops and civilian contractors in Iraq and Afghanistan, and by 2013 we spent about $1.5 trillion on the wars in Iraq and Afghanistan. In terms of legacy costs, more than 780,000 American soldiers have filed for permanent disability, and according to Bilmes (see the references), 671,299 of these claims have been approved. We also have more domestic violence and suicides in our armed forces than we had in comparable periods before the wars. The current Department of Veterans Affairs (VA) scandal only proves that these legacy costs are much more devastating than what is indicated by statistics.

I also point out that another cost is what we could have done with the lives and the money that we spent, had our foreign policy not been so misguided. Consider the fact that an average three-story, fifty-five-thousand-square-foot hospital that is constructed by union labor cost about $17.5 million in 2013. Our government could have built more than 180,000 such hospitals with the money that we have spent in these wars. Alternatively, we could have built 154,000 new two-story public schools—almost triple the number of public schools that we had in 2008. And, of course, what price can you put on the eight thousand lost lives?

So, chapter two serves as a discussion of how our failure to understand the Middle East, caused in part by this historically wrong view about the Middle Easterner, has had enormous and specific costs for us.

In chapter three, I begin with a discussion of how our American government textbooks currently cover our foreign policy and how the poor coverage in these textbooks leaves most of the students ignorant of how our foreign policy is made, and, more importantly, ignorant about the Middle East. In the section "Where Is Damascus?" I talk about some of the factors that contribute to this ignorance, the behavioral revolution in the social sciences, the lack of area studies and training in area studies, and the like. While I am very critical of the use of quantitative methods to study complex issues in foreign policy, I do believe that there is a place for such studies—when quantification and operationalization of variables makes sense. Yet, even then, such studies must be based on a qualitative understanding of the historical, cultural, and socioeconomic issues involved.

In chapter three, I also focus on the American roots of our intellectual thinking about foreign policy, and discuss in brief some of what the founding fathers had to say about foreign policy and how some of our leaders and groups think about foreign policy. Of course, one cannot discuss foreign policy without attempting to show how the policy is made. Therefore, a good part of chapter three focuses on models of decision making concerning foreign policy. I tend to favor the models that put the emphasis on the individual's beliefs and constraints, such as the bargaining model, not structuralist models such as neo-realism, but I discuss most if not all of these models in some detail.

Then, in chapter four, I bring all this together and show how the lobbyists, political action committees (such as the American Israel Public Affairs Committee [AIPAC]), the media, and think tanks have managed to shape an imperial foreign policy that does not serve the national interest of Americans. I argue that while some of these media figures and experts are indeed influenced—the Neo-Cons, for example—by the historically wrong views of the Middle Easterner, others are actually agenda driven, and their agenda isn't the American national interest.

The reason for the president of the United States having to use the State of the Union address on January 28, 2014, to promise that he will veto congressional efforts to impose more sanctions on Iran in the midst of diplomacy can be better understood when you read chapter four and my harsh criticism of AIPAC and its allies in Congress, the media, and think tanks.

Some might think that I am harsh in my criticism of some media figures who have the label "progressive." However, as you read my arguments, you might come to see my point of view that most of these so-called progressives are imperial progressives. That is, they want to maintain the American Empire and their progressiveness and respect for human rights and the like, stops at our shores or the shores of our repressive allies, such as Saudi Arabia and Israel.

Finally, I end the book with a discussion of US–Iran negotiations over the nuclear issues and the emerging unholy alliance of the Saudis and Israelis to make sure that Iran and America remain at each other's throats. I also make some policy recommendations that you might find interesting.

Why I Wrote This Book, My Worldview, and Who Should Use This Book

It was slightly over a year ago that I once again began teaching political science at the invitation of a local college. As I taught my classes, I shared my views on American foreign policy with my students. I told my students that I was born in Iran and lived there until I was seventeen years old, so my perspective might be very different from what they had previously been exposed to. But make no mistake: while my criticism of US foreign policy might have been influenced by my unique Iranian upbringing, my love of Iran, and my pride in my Persian heritage, I *chose* to become an American citizen because I love America, the values that she espouses in her traditions (if not in her foreign policy), and her people equally. Although I criticize the idea of *American exceptionalism*, I do believe that currently America is uniquely positioned to be a force for good in our world, and I want to teach my students why this is not so today. My hope is that if my students get to serve in the US Department of State or at the Pentagon, they would be better informed about at least one region of the world—the Middle East—and recommend policies that serve human rights, progress, and development for all people and not just reinforce the imperial edicts.

After teaching for a few months and sharing my thoughts with my students, I thought it would be a good idea to design a supplemental textbook where these thoughts are formalized, so I wrote this book. This book is based on my readings over the forty years since I first read Pirnia's books; my earlier published work on Iran, conflict, and even management;[5] my exposure to both American and Iranian cultures; my intellectual development and evolvement; and my training in political science and history at Kansas and Northwestern. And, yes, the book is even based on my MBA training at UC Riverside; my work in the business field; and my teachings at UCR, DeVry, Victor Valley College, and elsewhere—my students at these institutions have influenced my thoughts. I haven't, of course, listed or used all of the hundreds of books on Iran and foreign policy that I read over this forty-year span, and I can't possibly even begin to acknowledge all the influences that I have had in my life, but all these factors have shaped my worldview.

Therefore, true historians might find that this book needs more depth; political scientists might want more discussion of current events, the ruling elite, and models of foreign-policy decision making and international systems. Purely Middle Eastern experts might be disappointed about my focus on Iran and rather limited discussion of other countries. I am aware of these possible criticisms, but I have designed this book as a supplemental textbook that can be used in International Relations, Comparative Politics, and American Government classes (when discussing US foreign policy), not a comprehensive account. I also think this short book might be of interest to the general public; at least the people who have read it who are not students or political scientists have told me that it is interesting. Hopefully, they didn't lie!

I want to end this preface with an acknowledgment to a few people who merit acknowledgment. First, I want to thank my mother, Manizheh Moshiri, who instilled in me the love of learning and the love of Iran, its history, and its contribution to world civilization. There are many other family members and friends, such as my father, Hamid, my uncle, Taghi, and my older brother. Homayoon Moshiri, who have been major positive influences in my life. I also want to thank my girlfriend, Nicole Smith, who has been incredibly supportive and whose love has helped me cope with moments of writer's block and other setbacks.

---

5   My published work in political science includes *States and Social Revolution in Iran: A Theoretical Perspective* (1985) and a coedited volume with Ted Gurr and Jack Goldstone, *Revolutions of the Late Twentieth Century* (1991). My edited volume in management, *Management Communications: An Anthology* (2012), exposed me even more to the cultural misunderstandings that are an underlying theme of this work.

In particular, I would like to thank Dr. Mehdi Estakhr, associate professor of history at Alabama State University in Montgomery, who has been debating politics and history with me for more than twenty years and who has introduced me to many great works of history, a few of which I have used in this book. I also want to particularly thank Dr. Ray Maghroori, who has been a mentor and supporter since 1994 when I first took his class in UC Riverside's MBA program.

I also want to thank my students at Victor Valley Community College, who have been eager to listen to me and have shown to me, once again, that people, especially young people, are eager to learn only if we show them the relevance of what we are teaching to their lives.

Finally, I need to thank my publisher, Cognella, and its incredible staff—CEO Bassim, editor Jessica, acquisitions editor Marissa, and others who worked with me on this book and have been patient with my specific demands.

The Clash of Civilizations, which has become an intellectual foundation for neoconservative (neocon) thinking and American foreign policy, did not begin with the advent of radical Islam. Drawing on numerous historical and contemporary sources, we trace the mind-set of superiority, fear, and loathing toward the "barbarian Other" reflected in neocon thinking to Aeschylus's play *Persae* in 472 BC, and trace its development through the Roman Empire and the Crusades to contemporary times.

Map 1. The Middle East

Source: National Geospatial-Intelligence Agency / Copyright in the Public Domain.

Chapter One

Introduction

A young Iraqi girl cries as a British Challenger tank moves in on the Baath party office in Basra, April 8, 2003.

Source: Odd Anderson / AFP. Copyright © 2003 by Getty Images. Reprinted with permission.

Curzon's Persia

Among the "required readings" of a new staffer to the British embassy in Iran in the 1950s was an account of Iranians by George N. Curzon, the British undersecretary for India, who traveled to Iran in 1889. Curzon's writings, written in the true *orientalist* tradition and mind-set, portrayed the Persians as "consummate hypocrites, very corrupt and lamentably deficient in stability or courage."[1] In fact, the Persians were so lacking in courage that their own kings recognized their inability to defend their own frontiers and transplanted warlike tribes to defend the frontier.[2] Curzon's account of the Iranians was so negative that Peter King, the editor of *Curzon's Persia*, felt the need to pose and answer a question about why Curzon even bothered writing about people whom he viewed with "such contempt."

As professor Rashid Khalidi of Columbia University asserts, the British of the 1950s played a significant role in influencing American foreign policy with regard to the Middle East and, particularly, Iran.[3] In fact, it was the British, serving the interests of the Anglo-Persian Oil Company (today's BP), who convinced the Americans of the need to overthrow the democratically elected Mossadegh's government in 1953, which has ever since had so much impact on US-Iranian relations.

Curzon's views on Iranians, which in part shaped the mind-set of the British staffers in Iran and, through the British, the American foreign policymakers, are but anecdotal evidence that points out one of the main arguments of this book. Our foreign policy in the Middle East is so often disastrous and produces the wrong results because it is rooted in a misguided historical and intellectual reasoning that is based on wrong assumptions and views about the very people these policies deal with and goes all the way back to ancient Greece.

The premise of this book is that the current foreign policy of the United States is hegemonic; that is, the United States seeks to dominate various regions in the world—particularly the Middle East—to secure economics resources and to maintain its place as the premier political and military power. In doing so, the United States allied itself for years with repressive and authoritarian regimes in the region and sowed the seeds of today's militant Islamic movements in cooperation and conjunction with repressive governments like Saudi Arabia—a phenomenon that has now come to haunt the region and US interests.[4]

Of course, this is not a new argument. However, unlike most books and articles that use the words "hegemony" and "hegemonic," and discuss the role of the ruling class or "power elite" in shaping foreign policy, this book does not follow a Marxian approach. I don't believe that the history of the world and, for that matter, the history of US foreign policy, can be summarized by class struggle. Rather, the history of the world and the making of foreign policy is the history of the struggle of real people—people with emotions, feelings, beliefs, and faith who act out of passion, love, greed, and prejudices, and most often not purely for economic reasons. Surely, social and economic classes and social and economic structures have a role in shaping policymakers' views—views, but not the passions, feelings, and love of human beings that also influence and shape decision making. As Kenneth Waltz, in his classical work *Theory of International Politics*, wrote, "Economic considerations enter into most, if not into all, imperialist ventures, but economic causes are not the only causes operating nor are they always the most important one. All kinds of states have pursued imperialist policies."[5] Many of the world's largest empires were formed long before we witnessed the nineteenth- and twentieth-century capitalist mode of production and long before Hobson in 1902 and Lenin a few years later articulated a theory of imperialism based on insufficient demand and falling rates of capital in capitalist societies, which then necessitates creations of empires.[6]

This debate in social sciences over the importance of individuals and interest groups versus socioeconomic relations and structures is akin to the debate in *Strategic Management* over the importance of CEOs and organizational leadership versus trends in the general environment (e.g., the Great Recession of 2008) that affect businesses. Does it matter to have a Steve Jobs (Apple), Andrew Grove (Intel), or Jack Welch (GE) as your leader, or is it really the general demographic trends, consumer demand, government regulations, and technology that determine a corporation's success (Dess, et.al.,2014)?

The beauty of businesses, unlike social and political phenomena, is that you can easily measure significant changes in a corporation's fortunes almost immediately after a change of leadership. So, for instance, "when Carly Fiorina was fired as a CEO of [HP, there was] an immediate increase in its stock price of 7% ... and when [Carly's] successor Mark Hurd [who] had led the firm to five years of outstanding financial results ... abruptly resigned ... stock price dropped 12 percent almost instantly."[7] Hence, the market at least thinks that individuals and leadership matter. When analyzing prospects for a business (as elegantly discussed by Dess et al), all business analysts look at both general environmental factors that affect a business and internal capabilities and assets of a business, such as intellectual capital, leadership, culture, cash position, and so on, that enable the business to compete. What structural relationships and realities for a business do is to either limit or expand the strategic choices of its leadership, but it sure matters if you have a Steve Jobs making these choices or any number of failed business leaders.

We ought to take a similar approach to the study of political and social phenomenon. Yes, structures, social relationship, and positions within a system of states matter, but so do the people, ideas, and leadership who operate within these structures and are quite often capable of transcending and changing these structures.

Therefore, this is a book that highlights the role of ideas, mental frameworks, and filtering in formulating foreign policy. This book also emphasizes the role of interest groups, media, and opinion leaders. It is the combination of these factors, ideas, group politics, and economic interests that create this hegemonic foreign policy and this desire to maintain an empire. I also believe, and the opposition to the Syrian war is the best proof for my argument,[8] that in a representative democracy, grassroots public opinion that crosses class lines can affect foreign policy outcomes.

My other argument is that our current hegemonic foreign policy serves only the interests of a small power elite and particular interest groups and not the long-term national interests of the country, and that nowhere this is truer than in our policies toward the Middle East. This is also not a new discovery![9]

Scholars on the left and nationalists on the right have written boundless books and articles about this topic. All one has to remember is the voluminous publications by Noam Chomsky[10] or US army colonel and professor of history and international relations Andrew Bacevich's works. Here is how Bacevich summarizes the current *imperial* foreign policy:

> During the 1990s, at the urging of politicians and pundits, Americans became accustomed to thinking of their country as "the indispensable nation." ... [America's] chief responsibility was to preside over a grand projection of political-economic convergence and integration commonly

referred to as globalization. ... Globalization served as a euphemism for soft, or informal, empire ... creating something akin to a global Pax Americana. ...

[Therefore,] a political elite preoccupied with the governance of the empire paid little attention to protecting the United States itself. ... The institution nominally referred to as the Department of Defense didn't actually do defense; it specialized in power projection. ... Well-trained and equipped U.S. forces stood ready to defend Seoul or Riyadh; Manhattan was left to fend for itself.

Asserting control over the imperial periphery took precedence over guarding the nation's own perimeter. ... So for the United States after 9/11 war became a seemingly permanent condition. ... On the national political scene, few questioned that prospect. ... Americans were slow to grasp the implications of a global war with no exits and no deadlines. To earlier generations, place names like Iraq and Afghanistan had been synonymous with European rashness—the sort of obscure and unwelcoming jurisdictions to which overly ambitious kings and slightly mad adventurers might repair to squabble.

For the present generation, it has already become part of the natural order of things that GIs should be exerting themselves at great cost to pacify such far-off domains. For the average American tuning in to the nightly news, reports of US causalities incurred in distant lands now seems hardly more out of the ordinary than reports of partisan shenanigans on Capitol Hill.[11]

US Foreign Policy and Income Inequality in America

Michael Porter's Social Progress Index and Defense Spending

Professor Bacevich and many scholars who argue that our national policies, particularly our foreign policy, do not serve the national interest, or the interest of all Americans, don't rely just on logical argumentation. We have quite a bit of data to support this point. For instance, renowned Harvard business professor Michael Porter and his colleagues' Social Progress Index 2014 report ranks the United States sixteenth overall in the world in the index, where scores from each country on basic needs (sanitation, access to healthcare, etc.), foundations of well-being (access to

Social Progress Index		
Basic Human Needs	**Foundations of Wellbeing**	**Opportunity**
Nutrition and Basic Medical care	Access to Basic Knowledge	Personal Rights
Water and Sanitation	Access to Information and Communications	Personal Freedom and Choice
Shelter	Health and Wellness	Tolerance and Inclusion
Personal Safety	Ecosystem Sustainability	Access to Advanced Education

Figure 1.1. Source: The Social Progress Imperative. Adapted by Farrokh Moshiri.

knowledge, information, etc.) and opportunity (individual rights, access to higher education, etc.) are combined to produce a country ranking.

Because our economy at $17 trillion is by far the largest economy in the world, one would think that we would at least be among the top five countries in the world in the aggregate score of the index. Yet we don't even make the top-ten or top-fifteen lists, and on some indicators—health care (health and wellness), for example—we don't even make the top-fifty list.[12] So, what is the relationship between the United States' sixteenth-place ranking in the Social Progress Index and defense spending? Table 1.1 lists the values for the index and the three main categories of basic human needs, foundations of well-being, and opportunity as well as defense expenditures for all sixteen countries, both in actual dollars and as a percentage of GDP.

The United States spent forty-five times more, in absolute dollars, on defense than the average expenditure of the fifteen countries that achieved a Social Progress Index ranking *higher* than the United States did. Similarly, US defense expenditures as a percentage of GDP were also 3.5 times higher than those of countries that *did better* on the Social Progress Index.

Defense Spending and Income Inequality

If you are not yet convinced of the negative impact of defense spending on domestic tranquility, run a correlation coefficient function on the data above. You will get $R = -.60$, which indicates a strong negative correlation between defense spending and social progress. The more you spend on defense, the less you can improve the lot of your citizens. If you add France, with defense expenditures of $61 billion and

Table 1.1. Comparison of Defense Spending by the United States versus Fifteen Higher-Ranked Countries in Social Progress Index

	Defense Budget 2012–2013, in Billions of US Dollars	Defense Budget as a Percentage of GDP++	Social Progress Index	Basic Human Needs	Foundations of Well-Being	Opportunity
New Zealand	0.5	1.1	88.24	91.74	84.97	88.01
Switzerland	4.5	0.8	88.19	94.87	89.78	79.92
Iceland	.5	0.1	88.07	94.32	88.19	81.71
Netherlands	4.2	1.3	87.37	93.91	87.56	80.63
Norway	7.06	1.4	87.12	93.59	86.94	80.82
Sweden	6.3	1.2	87.08	94.59	84.71	81.95
Canada	22.6	1.3	86.95	93.52	80.31	87.02
Finland	0.96	1.5	86.91			
Denmark	4.4	1.4	86.55			
Australia	3.4	1.7	86.10	92.47	80.27	85.54
Austria	0.7	0.8	85.11	94.57	86.35	74.42
Germany	49	1.3	84.61	93.08	84.96	75.81
United Kingdom	58	2.4	84.56	91.90	79.47	82.29
Ireland	0.12	0.6	84.05			
Japan	51	1	84.21	94.72	79.25	78.67
United States	$613*	4.2	82.77	89.82	75.96	82.54

Sources: The data was obtained from a combination of sources, including http://www.socialprogres-simperative.org/data/spi; the World Bank at http:C17//data.worldbank.org/indicator/MS.MIL.XPND.GD.ZS and http://data.worldbank.org/indicator/PA.NUS.FCRF; the United Nations at http://data.un.org/Data.aspx?d=WDI&f=Indicator_Code%3AMS.MIL.XPND.GD.ZS; the US Department of Defense, Fiscal Year 2013 Budget Request, Index Mundi at http://www.indexmundi.com/facts/switzerland/military-expenditure; http://www.friedlnet.com/product/defense_spending_in_denmark; http://www.defensenews.com/article/20131014/DEFREG01/310140010/Departing-Norwegian-Government-Boosts-Defense-Spending-2014; European Defense Agency: National Defense Data 2012 of the EDA Participating Member States.

a Social Progress Index of 81.11, just a few notches below the United States, your correlation coefficient gets even stronger, $-.72$. If you add Russia and China, with expenditures of \$88 and \$188 billion on defense, respectively, and Social Progress Index values of 60.70 and 58, respectively, your correlation jumps up to $R = -.88$.

Of course, correlation coefficients don't prove causality, and as I indicate in chapter three, quantitative analysis of social and political phenomena can be problematic. This correlation is only as good as the meaningfulness of the operationalization of social progress using the indexed values. So, let's look at some more data and qualitative arguments and consider our R values in the context of trends in American society since we increased our empire-maintaining and expansion activities.

According to the data released by the US Social Security Administration, there has been a sharp rise in poverty in the United States since 2000, when our imperial foreign policy went into high gear with wars in the Middle East. In 2000, 31.1 million Americans lived in poverty—meaning that they earned less money than the official poverty thresholds. Currently, 46.5 million Americans live below the official poverty line of the US government, which is set at a ridiculously low level of \$11,011 for an individual. Consider that this is fifteen million people more now than in 2000, an increase of almost four percentage points as the percentage of total population. Furthermore, consider the fact that in many places in America, a gross income of \$11,000 does not even allow you to pay for basic needs, such as rent and utilities. A one-bedroom apartment in Los Angeles costs around \$1,000 per month or more, and the average family rental unit in Los Angeles County (which includes poor neighborhoods, such as Watts) costs \$1,435 per month. In New York, be prepared to spend at least \$1,600 per month to rent a one-bedroom apartment or \$1,500 per square foot if you want to buy an urban apartment.[13]

If our foreign and national policies really served the interest of all Americans, we would not have forty-six million people who live in poverty and can't even afford an apartment. If our foreign and national policies really served the interest of all Americans, we would have reduced poverty and scored high on all categories in the Social Progress Index report.

On the contrary, the continuation of our empire is making our average citizen's relative situation worse and is accelerating the growth of income equality in America. A recent *New York Times* article, based on a thirty-five-year-long survey, makes exactly the same observation about the largeness of our economy, yet the worsening conditions for the average American:

> While the wealthiest Americans are outpacing many of their global peers, a *New York Times* analysis shows that across the lower- and middle-income tiers, citizens of other advanced countries have received considerably larger raises over the last three decades. ...

Although economic growth in the United States continues to be as strong as in many other countries, or stronger, a small percentage of American households is fully benefiting from it that our middle class is in danger of disappearing.[14]

However, many would argue that the rise in income inequality in America has much more to do with domestic fiscal policy (e.g., declining marginal tax rates for the very rich) than our foreign policy and the maintenance of the empire. While it is certainly true that fiscal policies have had a large role in the decline of the American middle class and the rise of the super-rich, it is also equally true that our empire-building and -maintaining effort since the 1980s, and particularly so after 2001, have reduced our ability to invest in human capital—the investment in our children's education that have given America its competitive edge. As discussed in chapter two, the $4 to 6 trillion that we spend in Iraq and Afghanistan (after legacy costs are added) could have built thousands of schools in America and could have provided the necessary capital to improve our educational system in many other ways to maintain our competitive edge.

The great income gains for the American middle class and poor in the mid-to-late 20th century came after this country made high school universal and turned itself into the most educated nation in the world. As the economists Claudia Goldin and Lawrence Katz have written, "The 20th century was the American century because it was the human-capital century." Education continues to pay today, despite the scare stories to the contrary. The pay gap between college graduates and everyone else in this country is near its all-time high. The countries that have done a better job increasing their educational attainment, like Canada and Sweden, have also seen bigger broad-based income gains than the United States.[15]

Table 1.2. The Decline of Federal Spending on Elementary and Secondary Education

2005 Appropriation	2006 Appropriation	2007 Appropriation	2008 Appropriation	2009 Appropriation	2010 Appropriation	2011 Appropriation	2012 Appropriation	2013 Appropriation
37,530,257	39,762,172	36,830,689	37,933,513	38,830,088	38,921,047	37,906,168	37,361,393	35,359,335

Source: US Department of Education, Budget History Tables, https://www2.ed.gov/about/overview/budget/history/index.html?exp=6.

Republican policies at the domestic level (states controlled by Republican legislatures and governors) have worsened the educational picture and have substantially reduced the reach of this great equalizer. School closures because of lack of funds are common occurrence in the heartland of America (e.g., Marquette, Kansas), yet the federal expenditures on education are flat or declining.

Why is the federal government reducing its expenditures on the future of America? Because a good chunk of our the money is going into the defense budget. During the same period that federal appropriations for elementary and secondary education declined by $2 billion, federal spending on defense went up by $80 billion (see Table 1.3). Lack of educational opportunity is one of the major factors that contribute to the rise of income inequality in the United States.

There is a strong correlation between our foreign policy's empire-building goals and the rise of income inequality in the United States because of the siphoning of available national funds to military expenditures abroad. Between 2001 and 2011 our expenditures on defense doubled, and this statement holds true by and large even after adjusting for inflation.[16] At the same time, after an initial modest increase in federal expenditures for education, the spending on education, measured by appropriations for the Department of Education, actually decreased from 2006 to 2008. Currently the total spending on education, at $140.9 billion, which includes military and veteran education benefits, is only about 4 percent of the $3.5 trillion[17] proposed budget compared to defense spending, which is around 20 percent of the national budget.

As indicated earlier, education is still the best avenue of upward mobility for most Americans, and aside from fiscal policy, educating our children so that they can

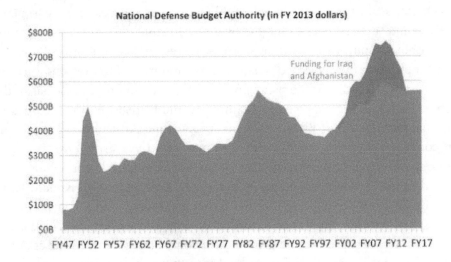

Figure 1.2. US Defense Spending-Budget Authority

Source: Center for Strategic and Budgetary Assessments.

compete in today's global economy is the best way to combat income equality. The point that I am making here is really rather simple. We have only so much money to spend, and when we spend so much of it on our military and the maintenance of the empire, we simply don't have enough money left to spend on education and the future of our children.

Professors James Morone (Brown University) and Rogan Kersh summarize the impact of the current large levels of military spending on our domestic institutions as follows: "Military primacy costs close to a trillion dollars a year. This is a high economic burden for any nation to bear. It means diverting spending from other needs—infrastructure, education and children's well-being. ... Finally, some on both the left and the right belief that too much emphasis on military power undermines liberty."[18]

If we perform a similar exercise to correlating our laggardness on the Social Progress Index with spending and instead correlate the rise in defense expenditures with the rise income inequality in the United States, we get a very strong .5 correlation, indicating that as defense expenditures rise, so does income inequality. We get .5, a strong correlation if we choose the period of 1980 to 2012 for our data set. What would happen if we make the connection between war and income inequality even stronger? What if we look at the correlation between the two factors from 2001, the start of our Middle Eastern wars (the invasion of Afghanistan) and 2012, when we basically pulled out of Iraq? We get an even stronger R, at .746! Below is the data that were used in this exercise.

So, we can make a case that the rise of income inequality correlates with our wars in the Middle East and the resultant increase in defense expenditures. By extension, our foreign policy mistakes have led to the growth of income inequality in the United States. Of course, historians could have told us that empires cost money to maintain and devour internal resources. One factor that contributed to exacerbating internal societal conflicts and problems that partly were responsible for the collapse of the Roman Empire was the shifting of resources to support military expenditures in the Eastern Frontier to confront the rising power of the Iranian Empire, the Sasanid (also written as Sassanid; see chapter four). Similarly, the British Empire disappeared by the gradual withdrawal of British forces from Asia and Africa once Britain realized that it could no longer financially afford to maintain these armed forces and grow its economy. More recently, the collapse of the Soviet empire in the 1980s has been attributed to the increased spending on defense to keep pace with Ronald Reagan's military buildup, an expenditure that the Soviet economy could not sustain.

Hence, maintaining empires is a burden on imperial society, and in the case of the United States it has led to the growth of income equality and slowness of social progress. But that is not all. What most observers don't mention is that this enormous military buildup and and our imperial adventures abroad are funded partly by increased borrowing and have contributed to a huge national debt as well. Currently 6 percent of our national budget simply goes to payment of interest on our national

Table 1.3. Connection between Defense Spending and the Rise of Income Inequality in the United States, Correlation R = .75 for 2001 to 2012 and Correlation R = .5 for 1980 to 2012

Year	Defense Expenditure in Billions of Dollars	Gini Coefficient of Income Ratio of Families by Race of Householder, All Races	Year	Defense Expenditure in Billions of Dollars	Gini Coefficient of Income Ratio of Families by Race of Householder, All Races
1980	$407.30	0.365	1998	$465.80	0.43
1981	$434.75	0.369	1999	$477.98	0.429
1982	$470.63	0.38	2000	$478.35	0.433
1983	$502.37	0.382	2001	$492.71	0.435
1984	$530.72	0.383	2002	$537.14	0.434
1985	$568.92	0.389	2003	$599.33	0.436
1986	$597.38	0.392	2004	$639.80	0.438
1987	$617.18	0.393	2005	$661.25	0.44
1988	$611.91	0.395	2006	$677.50	0.444
1989	$602.97	0.401	2007	$697.33	0.432
1990	$602.47	0.396	2008	$759.88	0.438
1991	$596.46	0.397	2009	$788.25	0.443
1992	$572.92	0.404	2010	$822.83	0.44
1993	$539.33	0.429	2011	$809.97	0.45
1994	$514.89	0.426	2012	$778.24	0.451
1995	$498.72	0.421	2013	$723.13	
1996	$490.41	0.425	2014	$697.11	
1997	$475.65	0.429			

Source: Data was compiled from Federal Reserve Economic Data (FRED), Federal Reserve Bank of St. Louis: Income Gini Ratio of Families by Race of Householder, All Races, http://research.stlouisfed. org/fred2/series/GINIALLRF and http://www.data360.org/dataset.aspx?Data_Set_Id=1189.

debt (see figure 1.3). Note that this is 1.5 times what the federal government spends on all educational programs. It is rather remarkable that the pundits on cable and network TV generally focus on mandatory social spending, not our tremendous defense budget, as a way of reducing the debt and balancing the budget. What we borrowed in fiscal 2013 is almost identical to what we spent on defense.[19]

Hence, the argument here is that we need to reduce defense spending to rebuild our infrastructure, strengthen our educational system, reduce budget deficits, and

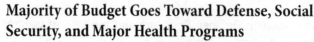

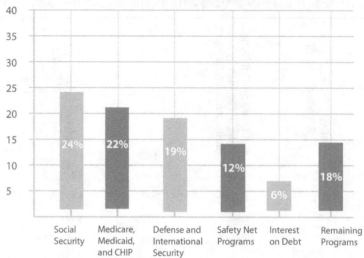

Figure 1.3. Defense Spending as Percentage of National Budget

Source: Center on Budget and Policy Priorities.

reduce our national debt. Reducing defense spending, however, does not mean that we have to lay off hundreds of thousands of troops, as critics might argue. Figure 1.4 clearly shows that biggest chunk of our expenditure goes to military operations (such as wars in Iraq and Afghanistan) as opposed to expenditure on personnel.

If a good chunk of our defense expenditures goes to operations, which include fighting the unnecessary wars in the Middle East, we can cut defense spending simply by fighting fewer wars! Our foreign policy toward the Middle East therefore becomes a key factor in not only reducing the violence and bloodshed that result from our foreign policy, but also achieving social progress at home, *in America*, and reducing income equality *in America*.

What Is New about My Work?

Of course, as stated earlier, the argument that our foreign policy is hegemonic and does not serve the interests of most Americans is not new. Neither is the argument that we spend too much money on defense.

Although I have not seen attempts to tie our defense expenditure directly to the growth of income inequality in America, what is really new about my work is that, in addition to making an explicit linkage between foreign policy and the growth of

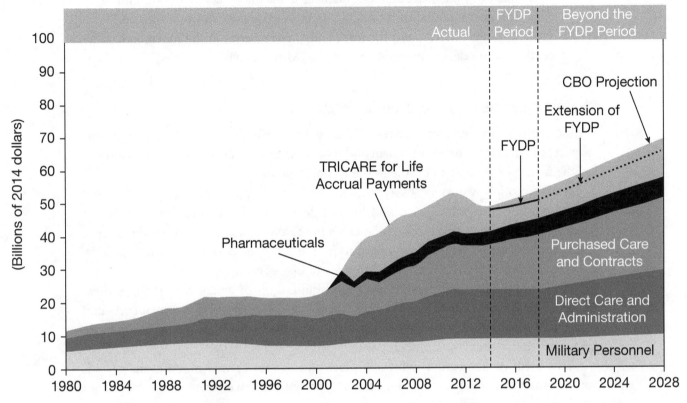

Costs of DoD's Plans for Its Military Health System

Figure 1.4. Categorical Costs of Department of Defense (DoD)

Source: Congressional Budget Office / Copyright in the Public Domain.

income inequality in the United States and the lack of social progress thereof, the discussion of the intellectual foundations of our foreign policy takes us back to ancient Greece, specifically to 472 BC and the famous Greek tragedy *Persae*. How the Greeks viewed non-Greeks after the Persian Wars and formed a view of the Persians and other Asiatic and African people as *genetically inferior, barbaric in customs and actions, and of lower moral character* and how that view was then transmitted through Greece's cultural and intellectual successors (e.g., Rome) through centuries is part of the story that is told here:

> [Aeschylus's tragedy *Persae*, 472 BC] … represents the first unmistakable file in the archives of orientalism, the discourse by which the European imagination has dominated Asia ever since by conceptualizing its inhabitants as defeated, luxurious, emotional, cruel, and always, as dangerous.

This [has had] an incalculable influence, from the Greek, Roman, and Christian characterization of Asiatic mystery religions, through the crusades, the renaissance, and the imperialist movements of the nineteenth century, to modern representation of the [Muslim] world.[20]

Ancient Athens and Its Impact on Our Views

While many draw parallels between today's American Empire and that of Rome, aspects of America's interventionism and its role within NATO are strikingly similar to the fifth-century Athenian role in the Delian League.

Athens, which was ruled by tyrants in the sixth century BC, switched to what might be called property-based and limited democracy in the fifth century BC—a democracy that excluded most of the city's inhabitants (including all women) from participation in the political process and had slavery as its economic foundations. Yet Athens has been hailed as the birthplace of democracy.

However, modern scholarship has found quite a bit of evidence that the earliest form of democracy, or what Thorkild Jacobsen calls *primitive democracy*,[21] had existed in Mesopotamia as early as the early third millennia BC and was much more inclusive than Athenian democracy was.

This form of democracy, which in places and at times was much more participatory than that of Athens—some cities apparently allowed women as well as all (fighting) men to participate in a bicameral legislative consultative structure (similar to the House of Commons and Lords or the House and Senate)—made decisions on a wide range of issues, from irrigation projects to going to war (e.g., the epic of Gilgamesh) to electing kings:

> Thorkild Jacobsen stated that ... myths are a form of allegory whereby ancient humankind projected the world around them onto the realm of the gods. ... In order for the people of ancient Mesopotamia to have attributed such complex democratic systems to their gods, they must have experienced analogous assemblies themselves ... primitive democracy seems to have functioned much like the aforementioned divine assembly.
>
> [Assemblies made] decisions regarding matters as diverse as irrigation projects, trade missions, land surveying, administrative issues and judging the serious offenses of citizens ... and formed the nucleus of municipal administration and allowed the collective resources of the community to be pooled in order to reach consensus for concerted action. The council further mirrored that of the gods by functioning as a bicameral assembly, divided between "an upper house of 'elders' and a lower house of 'men.'"

Although the elder men seem to have held most of the power, some research suggests that these assemblies also resembled those of the gods, in that "women as well as men took part in decision-making—sometimes with a dominating role." ... During an assembly each of the citizens had the right to express an opinion, and discussion would continue until virtual unanimity was reached; the final decisions were then announced by the elders.[22]

However, in *orientalist* discourse, and even mainstream academic scholarship, it is the slave-based, noninclusive, participatory Athenian form of government that has been hailed as the birthplace of today's participatory and universal form of democracy. For instance, a textbook on comparative politics frames its discussion of the "concept of democracy" in "the form of a Greek temple."[23] Another textbook on international relations (IR) finds the need to discuss today's scholars of IR who focus on gender roles in international relations in the context of Greek woman and the poet Sappho (612–570 BC), who "wrote love poems to women on the Island of Lesbos."[24] These textbooks and many others explicitly or implicitly argue that today's inclusive participatory form of governance owes its existence to Athens' fifth-century polity:

Many of these works on Middle Eastern democracy ... are based on a Western conception of democracy. This is the result of a discursive lineage that has its antecedents in the erroneous belief[25] that democracy miraculously sprang out of Greek civilization in the fifth century B.C. This superior system of governance ... arguably gave rise to those great moments in the construction and propagation of Western civilization. Democracy, in its modern, representative form, resurfaced later as a result of the major social upheavals that transformed Europe and America during the late eighteenth and nineteenth centuries.[26]

Not only are most writers and policy advisors influenced by this Western and what Arnold Toynbee called "egocentric" view of the Middle East; most also have "come from outside the region," so they idealize and glorify Greece and its successive Western culture and misunderstand the Middle East and its roles, challenges, and contributions.[27]

However, as world historians Peter Von Sivers, Charles Desnoyers, and George Stow point out, this is an idealization of the Greek role, and these Greek assemblies were similar to Mesopotamian or early Indian republic assemblies in the Ganges Valley area.[28]

Nonetheless, similar to today's justification for our intervention in the Middle East and elsewhere to support democratic movements, Athens also used the spread of democracy as a tool to galvanize its allies in the Delian League:

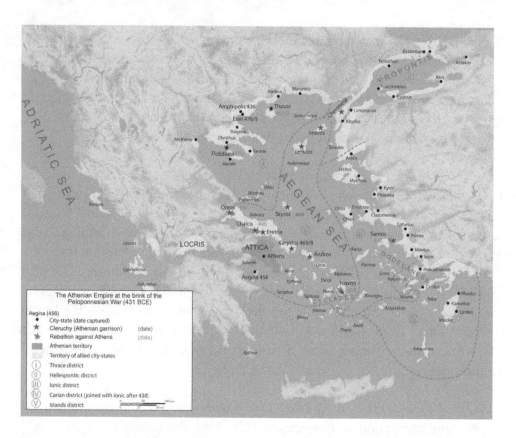

Map 2. Map of Fifth-Century Greece

Source: Adapted from: Marsyas & Once in a Blue Moon / Wikimedia Commons / CC BY-SA 2.5.

The defeat of the Persians in 480–479 was conceptualized at Athens not only as a triumphant affirmation of Greek culture and collectivity over alien invaders, but over the demon of tyranny … [this] ideology [tied together] the members of Delian league. … [While the stated aim was to push the Iranians back], the league under Athenian leadership soon began to look like an Athenian Empire. … The Athenians also sought to encourage democracies in the allied or subjugated states. A typical example is the case of Erythrae, [29] which … attempted to secede from the League and install a tyrant sympathetic to Persia. Athens intervened & imposed … a democratic institution.[30]

This work, besides tracing back the intellectual origins of our foreign policy to ancient Greece, also contains sections of detailed discussion of how our current foreign policy is formulated with regard to the Middle East that are buttressed by incorporation of new events and data.

I argue that our current policy posture and goals that view our role in the Middle East as a zero-sum game and force us to take unilateral actions not only serve to undermine our long-term national interests, but also are costly and bloody.[31] All one has to look at is our experience in Iraq, Afghanistan, Libya, and Somalia, and our current involvement in Syria.

Why So Much Focus on Iran?

For the reader who is unfamiliar with Middle Eastern history, it might be puzzling that so much of this manuscript is devoted to Iranian history and interactions with the West. The reason is really rather simple. From the establishment of the Persian Empire—the Achaemenids—in 550 BC by Cyrus the Great, to the end of the second Persian Empire—the Sasanians—in 651 AD, Middle Eastern history was essentially the history of Iranian empires who ruled the region that we know today as the Middle East, either in its entirety or in conjunction with Rome.

Cyrus captured today's Turkey, Iraq, Syria, and Palestine. His son Kambujiya II conquered Egypt in 525 BC, and Darius the Great added Northwest India and Central Asia in the 513–520 period.[32] Of course, the borders of the empire went back and forth during its two-century-long existence. In 480, when the Iranians sacked Athens, much of Northern Greece had become part of the empire. However, the Greek counterattack and the resulting Greco-Persian wars, which lasted until the Treaty of Callias in 447 BC, at times took parts of Anatolia from the empire. Similarly, Egypt broke away from the empire in 373 BC but was reconquered in 342 BC. Therefore, while the borders of the empire moved back and forth, by and large what we know today as the Middle East was ruled by Iran.

When Alexander the Great conquered the Persian Empire (334–330 BC), his conquests included the entire empire and therefore the entire Middle East. After his death, one of the states that divided up his empire was the Seleucid state. The Seleucid state, under Seleucus Nicator (312–281 BC), covered Mesopotamia, all of today's Iran, parts of Turkey and Syria, and Afghanistan.[33]

The Parthians, the successive Iranian state that emerged out of Northeastern Iran in 241 BC and eventually captured Seleucia in 146–141 BC, ruled much of Mesopotamia, Iran, the Caucasus, Afghanistan, and, at the zenith of their power, parts of Syria. The Sasanians, or, as I like to call them, the second Persian Empire, who overthrew the Parthians in 224 AD, even ruled greater parts of the Middle East, and their empire included long rules over Yemen, Oman, and the Arabian side of the Persian Gulf. At its zenith, in 602–621 AD, Sasanian armies were in control of Iraq, Syria, Egypt, Palestine, and much of today's Turkey, and had Constantinople under siege.

The Islamic conquest of Iran put an end to the Iranian military and political domination of the Middle East, yet post-Islamic, Iranian-centered empires continued to play a major role in the Middle East. While Iranian armies never again reached the Mediterranean shores or marched into Egypt, Iranian-centered empires continued to be the dominant power east of the Euphrates and continued to dominate the Caucasus, Iranian Plateau, Central Asia, and Afghanistan. Nader Shah Afshar, who

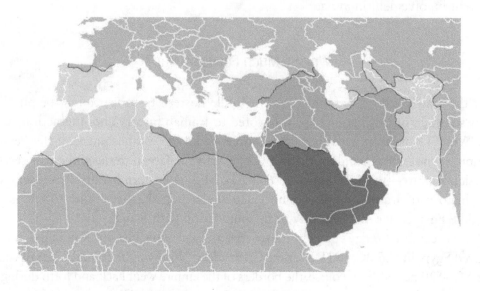

Legend:
  Expansion under the Prophet Mohammad, 622–632
  Expansion during the Patriarchal Caliphate, 632–661
  Expansion during the Umayyad Caliphate, 661–750

Map 3. Expansion of Islam and the Umayyad Caliphate

Brian Szymanski / Copyright in the Public Domain.

Map 4. The Abbasid Caliphate. Note that the Umayyad Emirate is what was left of the Umayyad Empire that was governed by remnants of the Umayyads.

Source: Copyright © 2013 by Khateeb88 / Wikimedia Commons / CC BY-SA 3.0.

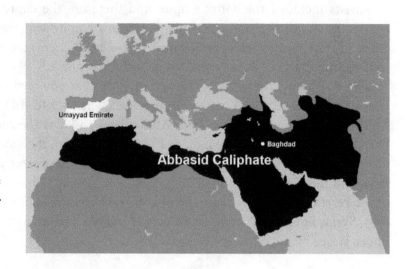

conquered Delhi in 1731 and brought the Peacock Throne to Iran, restored Iran to a preeminent position in the Middle East in the eighteenth century, and even as late as the nineteenth century, Iran ruled parts of Western Afghanistan, Southern Iraq, and nominally a good part of Central Asia.

However, there is no denying that after the Islamic conquest, Turkish and Arab civilizations, although heavily influenced by Iranian administrative and cultural traditions, played an equal or more important role in Middle Eastern history. All one has to do is take a look at the Umayyad (651–750), the Abbasid (750–1258), and the Ottoman empires and their domination of the Middle East from around 660 to 1850 AD to see the significance of Arab and Turkish roles in Middle Eastern history.

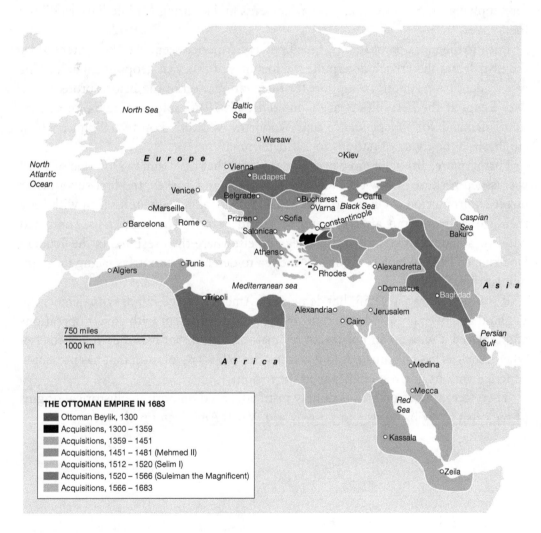

Map 5. The Ottoman Empire at Its Peak

Source: Atilim Gunes Baydin / Copyright in the Public Domain.

Yet the origins of *The Clash of Civilizations*, as asserted here, go back to 472 BC and Aeschylus's play *Persae*, when Iranian dominance in the Middle East was supreme. This book therefore focuses on pre-Islamic Iranian relations with Greece and Rome to outline the origins of neocon thinking, which I argue is rooted in the historical and cultural views of the Greeks and the Romans toward Persians or the face of the Middle East during their times.

When it comes to American foreign policy toward the Middle East, Iran again assumes a prominent role. Oil was discovered in the Middle East, first in Iran in 1908, and Iran became the first Middle Eastern country to export oil in 1913. American involvement in the Middle East began in earnest in 1942, when US troops joined Soviet and British forces in invading and occupying a neutral Iran to provide a route for supplying the Soviet Union with armaments and securing Middle Eastern oil for themselves.[34]

Prior to the invasion of Iran by allied powers, America seemed to be content to let the British and the French determine the fortunes of this vast geopolitical area. This was evident from American support for the continuation of the British protectorate over Egypt at the Versailles Peace Conference (1919) despite the Egyptian delegation's demand for independence and Woodrow Wilson's Fourteen Points, which emphasized the rights of nations to self-determination.[35]

Furthermore, although most historians assume that the Truman Doctrine of 1947 was issued because of Soviet challenges in Greece and Turkey, the first superpower direct confrontation occurred in Iran in 1946 over the Soviets' refusal to withdraw their troops from Iran after the end of World War II. The Iran crisis, combined with the situation in Greece and Turkey and elsewhere then resulted in the Truman Doctrine of 1947, which committed America to defending countries facing the communist threat.

It was first in Iran in 1953 that democratic America joined hands with democratic England and overthrew a democratically elected government with covert operations and replaced it with an authoritarian regime—a pattern that was then repeated elsewhere, such as in Guatemala. And it is Iran after 1979's revolution that has presented America with its greatest challenge in the region.

Therefore, a focus on Iran is doubly justified, based on both the historical origins of the clash of civilizations and post–World War II American involvement.

Chapter Two

Blood and Treasure

A military vehicle is hit by a deeply buried improvised explosive device while conducting operations just south of the Shiek Hamed village in Iraq.

Source: U.S. Army / Copyright in the Public Domain.

The Costs of a Misguided Foreign Policy: Blood and Treasure

Syria

Today, Syria is a picture of human suffering, misdeeds, and atrocities. More than one hundred thousand Syrians (by the United Nation's estimate) have been killed, and "atrocity crimes are being committed with complete impunity by all sides in the conflict, with no end in sight."[36] The situation is so bad that on May 15, 2014, more than one hundred civil groups from around the world asked the United Nations to pass a resolution and refer the Syrian situation to the International Criminal Court prosecutors.[37] Millions of people have become displaced, and as of now there are 742,000 registered refugees who are registered with the United Nations.

The Syrian conflict began during the Arab Spring's ending days in March 2011 with a protest against the Assad regime in the southern city of Dera. The protest gradually spread to the rest of Syria, and while protesters claimed that they were staging peaceful protests, government troops opened fire on several of these gatherings. The Syrian opposition then began to take up arms, and the conflict developed into a full-fledged war. Foreign actors—Saudi Arabia, Qatar, Turkey, Iran, the United States, Israel, and Russia—also became involved.

The Saudis and Qataris began to fund and arm the rebels, who mostly belonged to the Sunni sect of Islam. Fundamentalist Sunni Muslim fighters, who

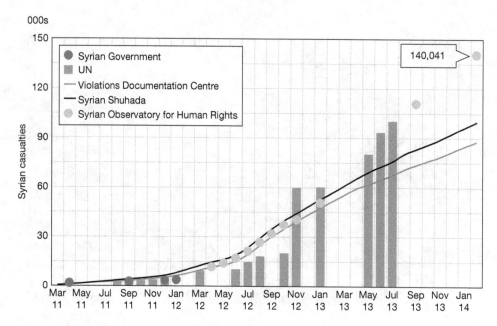

Figure 2.1. *Chart on Syrian Civilian Casualties*

Source: *http://www.bbc.com/news/world-middle-east-26116868.*

Total deaths over the course of the Syrian civil war

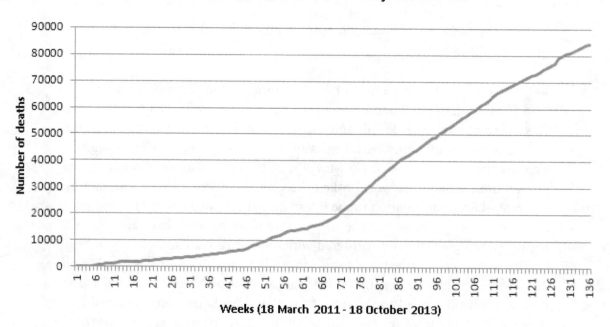

Figure 2.2. *The Syrian Civil War*

Source: *Copyright © 2013 by GraysonWiki & Futuretrillionaire / Wikimedia Commons / CC BY-SA 3.0.*

often belong to the ultra-orthodox Wahhabi movement (considered by some to be a branch of the ultraconservative Sunni Salafi school), then began to pour into Syria, primarily from Iraq with Saudi, Qatari, and Turkish support, to fight the Assad government. In fact, the British Broadcasting Corporation (BBC) reports that an entire battalion of rebel fighters, the Green Battalion, is composed of Saudi Arabians:

> The Green Battalion is based in the Qalamoun area of Damascus province and was founded in the summer by Saudi fighters who are of similar ideological orientation to ISIS and al-Nusra but had personal problems both groups.[38]

The most powerful, popular, and extreme elements of these rebel groups, whom we indirectly support with our opposition to the Syrian government, however, belong to our number-one enemy: "al-Qaeda's official Syrian affiliate, the al-Nusra Front."[39] Other extremists have gathered two other rebel groups, the Islamic State in Iraq and the Levant (ISIS). These two groups are also among the best funded and armed rebel groups. All these groups are Sunnis, as al-Qaeda actually does not consider Shiites to be Muslims and frequently targets them, as the civil war in Iraq has proven.

By contrast, the Assad regime is dominated by the Alawite sect of Shi'a Islam and has considerable support among Christians, other minority communities, and the business class in Syria, which is primarily Sunni. Working against Assad's enemies and their foreign backers are the Russians, the Iranians, and the Lebanese Hezbollah, who provide the government with funds and arms and, in the case of Hezbollah, fighters.

As indicated earlier, the United States also backs the fragmented coalition of the rebels, even though they include thousands of the Wahhabi fundamentalists, who often provide troops and recruits for al-Qaeda, our number-one enemy. This seems very similar to our support of fundamentalist extremists in Afghanistan against the Soviet Union, who gave birth to the Taliban, whom we have been fighting for the past decade and a half. As it has been argued in this book, our foreign policy sows the seeds of our problem in the region. Our 1953 overthrow of the democratically elected Iranian government changed the trajectory of Iranian politics and gave birth to anti-American feelings that were reflected in the 1979 revolution. Similarly, the United States positively viewed the overthrow of Qasim in Iraq[40] ten years later in 1963, in which the left, potential ally of the Soviet Union was decimated. Around five thousand suspected members of the Iraqi communist party were arrested and executed. Yet emerging victorious from this violent overthrow was the Ba'ath Party, which was Saddam Hussein's vehicle for his rise to power and his two wars with United States.

So we can see that US foreign policy, shaped either by Cold War calculations or by pure greed (i.e., opposition to the Iranian nationalization of oil in 1953), in Iraq, Iran, and Afghanistan resulted in the creation of the movements and political situations that came to challenge the United States years later and engaged the United States in three wars.

American support for Saudi and Qatari funding and arming of radical Islamists groups fighting the Syrian government is yet another instance of sowing the seeds of future foreign policy disasters. Nancy A. Youssef, in her article "Syrian Rebels Describe U.S.-Backed Training in Qatar," based on a PBS *Frontline* documentary (aired May 27, 2014), describes a US-based, multicountry effort that involves Turkey, the United States, and Qatar in providing training for the rebels. The multinational network operations begin with the rebels' traveling to Turkey, where they meet their "American handlers." They are then flown to Qatar, where they receive "three weeks of training in how to conduct ambushes, conduct raids and use their weapons. ... [This is despite the fact that,] officially, the United States only provides non-lethal aid, like food rations, clothing and first aid supplies."[41]

Our support, along with that of Saudis and other regional actors for the rebels, has been matched by increased Iranian and Russian support of the Syrian regime, which has resulted in a dramatic rise in levels of violence. So, when it comes to the slaughter of the innocent, the civilian casualties of more than one hundred thousand, and the destruction of cities, economies, and communities in Syria, all sides are to blame, *including us*.

While it is popular for media hacks and pundits to simply focus on an old tradition of animosity between the Sunnis and the Shi'as as the root cause of conflict in Syria, and there is an element of truth to that generalization, it is also true that our government fanned the Sunni fear of Shi'ite resurgence, starting in 2006, by encouraging Bahrain to crack down on its Shi'ite majority and by asking Saudi Arabia to finance and sponsor right-wing Sunni militant groups in Middle East, particularly in Lebanon as a counterweight to Syria and Hezbollah.[42] The massive communal violence that we witness today in Syria, just like the genocide in Rwanda and the massacres in Bosnia, was inflicted upon communities that did have a history of rivalry and distrust but had managed to live together in peace for decades and at times centuries, as was the case for Shi'as and Sunnis in Iraq and Syria under the Ottoman rule in the eighteenth, nineteenth, and early twentieth centuries. A political change, the assassination of a leader, the breakdown of the centralized state, the Arab Spring, and deliberate incitement by foreign actors such as the United States is what changed the coexistence of these communities into massive communal violence.

There are several opinion polls that support my contention. The University of Maryland's 2011 Annual Arab Public Opinion Survey, conducted by professor Shibley Telhami (principal investigator) in Egypt, Jordan, Lebanon, Morocco, and UAE (all strong majority–Sunni Arab countries) in October 2011 with a sample size of three thousand and a margin of error of +/–1.8 percent, indicated the following:

- Sixty-four percent of Arab respondents thought that the non-Arab and Shi'a Iran had a right to its nuclear program, an increase of 11 percent over the same poll's results in 2009.
- Only 35 percent of respondents thought that Iran's acquisition of nuclear weapons would be a negative outcome for the Middle East, a corresponding decline

of 11 percent from poll results in 2009. Half of the respondents felt that Iran's acquisition of nuclear weapons either would be a positive outcome for the region or would not matter, a 5 percent increase in these two categories compared with 2009.

- Only 18 percent of respondents in 2011 thought that Iran would be a big threat to their country. Seventy-one percent cited Israel, and 59 percent cited the United States. While this was an increase of 5 percent over the 2009 results, it means that the majority of Sunni Arabs do not consider Shi'a Iran to be a major threat (Telhami's interpretation notwithstanding).[43]
- Only 13 percent of the respondents thought of the then–Iranian president Mahmoud Ahmadinejad as the world leader whom they admired most, indicating that their support for Iran's nuclear program was independent of their thoughts about Iranian leaders.[44]

Similarly, on June 10, 2013, the Arab Center for Research and Policy Studies released the results of its 2012/2013 Arab Opinion Index, which was based on polls conducted in Yemen, Saudi Arabia, Kuwait, Iraq, Jordan, Palestine, Lebanon, Egypt, Sudan, Tunisia, Algeria, Morocco, Mauritania, and Libya. This year, Kuwait and Libya involved 20,350 individuals. The margin of error reported for the poll by the center is 2 to 3 percent. Except for Iraq, these are all majority-Sunni and -Arab countries. Here are some of the findings:

- Only 6 percent of these majority Sunni Arab respondents found the non-Arab Shi'a Iran to be the single biggest threat to collective Arab security. Israel, at 52 percent, and the United States, at 21 percent, constituted the biggest threats to Arab security. However, when asked about threat levels to specific home countries, the responses changed, and Iran was considered to be the biggest threat, by 12 percent of respondents.
- Sixty-three percent of the respondents indicated that they deal the same way with people of varying degrees of religiosity, and among these, 7 percent said that they actually prefer to deal with nonreligious people.
- In the aggregate, 67 percent of respondents opposed agitation against people of different religions by either agreeing or strongly agreeing with this statement: "No authority has the right to define as apostates those who hold varying interpretations of a religion, or to attack those from other religions."[45]

Finally, we should note that opinion polls indicated that in 2006, the Shi'a "Hezbollah leader Hassan Nasrallah was the most popular leader in the [predominately Sunni] region … [and] despite pro-Western Sunni attempts to construct a Shi'i/Iranian threat, only 11 percent feared Islamic Iran."[46] Although there is no denying that there are some among the Sunni Rebels in Syria who would be happy to slaughter Shi'ites, and there are those among the Shi'ites who would return the favor, most Muslims do not hold such hatred, as these opinion polls show. So, to simplify the civil war to simply a flare-up of centuries-old Shi'a-Sunny rivalry and to ignore all the associated geopolitical factors might serve the cable news experts' needs, but this is not a true reflection of the causes of the conflict.

In late August 2013, it appeared that our government was prepared to launch cruise missile operations to purportedly punish the Assad regime for its alleged use of chemical weapons. However, only about 9 percent of the American public supported military involvement in Syria at the time, and even the conservative Heritage Foundation had publicly opposed a proposed missile strike.[47]

Our erstwhile allies and our partners in crime, the British, however, apparently decided that they could not stomach yet another military engagement in the Middle East, and in a rare move, the House of Commons voted against military intervention in Syria:

> The MP's vote against military intervention in Syria marked a wonderful day for democracy in Britain, because at long last, the Parliament listened to public opinion and voted accordingly, casting a huge blow to the powerful British neo-con clique.

> In the great anti-war film *All Quiet on the Western Front* ... to Kantorek's horror Paul launches an anti-war tirade, and turns on his old teacher. '*He tells you go out and die, but it's easier to say go out and die than it is to do it and it's easier to say it than to watch it happen*'.

> In the same way that Paul had turned on his warmongering teacher, so British Parliamentarians—and the British public—have turned against the neo-con and '*liberal interventionist*' hypocrites who, like Kantorek, are so keen on war, so long as it's other people and their children who do the fighting and the dying.[48]

Interestingly, our government turned a blind eye to Saddam Hussein's repeated use of chemical weapons in the Iraq-Iran war against the Iranian army and Kurdish citizens in Halabja on March 16, 1988, which killed an estimated five thousand Kurdish civilians and wounded another ten thousand;[49] however, military intervention in Syria to punish purported use of chemical weapons is apparently now justified.

Our neocon and orientalists experts once again erred in their analysis of a Middle Eastern country and predicted a quick downfall for the Syrian regime. It now appears that the government that we oppose is actually winning the war, yet we continue to back the rebels who appear to be the losing without serious attempts at finding a peaceful solution that is acceptable to Damascus. Had the neocons and interventionists looked at the makeup of the Syrian opposition and the forces supporting the

Assad regime, they could have understood that a military solution that favors the United States' desired outcome, short of an American invasion, is unlikely. Professor Fawaz A. Gerges of the London School of Economics and Political Science explains the facts on the ground as follows:

> While Damascus and its allies—particularly Iran, Hezbollah and Russia—have been resourceful and ruthless in their war game plan, the anti-Assad coalition is deeply divided and suffers from a fatal disconnect between goals, means and ideologies. Beyond Assad's removal from power, there is little unity among the opposition front. In contrast, Assad and his partners share unity of purpose and ranks. ... It is doubtful if the ideologically and sociologically fragmented opposition can level the playing battlefield with the Assad coalition, let alone deliver a decisive blow. As things stand, the odds are against the opposition.[50]

Thankfully, now it appears that yet another American war in the Middle East has been postponed. While we don't know what our future possible involvement in Syria will eventually cost us in terms of blood and treasure,[51] we have a pretty good idea of the cost of war in Iraq, Afghanistan, and Libya.

A Treasure Poorly Spent

Libya

Our Libyan intervention, although much less costly than our involvement in Iraq and Afghanistan, still took more than $1 billion away from what could have been spent here at home on education, infrastructure, and other domestic needs. Worse, the fracturing of Libyan society and the continued inability of the new government to maintain law and order were contributing factors in the murders of an American ambassador and three other Americans in Benghazi on September 11, 2012. And, as in many cases before, the instability of post-Qadhafi Libya should not have come as a surprise to our decision makers. The United Nation's Human Rights Council prepared and released a comprehensive report on March 2, 2012, that warned of instability and lawlessness in Libya. The report highlighted the post-Qadhafi intermilitia (*thuwar*) fighting for territory and material goods, which included the wholesale arrest of the enemy town's population:

> Inter-*thuwar* clashes have occurred in the atmosphere of lawlessness that existed in several parts of Libya following the conflict. They were most pronounced in Tripoli where a number of *thuwar* brigades maintained a presence even at the time of writing. Following some clashes,

brigades have arbitrarily arrested those associated with other brigades. One such detainee who the Commission interviewed had been taken by a brigade from Wershafana on 11 November 2011 and detained there along with 64 others from Al Zawiyah. The Al Zawiyah brigade held about 27 men from Wershefana. The two brigades had fought over control of the "27 km" checkpoint which had led to several deaths between 10 and 12 November 2011. Both groups arrested residents of the "enemy town" in retribution. Several people were arrested in their cars apparently for no other reason that having Al Zawiyah license plates. Many, but not all were ill-treated.[52]

In addition to *thuwar* (anti-Qadhafi fighters), interfighting, carjacking, and killing of people for their property, the report in particular, highlighted the behavior of militias from Misrata and their brutal treatment of Tawerghans (Black Libyans from the town of Tawergha, forty miles south of Misrata), which included arbitrary arrests and routine beatings and torture.

> The Commission also notes the 22 interviews of Tawerghans detained in Misrata completed by Human Rights Watch, many of which describe Tawerghan detainees having their bones broken, being beaten around the head, suffering electric shocks, being beaten with a variety of objects including whips, rifle butts, metal bars, wooden sticks, rubber hoses and electrical cables. One man "displayed fresh gashes on his face and arms, and blood was visible inside his mouth. During the interview, the man lost consciousness for about one minute."

> The Commission notes that the Misratan *thuwar* have been open about their treatment of the Tawerghans. In one interview with the Commission, a *thuwar* said he thought that Tawerghans deserved "to be wiped off the face of the planet."[53]

Qadhafi forces also routinely engaged in torture and even mass executions. Yet the proceeding shows that the side we backed in the war is not so much better in terms of its human rights behavior, and it has added general banditry to human rights violations.

In addition to Misrata's militias, Libyan militias include a host of pro-al-Qaeda militant Islamic groups and militias composed and led by former Qadhafi aides and officers. On Friday, May 16, 2014, one such militia led by "General Khalifa Hifter stormed the parliament building in Tripoli ... after earlier attacking Islamist militia camps in Benghazi."[54] Bizarrely, the Libyan chief of staff called on Islamic militias to repel the general's forces, which might push the conflict into a full-fledged civil war. Our hands might yet be involved in the Libyan conflict, as the general Khalifa

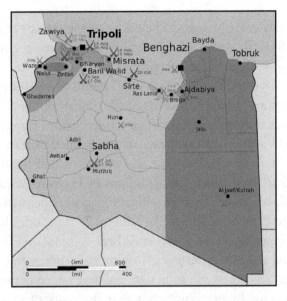

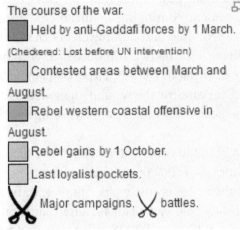

The course of the war.

Held by anti-Gaddafi forces by 1 March.

(Checkered: Lost before UN intervention)

Contested areas between March and August.

Rebel western coastal offensive in August.

Rebel gains by 1 October.

Last loyalist pockets.

Major campaigns. battles.

Map 6. The Libyan Civil War

Source: Copyright © 2011 by Rafy / Wikimedia Commons / CC BY-SA 3.0.

had fled to the United States after falling out of favor with Qadhafi and is reputed to have ties with the CIA. Our possible connections with the general raise an important question: Are we going to be dragged into the conflict yet again and add to our billion-dollar price tag and divert resources from our challenges at home?

Iraq and Afghanistan

It was, however, our wars in Iraq and Afghanistan that truly took significant resources from the American economy and diverted it to the war effort. The conservative estimate by the Congressional Budget Office (CBO) in 2010, which ignored accumulated interests and legacy costs (discussed below), put these costs at $1.4 trillion by 2012. In 2014, the CBO put a cap of $98 billion on overseas contingency operations, which is mainly for Afghanistan after the sequestration.[55]

However, Brown University's March 2013 report on the Iraq War put the monetary cost of that war alone at $2.2 trillion as of the time of publication and estimated that it would cost $3.9 trillion by 2053.[56] The report further stated that 7,888 American military personnel and civilian contractors were killed in Iraq and Afghanistan.[57]

When Afghanistan is added to Iraq, the monetary cost for the United States alone can go up to $6 trillion, says Linda J. Bilmes of Harvard University: "The Iraq and Afghanistan conflicts, taken together, will be the most expensive wars in U.S. history—totaling somewhere between $4 and $6 trillion. This includes long-term medical care and disability compensation for service members, veterans and families, military replenishment and social and economic costs."[58] Bilmes also notes that the costs of these wars account for about 20 percent of "total national debt added between 2001 and 2012."[59]

More importantly, Bilmes points out that the costs of these wars have a legacy component that will present continuing financial challenges for the United States: "This legacy is debt—promises and commitments that extend far into the future. The years of conflict have left America still burdened with heavy costs, even with the ground combat phase drawing to a close. These costs include the immediate requirements to provide medical care for the wounded, as well as the accrued liabilities for providing lifetime medical costs and disability compensation for those who have survived injuries."[60]

Already more than 780,000 American soldiers have filed for permanent disability, and, according to Bilmes, 671,299 of these claims have been approved. These veterans require care, and their care is costly (see figure 2.3). Based on the Congressional Budget Office data shown below, we can surmise that total Department of Defense health-care costs between 2008 and 2028 will be around $1.2 trillion (twenty years times the average yearly cost of $60 billion), and health-care costs for Department of Defense will reach around $70 billion per year by 2008.

But what do these figures mean in terms of what we could have done in America for American citizens? An average three-story, fifty-five-thousand-square-foot hospital that is constructed by union labor cost about $17.5 million in 2013. Our government could have built more than 180,000 such hospitals with the money that we have spent in these wars.[61] Alternatively, we could have built 154,000 new two-story public schools—almost triple the number of public schools that we had in 2008.[62]

The Human Cost

Yet, despite the large expenditures, the Veteran's Administration (VA) has shown itself incapable of dealing with large number of veterans that need care. Recently, the nation discovered that VA hospitals have been creating fake lists and have been

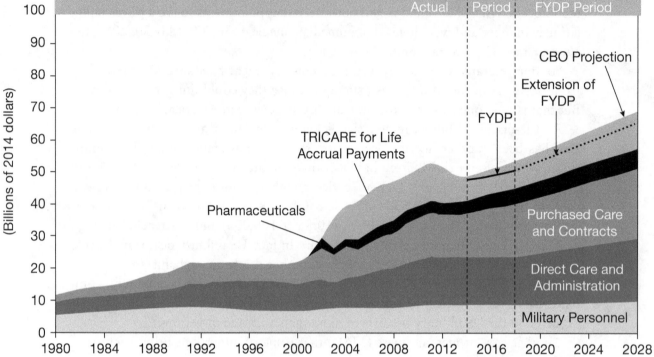

Costs of DoD's Plans for Its Military Health System

Figure 2.3. Defense Department's Projected Health-Care Spending

Source: Congressional Budget Office / Copyright in the Public Domain.

altering the wait times for appointments with doctors to show that they have complied with the maximum fourteen-day wait period mandated by the government. Meanwhile, some veterans, who had been waiting for at times longer than six weeks to see a doctor, have died, and it is not clear what has happened to the rest.

The timeline of the events published by *USA Today* shows that physicians began to warn the VA as early as 2012 about the lack of institutional capacity to deal with the influx of veterans from the wars that we fought by choice. For example, Dr. Katherine Mitchell, a VA emergency-room physician, warned her incoming director at Phoenix VA hospital that the "Phoenix ER is overwhelmed and dangerous," and that the Government Accountability Office had warned the VA that its recording of patients wait times is "unreliable."[63]

Dr. Mitchell was told that her "communication skills" were lacking and she was transferred, and nothing occurred as a result of complaints about other physicians and reports of other government agencies until April 2014, when the scandal broke wide open because of journalistic investigations and a House hearing. The scope of

the VA's failure became evident as more and more whistleblowers came forward and an internal VA investigation was completed. It turned out that in one facility alone, the Phoenix VA, 1,700 veterans had not received appointments to see a physician in a timely manner and were in need of immediate medical care. On May 30, 2014, the VA secretary, General Eric Shinseki, resigned.

So, our veterans who have served their country might have died after returning from our wars in the Middle East, simply because they could not get medical care. But that is only one aspect of the human cost of the war in America.

A little-discussed but extremely significant cost of American wars in the Middle East has been another horrible legacy effect: the mental anguish that US veterans suffer, which often exhibits itself in higher divorce rates and suicide.

Since 2001, among only active service members, more than 2,700 American soldiers have committed suicide. This is a rate (18 per 100,000 in 2012) that is significantly higher than pre-war levels (10.3 per 100,000) and has reached as high as 22.9 per 100,000 among Army personnel.[64] In fact, US military deaths by suicide in 2012 and 2013 surpassed the number of combat deaths in Afghanistan.[65]

While one may argue that these suicides cannot be directly associated with combat experience, they must be attributed, at least partially, to the cultural change that occurred in the US military because of more than a decade of warfare.[66]

Another cost of mental illness (PTSD) that some of our troops bring back from the front is the increase in domestic violence:

> The majority of studies of treatment-seeking veterans with post-traumatic stress disorder (PTSD) or combat-related mental health issues report that at least 50 percent of those veterans commit wife-battering and family violence. Male veterans with PTSD are two to three times more likely than veterans without PTSD to engage in intimate partner violence, according to the VA, which also found that the majority of veterans with combat stress commit at least one act of spousal abuse in their first year post-deployment.[67]

However, spouses are not the only victims of our soldiers' PTSD; children are often another set of victims, both indirectly because they are affected by the spousal abuse and directly as targets of the abuse. A 2010 *Stars and Stripes* article describes the rise in abuse and neglect of children:

> 2010 saw an increase in the number of substantiated child maltreatment cases reported to Family Advocacy, from 4.8 incidents per one thousand children in 2008 and 2009 to 5.7 per thousand in fiscal year 2010.

"That's a big jump," said David Finkelhor, a sociologist and family violence expert at the Crimes against Children Research Center at the University of New Hampshire. "It doesn't look like year-to-year bouncing around. It looks like it means something."

Substantiated child maltreatment cases include physical, sexual and emotional abuse and neglect. Nearly three quarters of the cases—72 percent—were classified as neglect or emotional abuse.

The report said 29 child deaths from abuse or neglect were reported to Family Advocacy last year. Twelve of them were under a year old.[68]

While divorce rates among military personnel are not that much different from civilian rates, some studies suggest that the military rates are higher, and some services have experienced their highest divorce rates in two decades.[69]

Of course, one can apply the *legacy* concept to Afghanistan and Iraq in yet another aspect. Anecdotal discussion (to follow) of Fallujah's birth-defect rates is just an example of the legacy costs and the price that the economies and peoples of these two nations and ours will continue to pay for decades to come. We need to look at the impact on Iraqi civil society as a whole that resulted from our intervention—both in terms of the complete fracturing of any civil order that we now witness and the economic costs of rebuilding war-torn countries.

One article by George Washington University compared our costs in rebuilding Iraq and Afghanistan to our efforts in rebuilding Germany after World War II. While we spent about $35 billion to rebuild Germany, we have already spent more than $60 billion in Iraq and more than $100 billion in Afghanistan.[70] Despite our best efforts, Iraqi civil society is broken, and Iraq is experiencing an uptick in civil strife, fueled in part by conflict in Syria. The current situation is best summarized in this passage from the *Nation*:

> The bombings—18 in all—are part of a wave of bloodshed that has swept across the country since April [2013], killing more than 3,000 people and worsening the already strained ties between Iraq's Sunni minority and the Shiite-led government. The scale and pace of the violence, unseen since the darkest days of the country's insurgency, have fanned fears of a return to the widespread sectarian bloodletting that pushed Iraq to the brink of civil war after the 2003 U.S.-led invasion.[71]

Between January and September 2013, an estimated five thousand Iraqis were killed and another twelve thousand wounded in the civil strife.[72] By September 2013,

Table 2.1. Iraqi Civilian Deaths, 2003–2014

Year	January	February	March	April	May	June	July	August	September	October	November	December	Yearly Total
2003	3	2	3,977	3,435	546	597	647	794	565	517	486	526	12,095
2004	610	663	1,004	1,303	654	901	825	874	1,033	1,016	1,652	1,112	11,647
2005	1,188	1,284	902	1,144	1,392	1,346	1,530	2,276	1,422	1,298	1,467	1,133	16,382
2006	1,544	1,570	1,946	1,799	2,271	2,571	3,283	2,851	2,559	2,977	3,064	2,886	29,321
2007	2,975	2,652	2,702	2,538	2,834	2,192	2,690	2,481	1,366	1,295	1,110	987	25,822
2008	847	1,072	1,637	1,299	890	747	643	682	606	590	535	582	10,130
2009	372	403	426	567	390	501	407	618	333	435	226	475	5,153
2010	263	304	336	385	387	385	443	516	254	312	307	218	4,110
2011	389	254	311	289	381	386	308	401	397	366	279	388	4,149
2012	524	356	377	392	304	529	469	422	396	290	253	275	4,587
2013	357	360	403	545	888	659	1,145	1,012	1,221	1,095	903	983	9,571
2014	1,076	930	1,009	1,013	558								4,586

Grand Total 137,553

Source: Data from Iraq Body Count, https://www.iraqbodycount.org/database.

Note: Title and column headings were altered by the author, and a grand total was calculated.

the situation in Iraq had become so bad that the government restricted traffic to alternate days to reduce the number of car bombs.[73] While these measures might produce results in the short term, the underlying sectarian conflict that was exasperated by our military involvement is unlikely to be resolved anytime soon.

Of course, Iraqi deaths overall since 2003 have been estimated in the hundreds of thousands, and even today Iraq suffers from the consequences of the policies of the United States and their aftermath. Regional actors, such as Saudi Arabia, Iran, and Turkey, also have contributed to the unleashing of the forces of sectarian violence. As table 2.1 shows, by May 2014 alone close to five thousand Iraqi civilians have been killed as a result of the aftermath of our invasion.

But also from the physical impact of the war on the environment:

> Ten years after the start of the U.S. invasion in Iraq, doctors in some of the Middle Eastern nation's cities are witnessing an abnormally high number of cases of cancer and birth defects. Scientists suspect the rise is tied to the use of depleted uranium and white phosphorus in military assaults.[74]

Fallujah's birth defects are said to be higher than Hiroshima's because of our use of white phosphorus and other chemical weapons in 2004.[75] Furthermore, our own troops' Gulf War Syndrome has been attributed to our use of chemical weapons (depleted uranium) in Iraq.[76]

Our involvement in Afghanistan, which dates back to before the attacks of September 11, 2001, and our support for the Islamic guerrillas who fought the Soviet Union continue to exact a human cost that goes beyond Afghanistan and have affected Pakistan and the Central Asian Republics of Kirgizstan, Tajikistan, and Turkmenistan.

The Taliban emerged onto the Afghani scene with Pakistani support in 1994. The Unites States (although at times reluctantly) and its erstwhile ally, Saudi Arabia, then joined the Pakistanis in support of the Taliban as a counterweight to Iranian and Russian support of the Tajik forces in Afghanistan. Furthermore, it was thought that the Taliban would play a key role in securing the route for "any southern [oil] pipeline from Central Asia that would avoid Iran,"[77] which has been a centerpiece of American foreign policy ever since the Clinton administration. It was only when the Taliban gave sanctuary to Osama bin Laden and al-Qaeda that the United States began to actively and firmly oppose the Taliban.

After the US invasion of Afghanistan, the Taliban and its supporters simply crossed the borders into Pakistan and established themselves in Northwest Frontier provinces and in the city of Quetta. The Taliban imposed Sharia law in territories that it held and attacked government offices and troops whenever the Pakistani government attempted to reassert some semblance of order. Some 1,500 Pakistani troops and countless civilians were killed by the Taliban by 2007, and in 2009, more than 2.5 million Pakistanis had to flee the Swat Valley region while the country was hit with a series of suicide bombings and attacks on its military bases. Pakistan continues to suffer from extremists' attacks, which were exacerbated partly as a result of our involvement in Afghanistan.[78]

Although comparatively small in numbers, civilian causalities in both Afghanistan and Pakistan, because of our use of drones and aerial bombardment, have been a major source of rising negative public opinion of the United States in the area. A United Nations report released in February 2014, "Afghanistan Annual Report, 2013: Protection of Civilians in Armed Conflict," states that just in the 2009 to 2013 time period, more than fourteen thousand Afghan civilians have been killed in the conflict. In 2013, 956 of these deaths were attributed to pro-government forces, and of these, 19 percent were caused by what is labeled as "air operations." Drone use alone accounted for forty-five civilian deaths and fourteen injuries according to the report.[79] While these numbers may not seem that alarming, when viewed in the overall context of the conflict, the fact that 45 percent of the victims are women and children adds to the negative perception of the United States.

The activities of Taliban in Pakistan and their cross-border incursions, similarly, resulted in our use of drone strikes and raids in Pakistan, which sharply turned the already negative Pakistani public opinion even more hostile. This negative public opinion is another cost of our constant military interventions in the Middle East and the support for Israel. This negative image has very long-term implications and potentially damages US credibility and interests in the Middle East.

> A year after the war in Iraq, discontent with America and its policies has intensified rather than diminished. ... Perceptions of American unilateralism remain widespread in European and Muslim nations, and the war in Iraq has undermined America's credibility abroad. ... In the predominantly Muslim countries surveyed, anger toward the United States remains pervasive. ... In the four predominantly Muslim countries surveyed, opposition to the war remains nearly universal. Moreover, while large majorities in Western European countries opposed to the war say Saddam Hussein's ouster will improve the lot of the Iraqi people, those in Muslim countries are less confident. In Jordan, no less than 70% of survey respondents think the Iraqis will be worse off with Hussein gone.[80]

These negative views of America persisted into and during the Arab Spring. A Pew Research Center poll taken in 2011 stated that these views had actually become more negative:

> A new survey finds that the rise of pro-democracy movements has not led to an improvement in America's image in the region. Instead, in key Arab nations and in other predominantly Muslim countries, views of the U.S. remain negative, as they have been for nearly a decade. Indeed, in Jordan, Turkey and Pakistan, views are even more negative than they were one year ago.[81]

American support for Israel has similarly produced a long-term negative view in the Palestinian territories. Fully 80 percent of Palestinians surveyed in 2009 held an unfavorable view of the United States.[82]

The opposition to American military interventionism in the region continues to be strong. A recent Pew Research Center poll revealed that in five out of six countries surveyed, a strong majority of respondents opposed US military intervention in Syria.[83]

Finally, our foreign policy and the maintenance of our empire have necessitated the creation of a vast military. Our military requires a continuing annual expenditure of more than $700 billion, $55 billion of which is simply devoted to the huge and ever-increasing security and intelligence apparatus that continues to err in its analysis.

To get some perspective on how much money we are spending on our military and intelligence efforts, consider the following facts. The money that we spend on

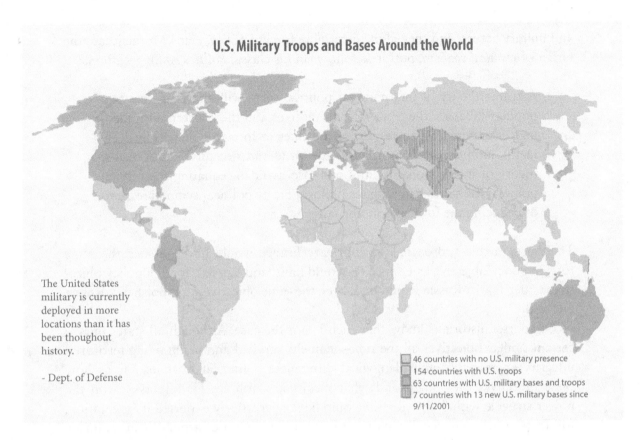

U.S. Military Troops and Bases Around the World

The United States military is currently deployed in more locations than it has been thoughout history.

- Dept. of Defense

46 countries with no U.S. military presence
154 countries with U.S. troops
63 countries with U.S. military bases and troops
7 countries with 13 new U.S. military bases since 9/11/2001

Map 7. US Military Deployment

Source: U.S. Department of Defense.

our intelligence apparatus alone is larger than the entire defense budget of Germany ($45 billion), and our total defense spending is more than twice of that of Russia, China, Britain, and France combined. We have more troops overseas (almost 260,000), not counting our personnel on aircraft carriers and ships, than the total military personnel of the British armed forces, or the French, the Germans, or the Japanese, each of which has about two hundred thousand troops.[84] Map 7 shows US military deployment around the world.

Why is our foreign policy so misguided and so costly? To understand that, we need to know how and by whom our foreign policy is formulated.

International relations theorists look at foreign policy formulation by using different levels of analysis. The *realists* use the interstate level of analysis and argue that foreign policy is the result of states' rational pursuit of their national interest as unitary actors. Power and its pursuit by states and the resulting interactions explain why states behave the way they do. In this approach, it does not matter who the decision makers are, and domestic groups have no role in the formulation of foreign policy. Regardless of ideology or decision makers' personalities, states are rational and unitary actors, and they alone determine foreign policy. Hans Morgenthau, the father of modern realism, puts it as follows in his classic *Politics Among Nations*:

> A realist theory of international politics, then, will guard against two popular fallacies: the concern with motives and the concern with ideological preferences. To search for the clues to foreign policy exclusively in the motives of statesmen is both futile and deceptive. ... A realist theory of international politics will also avoid ... equating the foreign policies of a statesman with his philosophic or political sympathies, and of deducing the former from the latter.[85]

Therefore, in this approach, Revolutionary France would have pursued the same foreign policy objective as Louis XIV would have, and Russian foreign policy objectives under Tsarist Russia would have been the same objectives that Bolshevik Russia pursued.

Of course, historians know that such is not the case. Although all states pursue certain similar objectives all the time—namely, survival and maintaining territorial integrity—personality and ideological differences matter, at least insofar as how these objectives are sought and what means are utilized. Had Trotsky won the power struggle with Stalin, Russia would have aggressively exported its revolution, for Trotsky believed that Russia must remake the countries around it in its image in order to survive. This is ironically similar to democratic peace theories, wherein world peace would be achieved only in a world full of democracies, because historically democracies have not attacked other democracies.

Stalin by contrast pursued the model of building socialism in one country as the avenue to achieving security objectives. Similarly, Revolutionary France was immediately engulfed in wars that culminated in the Napoleonic wars as a result of its revolution and the opposition of European monarchies to its message and government. Saddam Hussein attacked Iran in 1980 in part out of fear of the spread of the ideas of the Iranian Revolution among its majority Shi'a population, and Revolutionary Iran at the beginning attempted to export its revolutionary message across the Middle East.

Historians aside, today most international relations experts also do not buy into the realist arguments. Critics of realism argue that states are fictitious entities and that there is no such thing as a unitary actor who makes foreign policy. These critics, be they *constructionists*, *liberals*, or *democratic peace* theorists, explain foreign policy decisions based on the domestic institutions and structure of societies and the character and personalities of decision makers.[86]

Authoritarian states are said to behave differently than democracies do, and foreign policy formulation in democracies is subject to pressures brought forth by lobbyists, interests groups, bureaucracies, and other groups that pursue their own collective interests and attempt to mold the country's foreign policy so that it serves their interests. Foreign policy is made as a result of the clash of these groups and the personalities and abilities of their leaders.

This book similarly relies on the domestic and individual levels of analysis to explain our foreign policy formulation toward the Middle East. It is therefore argued here that our foreign policy in the Middle East is partly the result of the pressures applied by interest groups such as the pro-Israeli lobby and those who provide counsel to our decision makers. This latter group consists of four, at times overlapping yet at times distinct, groups who are involved in influencing and forming our foreign policy. These groups are the *orientalists*, *imperial progressives*, *agenda-driven pundits/lobbyists*, and *neocons*. But before we discuss these groups, let us discuss how typical academic textbooks on American government address the making of foreign policy.

Chapter Three

The Coverage
and Discussion of
American Foreign Policy
in Academic Textbooks
Where Is Damascus?

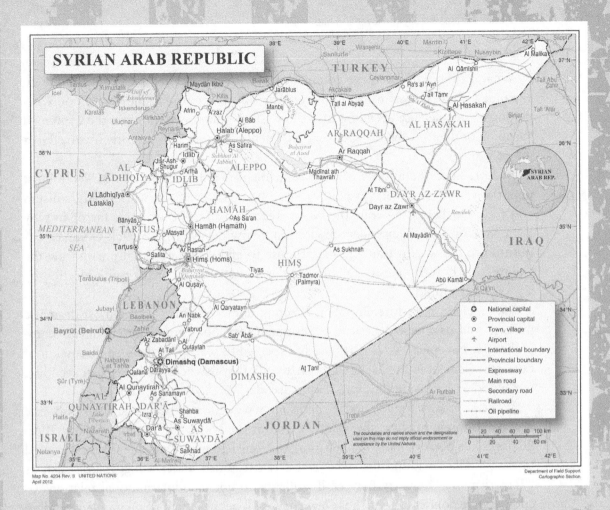

DoD Has Problems Locating Damascus in New Map Quiz

Source: Copyright © 2012 by United Nations. Reprinted with permission.

Where Is Damascus?

Back in the mid-1980s, I was attending a PhD program in political science at Northwestern University. One of my professors had just published a textbook on American government. He told me that if you capture 1 percent of the American government textbook market, it is worth $100,000. Of course, that was in the mid-1980s, and if the statement was correct then, the market for these textbooks should now be several times more valuable.

There are now dozens of textbooks on American government, each desperately seeking to differentiate itself from the pack of hungry competitors. As I was researching material for this manuscript, I looked at several of these books to see how our foreign policy is covered and discussed. I can't discuss the hundreds of books that are published on the subject, but I would like to discuss a few that are published by mainstream publishers. These are *We the People* by Patterson, *Am Gov* by Losco and Baker, *American Democracy Now*, by Harrison, Harris, and Deardorf, *Government Matters* by Maltese, and *By the People* by Morone and Kersh.[87]

What I expected, given the competitiveness of the market, was to see quite an expanded discussion of foreign policy. After all, we are today the world's only superpower, our defense spending of around $700 billion is more than the combined spending of the next ten big spenders on defense, and we are currently involved in a major war.

In fact, since the attacks of 9/11 until the Great Recession of 2008, the most important topic in American politics was our involvement in wars in Afghanistan and Iraq. Furthermore, while the Great Recession of 2008 was one factor in why John McCain lost the presidential election, many believe that Barack Obama's opposition to the war in Iraq and his promise to end it and eventually withdraw the troops from both Iraq and Afghanistan was a contributing factor to his election by a war-weary public.

So, here you have foreign policy affecting domestic policy in the most dramatic manner, and of course American government textbooks would surely devote comprehensive coverage to it. I particularly expected to see a very detailed discussion of our entanglement in the Middle East. After all, that is where we have been spending our blood and treasure for more than a decade.

What I actually found shocked me somewhat. All five books devoted only one chapter to foreign policy, always at the end of the book, and generally about 20 to 30 pages in a book of more than 650 pages. None had more than a few pages devoted to the Middle East, and that was generally subsumed under a bigger title such as "Terrorism" or "Military Power." If students do not take international relations or comparative politics classes, those few pages will be the extent of their understanding of our foreign policy and one of the most important areas of its focus: the Middle East. No wonder, then, that 43 percent of our officers in the Pentagon could not locate Damascus at the height of the Syrian crisis when we were ready to lob missiles at Syria.[88] Similarly, a *Washington Post* survey conducted between March 28 and March 31, 2014, at the height of Ukraine crisis, found that only one out of six Americans could find Ukraine on a map, and military households were no different from the general public. Only 16.1 percent of military households correctly identified Ukraine's location, which was almost identical to the percentage of the general public (16 percent) who correctly located Ukraine on the map.[89] This is despite the fact that two-thirds of 2,066 respondents were following the crisis "somewhat closely." Quite a few respondents thought that Ukraine was located in Canada; some even placed Ukraine in the Midwest! More interestingly, the less respondents knew about Ukraine and its location, the more they favored military intervention by the United States.[90]

This lack of coverage of various areas of the world and how our foreign policy is made and conducted toward the outside world is particularly shocking because most textbooks, even American government textbooks, now focus on globalization. Well, if you are going to travel to other countries and conduct business or entertain residents of other countries, it sure would help to know where these countries are

located, and it certainly wouldn't kill you if you knew just a bit about their customs, culture, and language.

Why is it that foreign policy and area studies, particularly for the Middle East, are so poorly covered in our American government textbooks?

Perhaps the authors think that because Congress and the presidency and the bureaucracy each are covered in some detail and all these institutions make foreign policy, there is little need to devote more space to foreign policy. After all, section 8, clause 3 of article I of our Constitution gives the right to regulate "commerce with foreign nations" to Congress, and clauses 11 and 12 of the same article and section give the right "to declare war" and to "raise and support armies," similarly enshrining Congress with said powers.

Perhaps it is that the detailed discussion of the interest groups, the media, and lobbying and political parties that shape foreign policy is assumed to be enough. Or, perhaps, American government professors don't write much about foreign policy simply because they themselves don't know much about it. Or it could be the commercial interests of the publishers that limit the discussion of foreign policy.

Whatever is the cause, I believe that our current American government textbooks and the training that our citizens receive from American government classes leave much room for improvement. Although this topic is covered more in depth in international relations and comparative politics textbooks, again, we need to be cognizant of the fact that many of our students never take another political science class, and then we end up in a situation where 43 percent of our officers in our national defense headquarters cannot find Damascus on a map, even at the height of a crisis and possible military confrontation with Syria.

Yes, math and science, the arts, sex education, and the like are important in their own rights, but as citizens of an increasingly integrated global economic network, we ought to know a bit about the world that we live in and who lives in it with us.

The Founding Fathers: Isolationism versus Interventionism; Idealism versus Realism

When explaining how our foreign policy is actually made, the obligatory chapter in American government textbooks discussed above focuses on the institutions of the presidency, the Congress, and, at times, the national security apparatus, interest groups, the media, and lobbyists. Each is discussed in brief, and here and there an occasional reference is made to the conflict between historically dominant yet competitive trends in American foreign policy: isolationism and interventionism and idealism versus realism.

Unilateralism, "a doctrine that holds that the United States should act independently of other nations," and *multilateralism*, "a doctrine that emphasizes operating together with other nations to pursue common goals,"[91] are competing approaches that can be used mostly under the interventionist philosophy, although conceivably one could be isolationist and unilateral in its approach. Similarly, Wilsonianism, a "belief that American values are to be number-one-consideration guiding [US] foreign policy"[92] can be considered a variety of interventionism. It is said that *neoconservatism* is an offshoot of Wilsonianism, albeit neocons, unlike Wilsonians, do not trust international organizations. In this work, I trace a much darker path for neoconservatism (see chapter four), and while I also consider neoconservatism to be an interventionist variety, I don't think that its ideological roots are Wilsonian. Rather, I make the argument that neocons owe their thinking to the thousands-of-years-old philosophy of Western superiority that was born during the Greco-Persian wars and transmitted by Greece's successor, Rome, and reinforced and expanded during the Crusades and colonialism. Neocons are also agenda driven, but their agenda is not a Wilsonian utopia, though that may be their claim—their agenda is shaping American foreign policy in the Middle East so that it serves the interests of Israel.

Another offshoot of interventionism is what Morone and Kersh call Hamiltonians—those who argue that American interventions should be based on economic interests, not ideals such as liberty. And, finally, there are Jeffersonians, who at once champion liberty and think that America should champion its spread, yet are wary of the military buildup that spreading liberty might require.

On the one hand, we have the *isolationist* tradition. The tradition of isolationism, exhibited now by Libertarians such as Ron Paul and his son, Senator Rand Paul, began with George Washington, who in his farewell speech warned about factionalism, a large and growing military, and foreign entanglements and permanent alliance. Washington urged an unbiased foreign policy that dealt with all nations equally: "Harmony, liberal intercourse with all nations, are recommended by policy, humanity, and interest." Washington specifically warned against foreign wars: "Why quit our own to stand upon foreign ground?" The empire that we maintain goes against everything that Washington believed in and warned us against on September 17, 1796, during his farewell address to the nation:

> The great rule of conduct for us, in regard to foreign nations, is, in extending our commercial relations, to have with them as little political connection as possible. ...

> Why forego the advantages of so peculiar a situation? Why quit our own to stand upon foreign ground? Why, by interweaving our destiny with that of any part of Europe, entangle our peace and prosperity in the toils of European ambition, rivalship, interest, humor, or caprice?

It is our true policy to steer clear of permanent alliances with any portion of the foreign world. ... I hold the maxim no less applicable to public than to private affairs, that honesty is always the best policy. ...

Harmony, liberal intercourse with all nations, are recommended by policy, humanity, and interest. But even our commercial policy should hold an equal and impartial hand; neither seeking nor granting exclusive favors or preferences; consulting the natural course of things; diffusing and diversifying by gentle means the streams of commerce, but forcing nothing; establishing, with powers so disposed, in order to give trade a stable course, to define the rights of our merchants, and to enable the government to support them, conventional rules of intercourse. ...

There can be no greater error than to expect or calculate upon real favors from nation to nation. It is an illusion, which experience must cure, which a just pride ought to discard.[93]

To me, Washington's isolationism means, simply, noninterference unless the nation's survival is at stake. I don't think it is fair to assume that our first president intended for the United States to isolate itself from the world. Rather, I think this farewell speech and similar thinking, such as Madison's warning about the dangers of wars, were simply advocating a cautious foreign policy that focused on American commercial interests by treating all nations with respect, or at least fairly and equally, as Washington had stated. Furthermore, foreign policy interventions that required a large standing army were viewed as dangerous to liberty at home:

Of all the enemies to public liberty war is, perhaps, the most dreaded, because it comprises and develops the germ of every other. War is the parent of armies; from these proceed debt and taxes, and armies, and debt, and taxes, are known instruments for bringing the many under the domination of the few. In war too, the discretionary power of the Executive is extended ... no nation could preserve its freedom in the midst of continual warfare.[94]

Similarly, Jefferson opposed war and thought that the aim of foreign policy should be to

[Protect] and [promote] individual freedom and well-being. ... No end of foreign policy can be morally autonomous, self-justifying, an end in itself. Instead, all the ends of foreign policy must be seen as means to the ends of society, which are in turn ultimately the ends of individuals.[95]

Yet even Jefferson was not isolationist, per se. He was a staunch advocate for American commerce, which at times required "coercive diplomacy." The Louisiana Purchase in 1803, which doubled the size of the United States, occurred during the presidency of Thomas Jefferson and with the active involvement of Jefferson. Jefferson and American leaders were worried about losing the shipping rights in Mississippi that America had gained in the Treaty of Paris in 1783. Spain, who had gained possession of the territory in 1762 from France, was transferring the land back to France, and Jefferson was now worried about what a new powerful neighbor, Napoleonic France, might do. He therefore instructed his friend James Monroe to act as minister extraordinaire in France and negotiate the purchase of all of the land west of the Mississippi, or, failing that, secure New Orleans and shipping rights. Monroe and Livingston (American ambassador in France) reached an agreement with Napoleon and his foreign minister, Charles Talleyrand, on April 30, 1803, to purchase the land for $15 million, and Congress approved the purchase on October 20, 1803.[96] Jefferson also believed in the expansion of America west of the Mississippi, and it was he who requested funding for an expedition to map lands from the Mississippi to the Pacific—the now-famous Lewis and Clark expedition, which set out in 1804, reached the Pacific in 1805, and returned to St. Louis in 1806.[97] Jefferson also ordered the American navy to engage pirates on the Barbary Coast of North Africa (Algeria, Morocco, Tunisia, and Libya) and signed a treaty with Pasha of Tripoli in 1805 that ended tributes that America had to pay to engage in shipping in Libyan waters—although the tribute payment that continued to other Barbary states was not settled until the second Barbary Wars in 1816. Incidentally, the Barbary Wars gave birth to a "line in the United States marine hymn: From the Halls of Montezuma to the Shores of Tripoli."[98]

In fact, it can be argued that Jefferson was also the father of American interventionism, insofar as he did advocate the spread of American ideals to the rest of the world:

> [America, the] solitary republic of the world, the only monument of human rights ... the sole depository of the sacred fire of freedom and self-government, from hence it is to be lighted up in other regions of the earth, if other regions of the earth shall ever become susceptible to its benign influence.[99]

American exceptionalism, the idea that America was somehow different and that indeed it was morally superior and had a unique role in world affairs, was born out of Jeffersonian thinking and has been used ever since to justify America's frequent intervention in world affairs and the empire. Zbigniew Brzezinski, national security advisor to President Jimmy Carter, criticized détente (rapprochement with the Soviet Union) on moral grounds and advocated a hard line toward the Soviet Union.

The Carter administration's support of human rights when applied to Eastern Europe was viewed by Brzezinski as keeping with "fundamental American traditions."[100] George W. Bush—the forty-third president—and neocons who advocated for, planned, and carried out the disastrous American invasion of Iraq in 2003 put much of their reasoning in the context of spreading democracy abroad and removing a tyrannical government. Bush began his speech to the nation on March 19, 2003, by announcing the invasion of Iraq and stating that military operations had begun to disarm Iraq and "free its people."[101]

However, statements that advocate "limited involvement in international relations"[102] have been interpreted as setting the stage for an isolationist foreign policy that is said to have dominated American foreign policy until World War II. In fact, it is said that it was the isolationist tendencies of the United States that prevented it from joining the League of Nations and therefore ensuring its doom and the onset of World War II.

Yet the reality is that American foreign policy, even as early as the nineteenth century, has had a very strong interventionist component. As discussed, the interventionist tradition in American foreign policy also dates back to our founding fathers and Jefferson's desire to spread liberty across the globe.

Historian Jeff Bloodworth argues that this interventionist trend dates even further back to pre-independence days and our history as a Puritan colony:

> The Puritans' Reformed Protestantism remains the alpha and omega of U.S. foreign policy and still shapes Americans' view of their role in the world.
>
> Key to understanding the connection between the seventeenth and twenty-first centuries is the Puritans' "destinarian" zeal. As a radical schism of a messianic outlier in Europe's Protestant movement, the Separatists saw their march into the wilderness as nothing less than a journey to save the world. Four centuries later, U.S. foreign policy still bears the destinarian imprint. ... Thomas Jefferson's political thought and presidential action reveal the sacred-secular mission fueling nineteenth-century U.S. foreign policy. The third president's "empire of liberty" amounted to more than acquiring the Louisiana territory for settlement. In his mind, it constituted a move toward the universal liberation of humanity. ...
>
> Initially catalyzed by the "teeming mass of ideas" linked to the American and French Revolutions, the humanitarian "association mania," as the *London Times* dubbed it, flourished in America. Humanitarianism was a decidedly liberal project premised on the Enlightenment's fundamental hypothesis that all human life is equal.

> The American and French Revolutions' emphasis on natural rights along with the emergence of the mass press, public opinion, and participatory government helped transform humanitarianism into a mass movement ... [and] made humanitarian intervention both politically possible and popular.[103]

The Monroe Doctrine of 1823 essentially declared all of Latin America within the American sphere of influence. Two decades later, in 1854, the Jeffersonian "coercive diplomacy" opened the Japanese ports and commerce to the United States, literally at gunpoint:

> On July 8, 1853 four black ships led by USS Powhatan and commanded by Commodore Matthew Perry, anchored at Edo (Tokyo) Bay. Never before had the Japanese seen ships steaming with smoke. They thought the ships were "giant dragons puffing smoke." They did not know that steamboats existed and were shocked by the number and size of the guns on board the ships. ... Matthew Perry ... brought a letter from the President of the United States, Millard Fillmore, to the Emperor of Japan. He waited with his armed ships and refused to see any of the lesser dignitaries sent by the Japanese, insisting on dealing only with the highest emissaries of the Emperor.

> The Japanese government realized that their country was in no position to defend. ... On March 31, 1854 ... Perry received what he had so dearly worked for—a treaty with Japan. The treaty provided for ... [the] opening of two ports to American ships at Shimoda and Hakodate.[104]

Of course, what the Naval Museum description of Commodore Perry's trip does not say is that Perry combined "vague threats of war with skillful diplomacy,"[105] and that the Japanese were threatened with destruction if they refused to open their ports to US commerce.[106] It is also said that Perry ordered his ships, "equipped with new Paixhans shell guns, cannons capable of wreaking great destruction with every shell to destroy some buildings in the harbor. [Ever since then] the term 'Black Ships' [is] used ... to symbolize a threat imposed by Western technology."[107]

The US war (or invasion, depending on your point of view) with Mexico in 1846 and the Spanish-American War of 1898 that took from Spanish control and gave to American control Cuba, Puerto Rico, Guam, and the Philippine islands, are also examples of this interventionist trend. The occupation of the Philippines was particularly brutal and reflected to some extent this battle between interventionist and idealist traditions in American foreign policy thinking:

The love-hate relationship between the Filipinos and Americans ... will probably never fade away. In 1898, the Aguinaldo republic had defeated the forces of Imperial Spain. In turn, after a bloody four-year war, the United States defeated Aguinaldo and hastily put together a colonial policy that, in its ambivalence, was to reflect the raging domestic debate between the imperialists and the anti-imperialists, the precursors of the doves and the hawks of the great Vietnam War debate.

To please the imperialists, the Philippines were converted into a U.S. economic vassal, the way the British treated India, the French Indochina, and the Dutch Indonesia. However, to please the anti-imperialists the Filipinos were extended a measure of political autonomy and personal freedom superior to that given to any colonial people perhaps in the whole of human history.[108]

Again, to say that American foreign policy before World War II was an isolationist one is a gross oversimplification. America's first declared and congressionally authorized wars were fought in 1798 (against France), 1801and 1815 (in North Africa's waters with Algerian, Libyan, and Moroccan Barbary pirates), and 1812 (against Britain), in the span of only a quarter of a century after the Constitution was ratified by the states. Thereafter, we have the war with Mexico (1846), the Spanish-American War (1898) and the Banana Wars (1912)—a number of limited military actions and interventions, largely on behalf of US commercial interests, particularly the United Fruit Company, in Central and South America. In the Banana Wars, US marines landed in (or invaded) and occupied Panama, Honduras, Nicaragua, Haiti, and the Dominican Republic until the Great Depression forced us to withdraw.[109] While we were still propping up pro-US governments or in effect occupying most of these countries, World War I broke out, and in 1917 our forces joined the Allied Powers.

American foreign policy has therefore always had a strong interventionist component to it. Yet this interventionist component has been driven at times by supposedly humanist motives (as in Jefferson's writings), while at other times, cold self-interest calculations, pursuit of power, and economic resources have clearly been the dominant forces in the shaping of our foreign policy. Mercantilism, realism, neorealism, and imperialism are various labels that have been associated with the latter or a foreign policy based on the use of force for the purpose of economic exploitation of other countries' resources.

Mercantilists and realists were represented early on in American intellectual thinking by another of our founding fathers, Alexander Hamilton, who, unlike Jefferson, thought that wars were caused by reasons independent of the form of government. Therefore, the Jeffersonian ideal of the Republican form of government's ending wars, an idea that we may now see expressed in democratic peace theory,[110] was preposterous.[111]

While our current American government textbook's obligatory chapter on foreign policy does occasionally mention in passing these competing traditions (isolationism versus interventionism and idealism versus realism), the coverage is in a few words, if coverage is offered at all, and there is rarely an attempt to construct models around these ideas or put them in broader theoretical terms.

Methodology of Studying Foreign Policy:
Behavioralist and Traditionalist Approaches

By contrast, international relations (IR) scholars love to model and theorize about foreign policy. At times, their discussions, even in the textbooks, get so theoretical that only the authors themselves might understand what they mean—certainly not the freshmen and sophomores who are supposed to read the textbooks.

For the most part, the problem arises from the rise of the behaviorist (or behavioralist) movement, which began in psychology and spread to the rest of social sciences in the 1950s and 1960s. *Encyclopedia Britannica* defines *behavioralism* as "the view that the subject matter of political science should be limited to phenomena that are independently observable and quantifiable."[112] Once you have the observable and quantitative data, you can empirically test various hypotheses, run regression analysis, model and predict behavior, and the like. While this might apply perfectly well to limited political phenomena, such as voting behavior, its application in international relations and comparative politics is highly questionable. While the math might make sense, the problem arises in operationalization of political variables. How do you operationalize the impact of a country's culture, history, and traditions on decisions made by a national leader? How do you account for your leader, who might be a Christian Evangelist who believes that his or her support for Israel will help bring about the end of days? How do you account for human ego, or the desire for revenge, or pride, for that matter?

Of course, you can come up with nominal categories of data and convince yourself that your operationalization and modeling make sense and call yourself a scientist and get some lucrative grants in the process:

> After the Second World War, the academic discipline of IR expanded rapidly. That was particularly the case in the United States, where government agencies and private foundations were willing to support "scientific" IR research which they could justify as being in the national interest. That support produced a new generation of IR scholars who

adopted a rigorous methodological approach. ... [The] term "behavioralism" ... signified not so much a new theory as [it] was a novel methodology which endeavored to be "scientific" in the natural-science meaning of that term.[113]

Furthermore, the advent of the Cold War and the growth of the defense industry and its associated think tanks meant that there was a lot of research grant money to go around. Governments and think tanks liked the promise of the behavioralist movement; namely, that their approach went beyond description and analysis and could—because of their scientific methods—actually predict events. So, these institutions began to shower political scientists with research money. Besides, political scientists who took this approach could now see themselves as on par with their colleagues in the natural sciences, which were called the hard sciences. The result was a generation of number crunchers who could come up with great R-squares but knew absolutely nothing about the world around them and how it worked. I obviously had the occasion to work with quite a few of them, and I vividly recall how surprised one such scholar of international relations, a decent fellow and a very smart person, was when I expressed an interest in playing basketball with him and few of the other departmental folks. He knew that I was from Iran, and he was absolutely thunderstruck that we had basketball in Iran and that I knew how to play (although, admittedly, not very well). Although I never asked him, I bet he could not find Damascus on a map!

But the reality is that all these models and math do not work well in explaining most international events, even if some people are so sold on them that the Nobel Prize could be awarded to its practitioners. In the process, you have lost your focus on things that really matter, such as knowing where Damascus is—basic geography, history, traditions of a country, the power of ideas, and the background and personality of decision makers and the people who surround them.

Finally, even if you put aside objections to operationalizations of variables in quantitative or so-called "empirical" studies of international relations, the fact remains that these studies have added very little to our knowledge of international relations. Consider, for instance, professor Fred H. Lawson's summary of "key findings from quantitative research."[114]

Lawson writes, "Arguably the most significant finding that has come out of the quantitative scholarship in international relations is the proposition that liberal democratic countries do not go to war with other liberal democracies."[115] I would argue that any college student or even a layperson with basic knowledge of post–World War I Europe could have told us that! If that is the most impressive finding of the quantitative approach—for which conceivably quite a bit of research grants were earned—what are some of the other findings? "Territorial disputes exhibit a particularly strong association with the outbreak of wars."[116] How surprising is it that conflicts over territory have been historically more likely to produce wars? Not surprising at all to people who have studied history.

Opposed to this trend were and are the traditionalists, among whom are international society scholars, constructionists, and postmodernists. This latter group approaches IR not as a value-neutral science, as behavioralists do, and does not believe that there is a law like regularity to international events or that those international events can therefore be easily predicted. Rather, they base their research on history and critical judgment of their own and take into account moral choices that leaders must make.[117]

International society scholars essentially argue that states live in a society of states that, while very different from our human societies, nonetheless has established *societal* norms of behavior, such as respect for the sovereignty of other states and the use of diplomacy to limit conflict. While one can agree that there are norms of behavior in international relations, the observance of these norms seems to vary with the nature and power of states involved in particular interactions. The United States and European powers seem to be constantly interfering in and, indeed, invading other countries, which is a clear violation of the sovereignty principles. Even lesser states constantly intervene in the internal affairs of their neighbors (e.g., Iran, Israel, and Saudi Arabia in Lebanon and Syria; Rwanda and Uganda in Congo; etc.). At times even the time-honored principle of respect for the embassies of other countries is on the verge of violation, as was the case with Britain's threat to arrest WikiLeaks founder Julian Assange, who had taken refuge in the Ecuadorian embassy in London.[118] Interestingly, the British threat, which was not carried through, was followed months later by another undiplomatic move over another leaker, this time Edward Snowden, by the coordinated action of several West European countries when the airspace of these countries was closed to the presidential plane of Bolivian President Morales, which sparked outrage in Latin America.[119] Hence, while there are norms of behavior, their observance seems to vary based on the relative power levels of the states involved and the particulars of the situation.

Constructionists argue that discursive power—a power given to the state by appeal of its culture and ideas to other countries—is just as important as military and economic power. Professor Lawson cites the example of Egypt's Nasser and Egypt's influence in the Arab world and the Middle East in the 1950s as an example of discursive power. Surely, Egypt was the most militarily powerful state, but its power was amplified by the appeal of its president, its culture, and its traditional role within the Arab world.[120] This discursive power is similar to Joseph Nye's concept of "soft power": "Soft Power does not rely on intimidation: it wins hearts and minds. It produces voluntary followers, not reluctant satellites."[121] Constructivists further argue that it is the interpretation of states' leaders of what the norms of behavior are and what to expect from other leaders that forms the basis of their behavior, not the size of their military: "state's actions and policies are based on how leaders, bureaucracies, and societies interpret or *construct* the information available to them. ... A serious threat for one state may not be an issue for another."[122]

Postmodernists challenge the very notion of international relations theory and argue that all these theoretical approaches, including Marxism, are partly created to maintain Western domination. Kevin Dunn, who considers himself to be a postmodernist, describes the problems with current IR theory as follows:

> Western-centric IR theory has created a system of dispositions that posits their historical experiences and cultural values are the norm for the international community. Their assumptions and experiences are passed off as "normal" and have enabled definitions and concepts that privileged this narrow segment of the world's population to become accepted as the norm within IR theory. Because most IR theory begins with ingrained assumptions about world politics based on Western experiences, thoughts, and desires, non-Western examples appear to be abnormal or aberrant and in need of explaining and, more often, fixing.[123]

Identity and our construction of it play a critical role in postmodernist thinking. Dunn, for instance, suggests that the American response to Russian intervention in Georgia in 2006 or the ongoing UN involvement in Congo is shaped in large part by the identities that we in the West have formed about the Russians and the Congolese:

> Can we not all agree that American and Western European responses to the conflict in Georgia have had as much, if not more, to do with their representations of Russian identity than with actual events on the ground? ... Over a century ago, Western representations of an "inherently savage" Congo enabled brutal conquest and colonization. Today, Western representations of an "inherently savage" Congo fuel apathy and inaction in one of the world's worst humanitarian crises, a crisis that the West has been complicit in creating for the last hundred years.[124]

The idea that most of our scholarship has ingrained Western assumptions and is biased is obviously one that this work agrees with and what Edward Said wrote about in his classic *Orientalism*.

Moreover, this book is written in a decidedly traditional approach, and obviously the explanation offered here is based on history, ideas, culture, and moral choices. To be sure, there is a legitimate place for quantitative analysis in the social sciences, particularly in business in marketing, consumer behavior, pricing, and inventory control; in economics and in political science in voting behavior; and even in group behavior, where at times you can use analysis of variance meaningfully. Yet when it comes to the making of foreign policy and predicting what nations and leaders might do, we need people who are area experts, people familiar with the language, culture, and history of countries, and people who are familiar with leaders to analyze their behavior and guide us.

Models of How Foreign Policy Is Made

Modeling of the decision-making process is, however, independent of whether one draws on history or runs multiple regression analysis. There are schools of thought—realism and its variants, liberalism/idealism and its variants, constructionism, gender theories, and Marxism—which have analytical frameworks that can be used by either methodological approach. Furthermore, the discussion within these schools of thought can also be explained, for the most part, in terms of three general models of decision making that are explained in detail in Graham Allison and Philip Zelikow's classic *Essence of Decision: Explaining the Cuban Missile Crisis*. These models are the rational actor model, the organizational process model, and the government politics model. We will look at these models in some detail below. For now, let us state that there is actually a strong connection between the models and levels of analysis and schools of thought. Let us begin with a discussion of *realism*, the oldest school of thought that discusses the formulation of foreign policy.

The realists view the international system as existing in a perpetual state of anarchy. There is no central authority or government that can give cohesion to the international system. Therefore, in this anarchical state, governments must look out for their own self-interest, which is often in conflict with other states. The difference between traditional realists, such as Hans Morgenthau, and neorealists, such as Kenneth Waltz, is that neorealists argue that it is the structure and nature of the international system that causes states to act selfishly and pursue self-interests, not the greedy, selfish nature of humanity.[125]

Furthermore, neorealists completely discard any ethical and moral considerations in this pursuit of power. In the neorealist view, states act as unitary, rational actors to achieve their primary goal, the pursuit and acquisition of power. Foreign policy and, for that matter, American foreign policy are made by rational calculations, devoid of moral and humanistic considerations, and aim to maximize state power. The rational actor model (RAM) fits this thinking very well. In fact Allison and Zelikow propose that the "hard core of classic realism begins with ... basic tenets from RAM,"[126] the *unitary actor* and *rationality* assumptions. This unitary actor is value maximizing and therefore has maximizing national security and the national interest as his core objectives. It follows, then, that states look at the foreign policy decisions through rational lenses with the aim of maximizing power. They look at alternative courses of action, calculate costs and benefits, and choose the alternative that best maximizes power. Yet the classical realist explanation of states' behavior is modified by *neorealist* or *structural realism*, which adds an emphasis on "system-level variables"[127]:

> In its strong form, The Structural Realist research program is similar to that of microeconomics. Both use the rationality assumption to permit inferences about actor behavior to be made from system structure. The Realist definition of interest in terms of power and position is like the economist's assumption about [firms seeking] to maximize profits: it provides the utility function of the actor. Through these assumptions, actor characteristics become constant, rather than variable, and systematic theory becomes possible.[128]

The rational actor model, therefore, fits nicely within either classical or new realist interpretations of state behavior. However, many observers of international relations find the realist approach to be too simple. International institutionalists and liberal critics of neorealism point out the growth of supranational organizations, such as the European Union, the United Nations, the Organization of African Unity, and others, to mock the idea of states as always blindly pursuing their own self-interests. Interdependence, globalization, and shared values, they argue, are increasingly reducing conflicts. States are acting much more on principles of reciprocity and identity than out of pure self-interest and dominance.[129]

But the most significant criticism of realism, and one that brings us to domestic and individual levels of analysis and the organizational process and government bargaining decision-making models, is the argument that the unitary actor nature of states is a product of fiction and vivid imagination. There simply isn't such a thing as a state actor. Rather, there is a multitude of organizations, groups, and people with diverging and often conflicting political and economic interests who make foreign policy decisions, not some unseen mysterious entity called "the state."

Particularly, the bureaucratic decision model, popularized by Graham Allison, argues that bureaucracies—the State Department and the Department of Defense, for example—have established organizational cultures, routines, and procedures that affect the outcome of decisions in which they participate:

> At any given time, a government consists of existing organizations, each with a fixed set of standard operating procedures and programs. The behavior of these organizations—and consequently of the government—relevant to an issue in any particular instance is, therefore, determined primarily by routines established prior to that instance.[130]

Unlike RAM, Allison and Zelikow point out here that the subject of analysis is not the unitary actor represented by the entire government; rather, the subject of analysis is the different organizations who must act in the situation. The organizational culture, capabilities, routines, and standard operating procedures "constrain" their behavior and influence both the "prioritization" of the mission and how tasks are translated into "operational objectives," which alters range of available policy choices and their implementations. Allison and Zelikow cite the example of the first Iraq war, when the political leadership wanted to find and destroy Iraqi scud missiles that were attacking Israeli cities, yet the military commanders did not see the military significance of the missiles and, more importantly, did not have the capability to find and destroy these missiles without diverting their operational plans.

Therefore, these bureaucracies "have their own goals," which is to maintain and expand their influence and promote their "institutional interest." So, the CIA will have different interests and operating procedures than the Department of State will and in its recommendation to the president would rely on its own worldview and earlier operations.

In the Bay of Pigs case, the CIA used the Guatemalan model—the operations "in which the CIA toppled a leftist [President Jacobo Árbenz Guzmán]_dictator with a handful of exiles [in 1954]" as a basis for the operational plan to topple Castro.[131] The CIA reasoned that the operation was a success in Guatemala and it would therefore again be successful in Cuba, another small Latin American country. This decision-making model, therefore, does not picture the decision as an act by a unitary, rational actor in pursuit of national interest. Rather, decisions are made by the combination of outputs of various bureaucracies, each of which has its own routines, culture, interpretation of mission and tasks, and capabilities and might be concerned mostly with the advance of its own institutional interest. Surely, the organizations might even convince themselves that their institutional interest is in the national interest.

This model, therefore, operates at an institutional level of analysis and looks at institutional interests and operating procedures within bureaucracies.

On the other hand, the governmental politics or bargaining model operates at the individual level of analysis and looks at the values and interests of individual leaders and key figures in the decision-making process. Allison and Zelikow point out that

> The leaders who sit atop of organizations are no monolith. Rather, each individual in this group is ... a player in a central competitive game. The name of the game is politics. ... Government behavior can thus be understood, not as organizational outputs, but as the result of bargaining games. ... Foreign policy is thus the extension of politics to other realms.[132]

The model's basic unit of analysis, therefore, is not the unitary actor or the organization; it is the result of interactions among "officials with diverse interests and unequal influence."[133] Allison and Zelikow therefore state that when using this model to analyze actions and behavior of a government, we need to ask very different questions than we do when we rely on RAM or the organizational process model. We need to ask, who are the key decision makers? How do we account for factors affecting their impact on the decision, and "what factors shape [decision makers'] perceptions, preferences and stance"?[134]

It is to the explanation of this latter issue, factors that shape decision makers' perception, preferences, and stance on our foreign policy in the Middle East, that I will now focus.

In the next chapter, I argue that many of the neocons, such as Dick Cheney, are influenced by a biased worldview that is the product of thousands of years of Western feelings of superiority.

Chapter Four

From the Greeks to the Neocons

The Intellectual Foundations of Our Foreign Policy: From Greeks and Romans to Orientalists, Imperial Progressives, Neocons, and Agenda-Driven Pundits

In the previous chapter, we discussed in some detail the thinking of the founding fathers on foreign policy. But where did the founding fathers get their ideas about foreign policy? Some ideas, such as Washington's avoidance of foreign entanglements, were uniquely American and were shaped by the historical experience of the War of Independence and the British and French governments' constant interference, wars, and pressures on the Americas, as well as America's geographic position.

Yet other ideas, particularly the interventionist thread, such as the Jeffersonian desire to spread democracy, have parallels in European thought and history. Athens and its Delian League similarly used the spread of democracy as a justification for the Athenian Empire. Similarly, the notion of America's moral superiority—expressed explicitly by Jefferson and champions of *American exceptionalism*—has parallels in the Greek, Roman, Crusader, and orientalist thought that shaped much of European justification for the invasions and occupation of the Orient.

In recent times, Bernard Lewis has been one of the main champions of orientalism. Lewis's publication of *What Went Wrong: The Clash Between Islam and Modernity in the Middle East* is in the true orientalist tradition. Because its publication was around the time of the tragic events of 9/11, Lewis's book made the circles of neocons, and he was then invited to the White House to share his biased wisdom with the Bush administration.[135]

Although we are not privy to what was discussed in that meeting, we can take a good guess at what kind of advice the administration received. In a later interview, speaking of Iran, Lewis told the interviewer that the mullahs of Iran "are religious fanatics with an apocalyptic mindset. In Islam, as in Christianity and Judaism, there is an end-of-times scenario and they think [it is] beginning or has already begun." So "mutually assured destruction is not a deterrent—it is an inducement."[136]

How would you negotiate with people who are fanatics and welcome the end of world? Of course, you cannot! One cannot fail to see a striking similarity and connection to Aeschylus's play and portrayal of Persians as emotional or the Roman view of the peoples of *Babaricum* (discussed below) again as emotional and governed by their base needs.

This idea that Iranian leaders are irrational and, therefore, we must attack an irrational Iran to prevent it from having nuclear bombs also happens to be a favorite theme of neocons and the pro-Israeli lobby, who want a war with Iran to advance Israel's agenda in the region at the expense of American blood and treasure.

Consider, for instance, Matthew Kroenig's piece in *Foreign Affairs*. Kroenig, who is a fellow at the Council on Foreign Relations, wrote in 2012, "The truth is that a military strike intended to destroy Iran's nuclear program, if managed carefully, could spare the region and the world a very real threat and dramatically improve the long-term national security of the United States,"[137] and he based his opinion in part on the dangers presented by an irrational Iranian leadership.

Of course, his work was immediately criticized and shown for the piece of propaganda that it was.[138] Furthermore, Kenneth Waltz, who was considered by many to be the most prominent international relations theory expert before his recent passing, argued that, on the contrary, a nuclear Iran would stabilize the Middle East, and Iran emerging with nuclear weapons would be the best possible outcome of the current standoff.[139] Waltz made his arguments in the same journal, *Foreign Affairs*, which sank to a new low by publishing Kroenig's article.

Whether Lewis and lobbyists such as Kroenig[140] are wrong because, as in the case of Lewis, they are caught up in their own orientalist worldview (Lewis thinks that syphilis is *still* called the "Frankish disease" in Persian)[141] or whether they are wrong, as in the case of American Israel Public Affairs Committee (AIPAC) and neocon lobbyists, because they want to advance an agenda favored by the right wing of Israeli policy is immaterial.

Then, of course, neocons are joined by those in our foreign policy establishment—liberal interventionists and imperial progressives—who simply seek American dominance and hegemony and would say anything to justify their agenda.[142] Some of these people may genuinely believe in American superiority, both in terms of the country's values and its historical role in the world. These liberal interventionists may truly see America as the champion of good democratic values (the Athens of the Delian League) whose mission is to spread its system across the globe, by force if necessary. If tens of thousands of the people whom we are trying to help by the imposition of our ideas are killed or maimed in the process, it is justified as the price of progress.

Centuries before Rudyard Kipling's 1899 poem "The White Man's Burden" was written to exhort the glories of colonialism and justify the British Empire, Roman historians justified their conquest of others in similar terms: "Many of Ammianus's references ... reflected a widely held belief in Rome's divinely sanctioned mission to establish order through the imposition of empire. ... This was Rome's imperial burden".[143] Consider what Kelly calls some of the most quoted lines of Publius Vergilius Maro (Virgil, 70 BC–19 BC), who is considered among the greatest Roman poets and whose "Aeneid" is a cornerstone of the Western canon:[144]

> Remember through your empire to rule Earth's peoples—
> for your arts are to be these:
> To pacify, to impose the rule of law,
> To spare the vanquished, and war down the proud.[145]

The liberal interventionists who share this view of a Roman imperial burden are joined by people whom I call imperial progressives. These are media talk show hosts (Chris Matthews is a prominent example)[146] who favor progressive ideas for the people who live within the territorial United States, but somehow stop being progressive when we move abroad. They do not question our alliance with an apartheid state such as Israel, which treats fully a quarter of its population as second-class citizens. Yet they are outraged (and justifiably so) if a small state such as Iowa attempts to disenfranchise a minority group by manipulating voting requirements.

Neither do they question or criticize the American alliance with repressive states such as Saudi Arabia, the Egyptian military, and various African and Asian autocracies. Imperial progressives, in general, support the American empire and throw out human rights, democratic values, international law, or any similar consideration if they conflict with what they consider to be the security interests of America—an interest that is the interest of the political and economic elite and not the average decent, hardworking American who does not even know what is happening abroad. These imperials support unilateral and American military action against potential rivals (for example, an unprovoked attack on Iran), while such action is quite illegal unless mandated by the United Nations or in self-defense in response to an imminent danger. Their support of international law ends at the border.[147]

The Clash of Civilizations

The continuity of a Greek sense of superiority, part of which was based on Greece's reliance on laws as opposed to the chaotic *barbaros*, is striking here.

Today, this attitude is best reflected in the writings of neocons who justify the American empire in similar terms: bringing democracy and civilization to the poor backward Asians, Africans, and Middle Easterners or as a bulk ward against the spread of Islam.[148]

Consider the thought process of Samuel P. Huntington, whose book *The Clash of Civilizations and the Remaking of the World Order* provides this astonishing advice: "The survival of the West depends on Americans reaffirming their Western identity … and uniting to preserve it from non-Western societies."[149]

Huntington's thoughts are in the true tradition of orientalist thinking immortalized in Edward Said's classic *Orientalism*: "Orientalism is a style of thought based upon an ontological and epistemological distinction between 'the Orient' and (most of the time) 'the Occident.' Thus a very large mass of writers … have accepted the basic distinction between East and West as the starting point for elaborate theories … and political accounts concerning the Orient, its people, custom, 'mind,' destiny, and so on."[150]

Although Said argues that this system of thought was largely the product of the French and the British colonial experience and was created in part to justify their actions, he does mention that "since World War II America has dominated the Orient and approaches it as France and Britain once did."[151] Underlying the orientalist thought system is a "relationship of power, of domination, of varying degree of a complex hegemony. … Orientalism depends for its strategy on this flexible positional superiority. … Now because Britain, France, and recently the United States are Imperial powers, their political societies impart to their civil societies sense of urgency."[152]

Huntington's writings and his concern about survival of the West provide a perfect example of the political society imparting the sense of urgency to its civil society that Said wrote about years before the publication of *The Clash of Civilizations*.

Yes, indeed! Islamic radicals are coming and want to impose Sharia law on us, at least according to Oklahoma's legislators and their proposed legislation HB 1060. The HB 1060's author, Frank Gaffney, who incidentally served in 1980s as deputy assistant secretary in the Department of Defense, says, "It is not to say that all Muslims are a threat. … It is the case, however, that those who embrace and submit to Sharia and insist on, according to its doctrine, making the rest of us submit to it, are a danger."[153]

This is a reflection of the thought process of Huntington translated and executed down to the local level.

Part of the result is a vicious Islamophobia that now permeates our society and manifests itself in several manners, from the aforementioned ridiculous passage of laws to prevent Sharia law from becoming state law, to opposing the construction of mosques, to attacking any American of Islamic background who is achieving national prominence.

This has gotten to the point that even faithful and trusted State Department employees who have an Islamic background are not immune. A recent example is found in the attacks on Huma Abedin, the wife of former Congressman Anthony Weiner. Abedin was born in Kalamazoo, Michigan, and is a graduate of George Washington University. Abedin served as the deputy chief of staff for Hillary Clinton, who might someday become the president of the United States. But even such high and exalted association does not preclude her from being accused of having a secret Islamic agenda, simply because her parents are from Saudi Arabia. A *National Review Online* article even went so far as to assert that Abedin's marriage is part of her secretive agenda to push a Muslim supremacist agenda in America:

> What a racket. The marriage to Huma Abedin, a Clinton insider, enables Anthony Weiner to resurrect a debased career and deflect attention from his psychotic antics even as he continues them. The marriage to Anthony Weiner, a prominent Jewish progressive, enables Huma Abedin to deflect attention from her associations with various Islamic supremacists even as, during her tenure as a top State Department official, American policy embraces Islamic supremacists.[154]

As Dr. Reza Aslan, an Iranian American professor of creative writing and a religious studies scholar at the University of California, Riverside, pointed out, if Abedin has a secretive Islamic agenda, she needs to rethink her strategy, because her husband is a pro-Israeli politician who denies that there is such a thing as an Israeli occupation of the West Bank and considered the Palestinian Authority's ambassadors to the United Nations to be terrorists.[155]

The most recent and vivid example of orientalism was demonstrated when Fox News interviewer Lauren Green interviewed Aslan. Green questioned how a Muslim scholar could possibly write an objective book about Jesus of Nazareth. The interview was so outrageous that it went viral, and Reza's book became an overnight best-seller.

Rachel Newcomb of the *Huffington Post* immediately made the connection to orientalism and after discussing Edward Said's work, she writes:

> For the past few hundred years, the most widely read books about Islam in the West have been written by non-Muslims. This is still largely the case: the authors whose bestselling books about Islam and Muhammad that you are most likely to read include Karen Armstrong, John Esposito, and even Deepak Chopra. To write about a subject and have many people read your words as authoritative pronouncements carries, in itself, a kind of power. It is for that reason that Aslan's Muslimness is threatening. Usually we write about them, and not the other way around. In response to the interviewer's repeated questioning of his background, Aslan replies, "It's not that I'm just some Muslim writing about Jesus—I am an expert with a PhD in the history of religions." But even Aslan's twenty years of academic study, plus the thousand references he uses to write his book, are not enough to convince Green that he has the right to be the one writing about us.[156]

However, attacks on Islam and Muslims in America are not limited to the conservative and right-wing sections of society and media outlets such as Fox. Chief among progressive critics of Islam is Bill Maher, who uses instances of outrageous actions by radicals and extremists who claim to be true Muslims as fodder for his anti-Islamic rants. The latest example of Maher's attacks was broadcasted on *Real Time with Bill Maher* on May 9, 2014.[157] Maher used the tragic kidnapping of innocent Nigerian schoolgirls by Boko Haram in March and April and the subsequent video rant of its fanatical leader Abubakar Shekau announcing his intention to sell the schoolgirls into slavery as an example of how evil and bad Islam is. Of course, Bill Maher did not mention that top Muslim scholars of world's largest block of Islamic countries (the Organization of Islamic Cooperation) unequivocally condemned this action. The Muslim scholars further said that "this "crime and other crimes committed by the likes of these extremist organisations contradicts all humanitarian principles and moral values and violates the provisions of the Koran and Sunna"—or teachings of the Prophet Muhammad."[158]

What Maher did in his show was akin to making the ridiculous argument that Christianity is an evil religion because a fanatic and opportunist Christian and former Catholic altar boy, Joseph Kony, and his Lord's Resistance Army "abduct children and force the boys to become fighters and keep the girls as sex slaves … [and force boys] to kill their own parents."[159] After all, Kony claims that he wants to create a government based on the Ten Commandments, a claim similar to Boko Haram's claim that they are fighting to install a government based on the Quran.

What Bill Maher and other liberal critics of Islam do here is use anecdotal evidence—horrendous actions by a few Muslims—to paint all Muslims in a negative light. This is guilt by association and should be dismissed for the bigotry that it is. Unfortunately, when these views are repeatedly expressed by media figures and talk show hosts and even appear in print, the public opinion of Muslims, including hardworking and law-abiding Muslim citizens of America, is negatively affected.

American foreign policy advisors and decision makers also come from this public, and this negative image of Muslims that is constantly broadcasted even on the progressive shows might affect their worldview and decisions. Of course, in civil society itself it has and will continue to create stereotypes for Muslim Americans and increase bias and discrimination against them.

Barbaros: The Origin of Orientalism

I argue that this intellectual trend, the belief in the heroic role of the *good and superior* Western civilization against the evil of Easterners, however, predates eighteenth- and nineteenth-century colonialism and Islam and goes even further back in history than Rome to its intellectual source: Ancient Greece. The actual clash of civilizations does indeed seem to go back a long way. Have you ever seen an Olympic event called the marathon?

> The fight at Marathon went on for a long time, and in the center the barbarians won, where the Persians themselves and the Sacae were stationed. But on each wing the Athenians … were victorious. … As the Persians fled, the Greeks followed them … until they came to the sea. With the rest of the fleet, the barbarians rounded Cape Sunium, because they wished to get to Athens before the Athenians could reach it.[160]

Note how Herodotus refers to the Persians of the storied Persian Empire as "barbarians," which gave us the first declaration of human rights (the Cyrus cylinder), the first highway system (the royal highways connecting Susa, Persepolis, and Sardis), and the origins of our postal system. Furthermore, setting aside the dispute over the causes of the Persian withdrawal (did they withdraw to capture Athens, or were they defeated?), the fact remains that every four years with a marathon at the Olympics, we continue to celebrate the Athenians' successful run back to their city.

The battle of Marathon is, of course, only one instance where a Greek battle with the Persians has been deemed as crucial to the survival of Western civilization. Amazingly, even the Greeks' defeat at the battle of Thermopylae (480 BC) has been described as a savior of all things good,[161] and, of course, Hollywood had to get into the act by creating a bizarre portrait of the Persians and romanticizing militaristic and fascistic Spartans as the saviors of democracy (Farrokh).

Herodotus traces back the East-West divide to the battle of Troy:

> [The Persians say] it is the work of unjust men, we think, to carry off women at all … [but the Persians] made no accounts of the women carried off from Asia but the Greeks, because of a Lacedaemonian woman, gathered a great army, came straight to Asia, and destroyed the Power of Priam.[162]

Some may argue that the first work that portrayed the Persians as the enemy was *The Capture of Miletus* (499 BC) by the Greek playwright Phrynicus, who was fined for the negative impact on the Athenian population. It is said that the whole of Greece mourned the fall of the city.[163] However, Hall argues that it goes back to Aeschylus's play *Persae* in 472 BC. Hall points out that while in archaic Greece, during the Trojan War, such an us-versus-them attitude did not exist yet, even the Trojan War could now be reinterpreted:

> Priam was a King, Hector a hero, Memmnon the Son of Dawn, and Medea a sorceress; to the fifth century theatre goer an essential aspect of such figures identity was that they were barbarians (Hall, 1989, p. 54). [Therefore, later

on], the story of the Trojan War could now be interpreted as a precursor of recent history, a previous defeat of Asia by Hellas. [In fact] the Polygnotus' mural in the Stoa Poikile[164] [depicts] the victory at Marathon. ... Alongside the victories of Theseus & Heracles over the Trojans.[165]

Admittedly, Greek and Persian relations were complex. Many Greeks served as mercenaries in Persian armies (immortalized in Xenophon's *Anabasis* and his account of the retreat of survivors of a Greek mercenary army), and Persian gold often bought Greek heroes.[166]

> Greeks and Persians had a long history of official and casual intercourse. Warfare, at every temperature from outright hostility to diplomacy in times of uneasy peace, played a large part in their interactions, but there were also many cultural contacts. ... In the fifth century heyday of Athenian interest in Persia, eastern artistic motifs and styles decorated Athenian pots, clothing and luxury items, and references to the Persians, especially to Greek victories over them, abounded in all forms of entertainment—in literature, sculpture, painting and rhetoric. ... The Greeks learnt (or relearnt, after the Dark Ages) from the east how to work bronze and construct monumental buildings. ... [167]

Furthermore, not all Greek works about Persians were unsympathetic. It is said that many scholars view Aeschylus's play *The Persians*, also known as *Persae* (472 BC), as sympathetic, or, as Edward Said puts it in "The Persians," "The Orient is transformed from a very far distant and often threatening Otherness into figures that are relatively familiar."[168]

Nonetheless, Greek historians such as Herodotus and Xenophon had this sense of Greece as a nation different from and *superior to* the Asiatic that began perhaps with Troy, continued with the fall of Miletus in 499 BC and the battles of Marathon (490 BC) and Thermopylae (480 BC), and continued to the fall of the Persian Empire in 330 BC (map 8 shows the Persian Empire). In fact, Hassan Pirnia, who drew largely on the work of Greek and Roman historians to write his three-volume history of Iran, *(Tarikh-e) Iran-e Bastan* ([History of] Ancient Iran), says of the Greek historians that Herodotus did not like Pars or Parsi (Persia and Persians), and Plutarch in particular was so pro-Greek that his writings are full of sorrow whenever the Persians got the better of the Greeks.[169]

Edith Hall, in *Inventing the Barbarian: Greek Self-Definition Through Tragedy*, provides further evidence that the East-West divide, particularly the view of Easterners as *genetically inferior, barbaric in customs and actions, and of lower moral character*, solidified during the fifth century as the result of the Persian wars:

> The polarization of Hellene & barbarian was invented in specific historical circumstances during the early years of the fifth century B.C.,

partly as a result of the combined Greek military efforts against the Persians. ... The image of an enemy extraneous to Hellas helped to foster a sense of community between allied states. ...

It was the fifth century which invented the notion of the barbarian as the universal anti-Greek against whom Hellenic—especially Athenian—culture was defined. ...

[After Aeschylus's *Persae*] *barbaros* at first primarily [referred] to the Persians, but because their empire covered so many of the people with whom the Greeks had contact—the Egyptians, Phoenicians, Phrygians, Thracians—it was soon to acquire the generic sense of denoting all non-Greeks which was to reflect and bolster the Greeks' sense of their own superiority. ... [170]

What is even more startling is that the Greeks' sense of superiority was not confined to the cultural and political realms. Hall argues that because the economic foundation of the Athenian polity was slavery and because the majority of the slaves were non-Greek or *barbaros*, a class division along ethnic lines emerged "which provided stimulus for the generations of arguments which supported the belief that barbarians

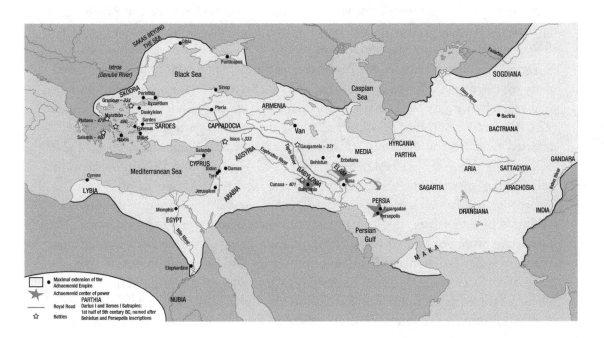

Map 8. Map of the Persian Empire

Source: Copyright © 2006 by Fabienkhan / Wikimedia Commons / CC BY-SA 2.5.

were genetically inferior, even slavish by nature."[171] One cannot help noticing how similar this view is to Curzon's view of the Persians (discussed above) as timid.

Thereafter, after about two centuries of interruption, another Iranian power rose in Iran that *threatened the Greek cultural successors: the Romans*.

In the Battle of Carrhae in 53 BC, a year before Eburones, in the deeply wooded forests of *barbaricum* in Eastern Belgium, had wiped out a legion and five additional cohorts[172] of the Roman army, thousands of miles to the east, in the deserts of Mesopotamia, an Iranian (Parthian) army of nine thousand light cavalry and one thousand heavy cavalry routed a Roman army four times its size. The Romans were under the command of Marcus Lucinius Carssus, who had defeated Spartacus twenty years earlier and who, along with Julius Caesar and Pompey the Great, was a member of the First Triumvirate. The Romans lost twenty thousand legionnaires, and the Iranian forces took another ten thousand Roman prisoners and several legion standards and executed Crassus. Rome was humiliated.

In 2 BC, the Roman emperor Augustus ordered the reenactments of the Persian Wars in *Salaminian Naumachia* to symbolize Rome as the inheritor of the Greek legacy and as a champion of that culture, and to equate Arsacid Iran with Achaemenid Iran and prepare Rome for an Eastern campaign. However, by 20 BC, Augustus had recognized that Rome had met its match in the Parthian Dynasty and agreed to settle on the Euphrates as the permanent border between the two empires. Nonetheless, Augustus had to ideologically explain why the superior Romans had renounced the capture of territories beyond the Euphrates. Augustus therefore redefined Iran as the *alter orbis*, "a degenerate world, whose conquest was undesirable for Rome," and equated the Arsacid Iran with Achaemenid Iran, from whom the Parthians inherited their degeneracy, despotism, and love of luxury.[173]

Despite the Augustan peace, the Parthians and the Romans continued to war intermittently over Armenia, Mesopotamia, Syria, and other territories for more than four hundred years. However, it was the rise of Parthian's successive Persian dynasty, the Sasanid (224 AD to 651 AD) that drastically changed the picture, particularly after Shapur I defeated three Roman emperors (Gordia III, 238–244 AD; Philip the Arab, 244–249 AD; and Valerian, 253–259 AD). Shapur captured Valerian, and Valerian became the only Roman emperor who was ever captured and kept as a "prisoner of war."[174]

Because the Romans, similar to the Greeks, viewed the Iranians like other inhabitants of *Babaricum*, the Iranian victories once again presented a dilemma. The barbarians were considered to be "lesser human beings," whose bodies ruled their minds. The barbarians were irrational and were "always being blown all over the place by chance events. ... [The] barbarian society was collectively inferior: a world where might equaled right. The Barbarians thus provided the crucial other in the Roman self-image: the inferior society whose failings underlined and legitimized the superiorities of [Rome]."[175]

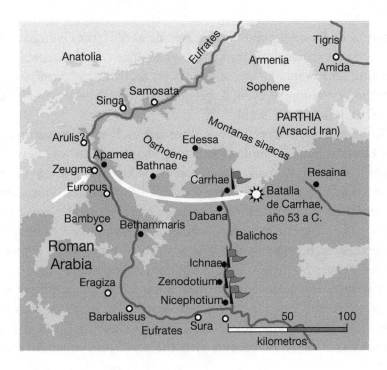

Map 9. The Battle of Carrhae and the Parthian Empire

In fact, these barbarians were subhuman. Therefore, not only was it right for Rome to conquer their lands; it was also quite acceptable for the civilized Romans to slaughter the "Other." It was all right, for instance, for Romans to slaughter more than thirty-nine thousand inhabitants of Avaricum, a Gallic city of forty thousand, as Julius Caesar did in 52 BC, or to feed the captured German Frankish kings Ascaricus and Merogaisus to wild beasts, as Constantine did in 306 AD.[176] After all, barbarians were not really rational, thinking humans like Romans were.

More importantly, notice how strikingly similar Roman views of the *irrational* barbarian are to today's political discourse by American officials about the "madmen" of the Middle East and North Korea, and Bernard Lewis's view that you cannot negotiate with irrational Iranians. And note how strikingly similar the Romans' view of their own superiority in justifying their empire is to our self-assigned American exceptionalism and belief in the superiority of our political system to those of countries we count as adversaries.

Just like Rome had divine favor behind its efforts, we seem to think that God has indeed blessed us—in fact, our presidents end their speeches with "God bless America." We, just like Romans, believe that as a superior society we should always emerge victorious, and we cannot cope with resistance and setbacks.

So, then, how does one explain the repeated defeats of (the civilized and superior) Romans by a single (barbarian) Iranian king? Shapur's victories could not be dismissed as a one-time event, a fluke of history, as the Romans dismissed Ambiorix's victory over the Romans in 54 BC in Belgium or Arminius's destruction of the Roman army in 9 AD at Teutoburger Wald.

Worse, Roman armies facing Shapur were led by Roman emperors, and unlike Ambiorix's Eburones and Arminius's Bructeri, Shapur's Iran was never conquered by Rome and in between Roman victories continued to inflict defeat after defeat on Rome. How would you then explain these defeats to the citizens of the empire?

The solution that the Romans found was the method used by governments from time immemorial to explain the inexplicable: they simply lied. When, in 363 AD, another Iranian king (Chosroes) defeated and killed the Roman emperor (Julian) and forced his successor (Jovian) to sign a humiliating treaty so that the remainder of the Roman army could escape with their lives, the Roman emperor simply produced coinage that read PERSIAN PEACE as a victory. The emperor then sent out his spokesperson Themistius to reinforce the point by claiming that the Persians had accepted Jovian as an emperor, because after the peace proclamation, they put aside their spears.[177]

Although it is hardly ever discussed in history textbooks and classes, the rise of a new Iranian power in the East had profound consequences for Rome:

> Nothing could better symbolize the new world order. The rise of Sasanians destroyed what was by then more or less a century of Roman hegemony in the East. Rome's overall strategic situation had suddenly and decisively deteriorated, for the Sasanian superpower, this new Persian dynasty ... marshaled the resources of Mesopotamia and the Iranian Plateau much more efficiently. ... The rise of a rival superpower was a huge strategic shock ... for the [Roman] empire as a whole.[178]

One consequence for Rome was an increase in the size of its standing army from around three hundred thousand to around four hundred thousand. Obviously, the army needed to be paid, and that necessitated tapping all financial sources, which in turn necessitated a complete and "massive restructuring of the Roman Empire."[179]

The second consequence of the rise of the Persian superpower was that Rome had to marshal its resources for the Eastern front, which resulted in the absence of emperors and their accompanying ability to create and support a patronage system in the West. As historian Peter Heather mentions, the breakdown of the patronage system created a form of "military anarchy" in the Western parts of the Roman Empire.[180]

The two superpowers continued to battle until the very end of the Sasanian Dynasty (629 AD) and the advent of the Islamic conquest of Iran.

At times, the Iranians won victories and even at one point reached and surrounded Constantinople (625–627 AD). At times the Romans won, and under Heraclius (627 AD), the Romans broke the siege of Constantinople and pushed to the heart of the Sasanid Empire. Heraclius's victory ended the last war between the empires. Yet, the war had taken thirty years and left both exhausted and vulnerable to the Arab armies advancing from Saudi Arabia under the banner of Islam.

As discussed earlier, one would think that the numerous Roman defeats at the hands of the rival Persian superpower might change their inherited superior Greek view of themselves and that the Romans might have come to view the Persians on equal cultural terms. However, that did not turn out to be the case. The Romans referred to both mostly illiterate and pastoral Germanic tribes and the highly advanced, sophisticated Persians as barbarians.[181]

By Constantine's time and his conversion to Christianity, another factor reinforced the negative views that the Romans held for their neighbors. It is important to note that the "Other" by now had an additional element to be frightened of: the Zoroastrian religion. While, unlike in Augustus's time, the Romans could no longer deify their emperors, their "divine status was retained in Christian-Roman propaganda's portrayal of God as handpicking individual emperors to rule with Him. ... At the top end of Roman society, the adoption of Christianity thus made no difference to the age old contention that the Empire was God's vehicle in the world," and, therefore, Roman imperialism and superiority were justified.[182]

Furthermore, while it is now the established consensus that the Achaemenids of the Persian Empire were followers of Zoroaster, they were quite tolerant of the religions of others. The Sasanids, however, made Zoroastrianism the state religion and considered the Iranian Christians to be a fifth column for a Christian Rome, and that fueled the rivalry between the empires even more.

The famous *Naqsh e Rustom* inscription by Shapur I begins with religious references and ends with religious references, while discussing the annihilation of Roman legions:

> I, the Mazda worshipping lord Shapur, king of kings of Iran and non-Iran, whose lineage is from the Gods, son of the Mazda worshipping divinity Ardashir, king of kings of Iran, whose lineage is from the Gods, grandson of king Papak, am ruler of Iranshahr, [I hold?] the lands:
>
> Persis, Parthia, Khuzistan, Mesene, Assyria, Adiabene, Arabia, Azerbaijan, Armenia, Georgia. ... [183]

[...]

In the third campaign, when we attacked Carrhae and Urhai [Edessa] and were besieging Carrhae and Edessa Valerian Caesar marched against us. He had with him a force of 70,000 from Germany, Raetia. ... [184]

And beyond Carrhae and Edessa we had a great battle with Valerian Caesar. We made prisoner ourselves with our own hands Valerian Caesar and the others, chiefs of that army, the praetorian prefect, senators; we made all prisoners and deported them to Persis. And Syria, Cilicia and Cappadocia and men of the Roman Empire, of non-Iranians, we deported. We settled them in the Empire of Iran in Persis, Parthia, Khuzistan, in Babylonia and in other lands where there were domains of our father, grandfathers and of our ancestors. [185]

Besides the religious identification, there are several other interesting observations from this passage, which, despite the length of the quotation here, is much longer in the inscription.

First, a single Iranian king defeated the legendary Roman army on three separate occasions, in a span of several decades and captured or killed several Roman emperors. As discussed earlier, this had enormous ramifications for Rome and resulted in a restructuring of the empire.

Second, the use of the words "Iranshahr" (Iran city), "Iran," and "non-Iran" is quite significant. Despite the erroneous assumption by many so-called Iran experts who, as is the case with most neocons and orientalists, are ill informed and who think that the current territorial Iran was called Iran only after 1935, the truth of the matter is that Iranians themselves always called the country Iran. Even before Shapur's times, we can find evidence of the reference to the land as Iran Avej (the land of Aryans) as far back as Achaemenids in the sixth and fifth centuries BC. This fact further implies that Iranians have always had a sophisticated view and understanding of nationhood and of their own identity, and that in turn has implications for current US foreign policy.[186]

While the passage portrays the importance of religion for Sasanian kings, and that exacerbated the conflict with Christian Rome, it is noteworthy that the Romans returned the favor and not only prosecuted Zoroastrians but also manipulated the religion to portray a worse image of the Iranians.

Dr. Mehdi Estakhr's monumental two-volume work *The Place of Zoroaster in History* makes precisely this point:

[This] study serves in part as a contribution to the general theme of "Orientalism" and the concept of the "Oriental Other," as it will show that the ideas ascribed to Zoroaster, when politically conditioned, as they were for most of the Period in the Christian Eastern Roman Empire, were manipulated to form public opinion against the "Other."[187]

When Iran was overrun by Islamic armies and converted to Islam in the seventh century, the religious division was still there—Zoroastrianism was simply replaced by Islam. Although modern scholarship portrays a somewhat more complicated picture of the Islamic conquest of Iran and suggests that the Parthian noble families who were running Iran before the Sasanians continued to hold sway in Eastern and Northern Iran as client rulers of the Umayyads (see map 10),[188] the picture from the Christian West would not have included these internal differences.

It was then that the armies of Islam began their advance in Christian Europe and North Africa, a series of wars that later on included the Crusades and the Spanish re-conquest.

The Crusades

It was in 1095 that Pope Urban II called on the faithful of Europe to go to the rescue of the Byzantine Empire and to exterminate the enemies of Christianity—the Seljuk Turks. The Turks were "an accursed race," and "it was Christian duty to 'exterminate this vile race from our lands.'"[189]

The first Crusader army, composed of several smaller armies and numbering forty thousand to sixty thousand, began its march soon after Urban's speech and started the extermination process, not by killing Muslims in the Middle East, but by persecuting long-established Jewish communities in France and Germany. At times, the Jews were simply slaughtered. At other times they were given a choice between conversion to Christianity and death, or if they were truly lucky, the Jews managed to escape with their lives and faith intact, in return for payments to Crusader leaders such as Peter the Hermit. This first Crusader army never reached the Holy Land and was annihilated in Hungary or further east by Turkish armies.[190]

Three years later, the Crusaders (who sent in two armies of sixty thousand and one hundred thousand) captured Jerusalem and began the extermination process by slaughtering forty thousand innocent Jews and Muslims who had lived there in harmony with Christians for almost five centuries after the Islamic conquest.[191]

This was the opening salvo in a war fueled by religious bigotry that forever changed the composition and politics of the Middle East and helped shaped to this day Western views on Middle Easterners. The barbarians were still in the East, only now they were called Muslims, and their subjugation—and, indeed, extermination—had received divine blessings. To this day, as Karen Armstrong points out, the word "crusade" has a positive connotation in Western dialogue, as in "the crusade against poverty."[192] Our culture still views this bloody and sad episode in history of humanity with approval—at least subconsciously.

The Crusader mentality continues to shape our politicians', academics', and anchormen's and anchorwomen's views. As Julian Glover of the *Guardian* wrote in 2009,

> The great Crusader forts, 9/11, Iraq and Afghanistan are all part of the same thing, an unresolved conflict between the Christian and Islamic worlds—a war that has at times been hot, at times cold, which has often been fought in a secular disguise and in which the west has frequently been the aggressor. ... John Burton, Blair's former constituency agent, says, "It's very simple to explain the idea of Blair the warrior. It was part of Tony Blair living out his faith." In the prime minister's eyes, Iraq "was all part of the Christian battle; good should triumph over evil."[193]

Nothing reflects the Crusaders' mentality in the thinking of our leaders better than the words of Lt. Gen. William G. "Jerry" Boykin, who was the deputy undersecretary of defense for intelligence in 2003 and who cast his pursuit of Osama bin Laden in Crusader terms:

> [Boykin appeared] before a religious group in Oregon in June [2003] to declare that radical Islamists hated the United States "because we're a Christian nation, because our foundation and our roots are Judeo-Christian ... and the enemy is a guy named Satan."

> Discussing the battle against a Muslim warlord in Somalia, Boykin told another audience, "I knew my God was bigger than his. I knew that my God was a real God and his was an idol."

> "We in the army of God, in the house of God, kingdom of God have been raised for such a time as this," Boykin said last year.[194]

Christian evangelism in the United States armed forces is not isolated to General Boykin. The cadets at the Air Force Academy in Colorado Springs, where the elite of the American Air Force are trained, have reported considerable religious pressure, "mostly from evangelical Christians at the school, and are afraid to complain for fear of reprisals."[195]

Regardless of how far back in history one might want to go—the *Ancient world*, the *Crusades*, or *The White Man's Burden*—this idea of West versus East and the superiority of Western ways has long roots and has at its core the faulty analyses of

Map 10. Map of the Sasanid Empire at Its Height around 610–627 AD

Source: Copyright © 2013 by Gabagool / Wikimedia Commons / CC BY 1.0.

orientalists and neocons that have shaped so much of our misguided foreign policy in recent years.

The bottom line is that these analysts have been consistently wrong about events in the Middle East (think Iraq, Afghanistan, and the not-so-fast attempted regime change in Syria). Yet they do advise the executive branch and therefore push successive US administrations to adopt foreign policy initiatives that are not only immoral but actually hurt America's national security in the long run.

Neocons and Agenda-Driven Pundits

There is considerable overlap between the names of orientalists such as Huntington and agenda-driven pundits and neocons. But who are these people?

Professor Flynt Leverett, who served in the Department of State, the CIA, and the National Security Council (NSC), and his wife, Hillary Mann Leverett, who also served at the Department of State and the NSC and also actually met and conducted negotiations with Iranian officials, have put together a list of these people and a lucid discussion of their thinking:

> Neocons argued ... the case for ... American pursuit of empire like hegemony, largely through military action. ... [These] proponents ... linked by ties of family, education, and mentorship—included Elliott Abrams, John Bolton, Max Boot, David Brooks, Eliot Cohen ... Francis Fukuyama ... Robert Kagan, Fredrick Kagan, Zalmy Khalizad, Charles Krauthammer, William Kristol ... Richard Perle ... Paul Wolfowitz, James Woosley and David Wurmser. ... Their efforts to shape public debate have been reinforced ... by Niall Ferguson and Robert Kaplan who ... advocate the creation of a new "Liberal empire."
>
> The Middle East is a special focus for neocons, who believe ... Western civilization [is] embodied by Israel. ... They have urged ... Washington ... [to use] assertive application of hard power to root out bad regimes and replace them with ones prepared to accept American hegemony and Israel regional dominance.[196]

There are several very important points in this short passage.

First, note that the architects of the Iraq War, Paul Wolfowitz and Richard Perle, the so-called intellectual fathers of the war, and their propagandists on Fox News, Charles Krauthammer and William Kristol, are on this list.

Second, add Donald Rumsfeld to this list. He worked with Dick Cheney and Anthony Scalia while he was the chief of staff for President Gerald Ford, and met others during the Reagan administration when he was appointed as special envoy to the Middle East, where in 1983 he met Saddam and they shook hands.

Third, note their allegiance to Israel and their view that Israel must achieve regional hegemony with the support of the United States. Of course, they have their allies in the media who help propagate their message. Chief among them is Wolf Blitzer, who is now a central figure in the supposedly objective CNN. Blitzer has been a member of the American-Israeli Public Affairs Committee (AIPAC), the most aggressive pro-Israeli lobby in the United States. And what was Blitzer doing at

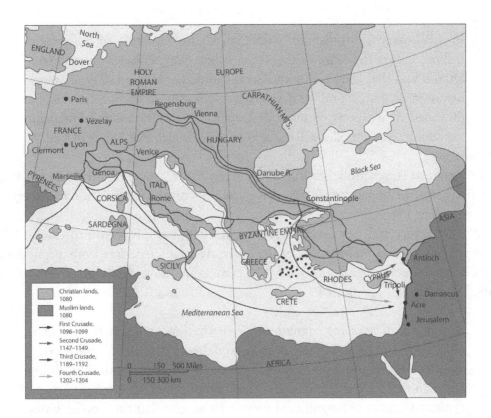

Map 11. Map of the Crusades

AIPAC? "While at AIPAC, Blitzer's writing focused on Middle East affairs as they relate to United States foreign policy."[197]

These are the same people who called for a military strike against Syria, purportedly in retaliation for Assad's using chemical weapons, while in the 1980s they supported Saddam Hussein in his use of chemical weapons against Iran and the Kurds. It is not that their humanity (or lack thereof) is offended by the slaughter of innocent civilians. It was perfectly OK with them if Saddam gassed Iranians and Kurds. Rather, their aim is to degrade Syria's capability and, as the Leveretts have pointed out, help Israel achieve regional hegemony.

AIPAC came out openly for an American strike on Syria, and that pushed some members of Congress who are generally afraid of AIPAC but were in doubt about the wisdom of an attack on Syria to lean toward a strike and used 250 lobbyists to convince others.[198]

One can make a solid case that the main patrons of our disastrous foreign policy are Israel and its domestic allies. In 2003, long before the Syrian civil war and Assad's purported use of chemical weapons, the Israelis pushed for US action molded after the invasion of Iraq that would target, Libya, Syria, and Iran:

In a February 2003 meeting with then Under Secretary of State John Bolton, before the start of the second Gulf War, Prime Minister Ariel Sharon said that Iran, Libya and Syria should be stripped of their weapons of mass destruction. "These are irresponsible states, which must be disarmed of weapons of mass destruction, and a successful American move in Iraq as a model will make that easier to achieve," Sharon said.[199]

The role of pro-Israeli lobbyists, and particularly AIPAC, deserves attention when we are discussing the impact of agenda-driven pundits on the formulation of American foreign policy.

Writing before the presidential elections of 2008, two Harvard professors, John J. Mearsheimer and Stephen M. Walt, correctly predicted that both presidential candidates, Barack Obama and John McCain, would have total agreement on one subject, Israel:

> Serious candidates for highest office in the land will go to considerable lengths to express their deep personal commitment to one foreign country—Israel—as well as their determination to maintain unyielding U.S. support for the Jewish state. ... None of the candidates is likely to criticize Israel in any significant way or to suggest that the United States ought to pursue a more even handed policy in the region. Any who do will probably fall by the wayside.[200]

Of course, we know that such was indeed the case in 2012, and then again in 2013. In 2008, the Democratic and Republican candidates for president competed with each other to appear more pro-Israeli than the others. Speaking in front of AIPAC, Hillary Clinton, the presumed frontrunner for 2016, referred to Israel as a "beacon of what is right in a neighborhood overshadowed by the wrongs of radicalism, extremism, despotism, and terrorism," and Obama asserted "that she would do nothing to change the US-Israeli relationship."[201]

Mearsheimer and Walt's view of US politicians is confirmed by former president Jimmy Carter:

> It would be almost politically suicidal for members of Congress to espouse a balanced position between Israel and Palestine, to suggest that Israel comply with international law or to speak in defense of justice or human rights for Palestinians. Very few would ever deign to visit the Palestinian cities of Ramallah, Nablus, Hebron, Gaza City or even Bethlehem and talk to the beleaguered residents. What is even more difficult to comprehend is why the editorial pages of the major newspapers and magazines in the United States exercise similar self-restraint, quite

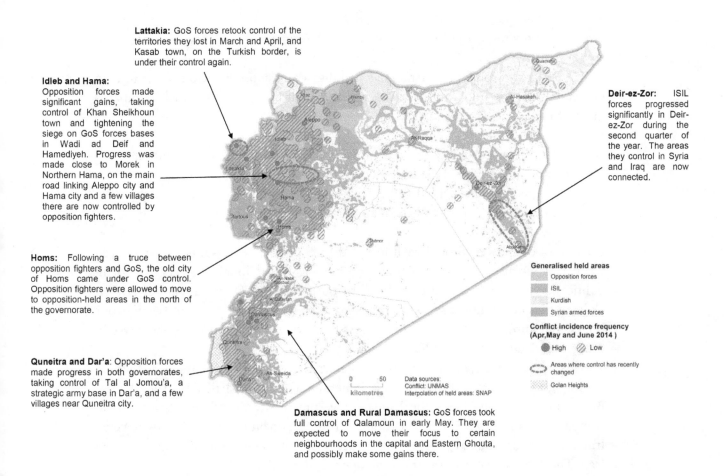

Lattakia: GoS forces retook control of the territories they lost in March and April, and Kasab town, on the Turkish border, is under their control again.

Idleb and Hama: Opposition forces made significant gains, taking control of Khan Sheikhoun town and tightening the siege on GoS forces bases in Wadi ad Deif and Hamediyeh. Progress was made close to Morek in Northern Hama, on the main road linking Aleppo city and Hama city and a few villages there are now controlled by opposition fighters.

Deir-ez-Zor: ISIL forces progressed significantly in Deir-ez-Zor during the second quarter of the year. The areas they control in Syria and Iraq are now connected.

Homs: Following a truce between opposition fighters and GoS, the old city of Homs came under GoS control. Opposition fighters were allowed to move to opposition-held areas in the north of the governorate.

Quneitra and Dar'a: Opposition forces made progress in both governorates, taking control of Tal al Jomou'a, a strategic army base in Dar'a, and a few villages near Quneitra city.

Damascus and Rural Damascus: GoS forces took full control of Qalamoun in early May. They are expected to move their focus to certain neighbourhoods in the capital and Eastern Ghouta, and possibly make some gains there.

Map 12. Map of the Syrian Conflict

Source: Copyright © 2014 by ACAPS / CC BY-ND 3.0.

contrary to private assessments expressed quite forcefully by their correspondents in the Holy Land.[202]

Mearsheimer and Walt ask why there is such unanimity of views on Israel among US politicians. They argue that the Cold War is over, so Israel does not have the same strategic value for the United States as it once did. Indeed, Israel today is a "strategic liability" for the United States. Furthermore, American support for Israel makes fighting terrorism more difficult, not easier. Mearsheimer and Walt's answer is the power of the Israeli lobby, particularly AIPAC.

They assert that this lobby is not a "conspiracy." Rather, it is an interest group composed of both Jews and Gentiles whose purpose is to influence American foreign policy so that it serves the interests of Israel. While American involvement in the Middle East was virtually nonexistent before World War II, security issues, oil, and the United States' relationship with Israel, particularly after the Six-Day

War, have now made the Middle East the prime consumer of American blood and treasure.

The American support for Israel has had disastrous consequences for our foreign policy. Besides the Iraq War, Mearsheimer and Walt use the 2006 Israeli bombardment of Lebanon as an example:

> Almost every country in the world harshly criticized Israel's bombing campaign[, which killed over one thousand, most of whom were civilians. ... The United States] instead supported Israel ... [which] undermined the pro-American government in Beirut.[203]

Because of the power of the Israeli lobby, the US political elite supports Israel even when it is violating American values and hurting US national interests. American politicians are simply afraid of AIPAC, to the point that Steven Rosen of AIPAC claimed that he could get seventy US senators to sign a blank paper in twenty-four hours, and another staffer told a journalist that 250 to 300 House members would "reflexively" do "whatever AIPAC wants."[204]

This is not mere speculation; AIPAC has indeed been a major force in shaping US foreign policy toward the region in general and Iran in particular, at least since Bill Clinton's era. In 1995, the Iranian government invited several American oil companies to once again begin operating in Iran. President Clinton not only rejected Iranian overtures but also began the process of imposing economic sanctions on Iran. The 1996 Iran-Libya sanctions were drafted by AIPAC.[205]

Robert Dreyfuss considers AIPAC to be the most powerful lobbying group in Washington, even more powerful than the National Rifle Association (NRA). Dreyfuss paints a picture of AIPAC's power in his description of its 2009 three-day conference:

> The occasion, the gala banquet capping the annual three-day conference of Washington's most powerful lobbying group, the American Israel Public Affairs Committee. With more than half of Congress attending, and America's top politicians fumbling to score crowd points with awkwardly delivered Hebrew phrases and fulminations concerning Iran, the reading of the names has become a yearly demonstration of AIPAC's clout. Banquet speakers included Joe Biden, Newt Gingrich, and John Kerry, looming on gigantic screens that lined the hall. Representing Israel were President Shimon Peres (whose address was interrupted by a half-dozen Code Pink activists) and, via satellite link, Prime Minister Benjamin Netanyahu. It was a dog and pony show no other group—not the American Medical Association, not the National Rifle Association, not AARP—could hope to match.[206]

The University of Southern California's (USC's) Annenberg School for Communication and Journalism blog, News 21, reports that this three-day 2009 banquet cost AIPAC $9 million. In addition to throwing lavish parties, AIPAC pays for luxurious one-week trips for US congressmen and congresswomen that cost $28,000. Finally, AIPAC uses about thirty political action committees to fund campaigns of its supporters in Congress (see appendix B).[207] Members of Congress who are beneficiaries of AIPAC's financial support frequently sponsor legislation to support Israel and force the White House to take a harsher view of Middle Eastern countries that oppose Israel. Senator Mark Kirk, who received more money from AIPAC than any member of Congress from 2007 to 2012, and Senator Lindsey Graham, who ranks fifth on the list of recipients, are frequent sponsors of these bills. These senators attempted to torpedo negotiations with Iran by sponsoring additional sanctions legislation that would kill any chance of an agreement between the United States and Iran:

> At the forefront of those efforts was a US Senate bill outlining oner-
> ous new sanctions, should the talks fail, and presented as a "diplomatic
> insurance policy" to strengthen President Barack Obama's negotiating
> hand. … Instead, administration officials feared it would set him up for
> failure.

> The pro-Israel lobby brought its considerable bipartisan influence to
> bear in pushing heavily for the bill, to the extent that one of its co-
> authors, Republican Senator Mark Kirk, called it a "test issue for the
> pro-Israel community." … But with the White House characterising the
> move as a "march to war", most Democrats dropped their support and
> the bill was shelved.[208]

In addition to having the support of senators and members of Congress congress-persons, the lobby's attack dogs, such as Alan Dershowitz, who is a frequent guest on CNN and other networks, are quick to attack anyone who criticizes anything Israel has done as being anti-Semitic, even if the person is former president of the United States Jimmy Carter, who wrote *Peace: Not Apartheid*.[209] Dershowitz is so biased and tells so many half-truths and misleading statements that even Jewish groups criticize him. Dershowitz's latest propaganda work is an attempt to sabotage the ongoing negotiations between Iran and America. Here is how J Street, a liberal Jewish advocacy group, summarizes his attacks:

> It is … irresponsible for Dershowitz to advocate throwing a spanner in
> the works of diplomacy, which provides the best, if not the only path,

to ensuring that the U.S., Israel and the world never have to deal with a nuclear-armed Iran.

Dershowitz buys into the boogeyman of "the bad deal" when in fact, there is no actual deal to attack. With the precise contours, terms and mechanisms of a first step agreement impossible to know—because it does not yet exist—Dershowitz and other opponents of the administration's efforts conveniently assert that they will be unacceptable. He should give the real experts who are handling these highly technical issues a chance to succeed, rather than assuming he knows their bottom line better than they do.

It's easy to build straw man arguments and throw out insults. Yes, Neville Chamberlain's appeasement failed to protect Czechoslovakia and Poland from Nazi aggression and prevent World War II. Does that make anyone who tries to avoid war another Chamberlain, and every war proponent another Churchill? Was George W. Bush another Churchill when he invaded Iraq in 2003?

Let's get beyond the name-calling and treat each crisis and each challenge on its own merits. Diplomacy leading to a tough, verifiable deal with Iran would be good for Israel, good for the United States and good for the world.[210]

Of course, you won't see this criticism of Dershowitz on CNN, where he is a frequent guest, or on the "progressive" MSNBC. You have to go to the Israeli media and the *Haaretz* newspaper to read it. In fact, you hardly ever see any mention or analysis of the role of pro-Israeli groups in shaping US foreign policy toward the Middle East. But the involvement of the media doesn't just end in their sheepishly following Israeli lobbies' pronouncements.

Of course, media personnel have good reason to be afraid of the lobby. When in January 2014 an *Economist* cartoonist captured the essence of difficulty that President Obama faces in congressional opposition to his rapprochement to Iran by depicting the president "shackled to a congress emblem embossed with Stars of David ... critics blasted the cartoon for suggesting that the US is controlled by Jews and Israel," and the *Economist*, perhaps the leading and "the most influential" weekly news magazine in the world, had to remove the cartoon and issue an editorial apology.[211] The idea that a cartoon in this leading magazine had to be removed simply because it captured the truth of the power of AIPAC's hold on Congress—a fact mentioned in a number of leading mainstream American government textbooks, whose authors are certainly not anti-Semitic nor conspiracy theorists, and routinely confirmed in surveys of members of Congress and their staffers—is the best testimony about AIPAC's power. Philip Weiss of *Mondoweiss* commented a few days later,

> Economist cartoon, since removed [the cartoon] … [the *Economist* said,] "The print edition of this story had a cartoon which inadvertently caused offense to some readers, so we have replaced it with a photograph."

> The Anti-Defamation League's Abe Foxman called on the *Economist* to issue a "full-throated apology" for publishing the cartoon. … Foxman smeared political scientists Steve Walt and John Mearsheimer [of Harvard University] and former president Jimmy Carter for talking about the Israel lobby.

> While he's at it, why doesn't he land on Jon Stewart for being anti-Semitic? As *The Washington Post* explains Stewart's sketch last week:

> He asks, reasonably: Why are 59 senators pushing for a sanctions bill that most observers seem to think will actually set back the bill's goal? He argues that this is explained by the nefarious behind-the-scenes lobbying of pro-Israel groups such as the American Israel Public Affairs Committee.[212]

Below is the "offending" cartoon, although my aim in printing it here is not to offend anyone; rather, it is intended to stimulate debate, champion freedom of thought and expression, and exercise academic freedom. A picture, at times, is truly "worth a thousand words," and this cartoon smartly shows that both the Iranian and American governments must overcome domestic opposition in their attempted reconciliation.

The Role of the US Media in Perpetuating Orientalism

Historically, we know how powerful the media can be in shaping public opinion and affecting foreign policy decision making. Some scholars go as far as arguing that the Spanish-American War (1898) was caused largely by "war hysteria generated by influential newspapers of the time who took up the cause of Cubans battling Spanish authority as a way of selling newspapers."[213] One reason for the distorted view of our supposed adversaries is that many of the influential media personalities who help shape public opinion are themselves either neocons or orientalists or have been trained and mentored by these imperialists.

This is particularly important, for through their airtime on TV and radio talk shows, their "expert" appearance on news programs, and their commentary in newspapers and journals, the neocons can shape the opinion of Americans who do not have strong political commitments and are "open to influence by the media."[214] Furthermore, as professors Morone and Kersh point out, the media has an even more important way to influence the public—by setting the agenda:

> Setting the agenda is one of the most important influences the news media has on American politics. ... Large demonstrations in major American cities against the Iraq war in 2003 got scant mention. Three years later, another set of demonstrations in support of immigrant rights caught the media's attention. As the news reverberated, the demonstrations multiplied and grew. The coverage put immigration issues squarely on the national agenda.[215]

Who are the people who set the agenda and decide that the opposition to the Iraq War does not deserve much attention and news coverage and should not be placed on the national debate agenda? Of course, these are the editors, producers, and media personalities who anchor the shows. These are the same people who by and large support the empire and its policies in the Middle East, particularly what is called a "special" relationship with Israel. A few are outright neocons, as you would see on Fox News and hear on right-wing talk shows. Most reporters and editors, however, consider themselves to be Democrats and liberals. Unfortunately, they are the CNN and MSNBC variety of Democrats and liberals—those whom I call imperial progressives. *Imperial progressives* are people who support democratic rights and progressive issues within the borders of the United States but somehow forget about these values and issues when it comes to the rights of other human beings who live outside the United States. They hardly ever criticize our imperial foreign policies (e.g., they were mostly silent in the period leading up to Iraq War). They hardly ever question our support for Israel, and whenever an issue regarding Israel is discussed, their guests are by and large pro-Israel and spouse Israeli views. So, when in April 2014 Secretary of State John Kerry correctly called Israel an "apartheid state," most shows and media analysis focused on what Kerry should have said.[216]

We already mentioned how one host of several CNN programs, Wolf Blitzer, worked for AIPAC. Another influential CNN commentator is Farid Zakaria, who is currently the host of CNN's *GPS*. Zakaria received his PhD from Harvard in 1993 and studied under Samuel P. Huntington, whose orientalist views have been known for decades. Zakaria often acts as a propagandist for US foreign policy, a role shared by many media hacks. "When a Washington official makes a statement, even a false one, the major media dutifully report it with few opposing sources."[217]

Cartoon 4.1. Congressional Opposition to the President's Rapprochement with Iran

Source: Copyright © 2014 by Peter Schrank.

Some of the remarkable instances of Zakaria's propaganda include his response to the Iranian envoy's statement that US policy has victimized Iran. Zakaria pointed out the hostage crisis as an example of Iran's victimization of the United States. In his interview with Ahmadinejad, he spent six minutes grilling him about Iran's supposed intention to wipe Israel off the map, and he referred to the United States' support of Saddam Hussein against Iran on another occasion as merely "providing agricultural assistance."[218]

The other part of the media's reasons for propagation of the empire is that they are owned by corporate owners whose interest is to maintain the empire:

> These days, six companies own the large majority of news and entertainment media in the United States: Time Warner (CNN), Disney (ABC), Murdoch's News Corporation (Fox), Bertelsmann of Germany (Doubleday publishing), Viacom (CBS) and General Electric (NBC).

> These companies have vested corporate interests to protect. None wants to see critical stories about its own holdings, which in some cases include war industries. And corporate executives certainly don't want to alienate government officials who handle antitrust matters, renew Federal Communication Commission Licenses, and offer lucrative government

contracts. No one wants to be seen as undercutting national security by publishing embarrassing articles.

> In subtle and not so subtle ways, owners make clear [that] their media enterprises should avoid certain topics. If writing critical stories, reporters must keep the stability of the empire in mind.[219]

Finally, the media relies on national experts to analyze foreign affairs. Some of these so-called experts neither write nor speak the language of their country of expertise, nor have they ever been to that country, yet somehow they get to serve on the National Security Council and are frequent guests on talk shows and/or write books on the subject.[220]

Worse, many are from institutions and think tanks, such as the Washington Institute for Near East Policy, that have been founded by Israeli lobbyists, the orientalists, and other interest groups, and have no interest in offering an unbiased and objective assessment of the current affair issue at hand. The Leveretts name the American Enterprise Institute, the Hudson Institute, the Foundation for Defense of Democracies, and the Foreign Policy Initiative, among other institutions, which have been founded by neocons or have been taken over by them.

These are the institutions that often provide the so-called experts on TV talk shows and help shape American public opinion. Among these "experts" is Fouad Ajami, a frequent guest on Anderson Cooper's *360* shows on CNN, *Charlie Rose*, and other prominent TV talk shows.

Ajami, along with another neocon hero, Bernard Lewis, has consistently opposed negotiations with Iran and has cofounded the Association for Study of the Middle East and Africa to support the Israeli and neocon agenda.[221]

Another favorite guest of CNN, mostly on Farid Zakaria's *GPS*, is Bret Stephens, who, like Wolf Blitzer, spent part of his career in Israel. Stephens was the editor-in-chief of the right-wing *Jerusalem Post* newspaper, which used to have a news tab titled "The Iranian Threat." Stephens now peddles these same ideas in America at the conservative but respected *Wall Street Journal* as its foreign affairs columnist and deputy editor.

These individuals and think tanks have been involved in a decade-long project to shape American public opinion and American foreign policy to both support Israel and favor the use of American power to strike down Israel's enemies, even if that is not in the national interest of the United States.

At times, this attempt to shape US public opinion and foreign policy takes an explicit form and is surprisingly unabashed. Among the best examples is the way in which Congress, particularly the Republican-dominated House, questioned Chuck Hagel. Quite a few questions were focused on Hagel's support for Israel, and very few Republicans bothered to ask Hagel questions that directly concerned the national interests of the United States or his intended goals and policies for US defense.

A subtler example is the oft-repeated criticism of the Obama administration for its attempt to change the terminology of combating extremism to soften the image of the United States abroad, particularly in the Middle East. Yet these efforts were sharply criticized by neocons, the Israeli lobby, and orientalists. Could it be that these groups believe that the existence of tension between the United States and the non-Israeli part of the Middle East and the resultant hostility on both sides would assure the continued support of the American public for Israel?

If one ever had any doubts about the accuracy of the latter statement, the current opening and possible diplomatic breakthrough between Iran and the United States provides a compelling statement. As the newly elected Iranian government is apparently attempting to seek a diplomatic solution over the nuclear proliferation issue, the Israeli right wing, spearheaded by Benjamin Netanyahu and aided by neocons and media pundits, has launched an offensive to kill any chances of a rapprochement between Iran and the United States. Minutes after the new Iranian president, Hassan Rohani, delivered his UN speech, in which he reaffirmed Iran's contention that its nuclear program is peaceful and invited talks and diplomacy, Netanyahu called his speech "a cynical speech that was full of hypocrisy."[222] Paul Wolfowitz, a leading neocon, and his colleagues, who did serious damage to the United States by shaping the Iraq agenda of the Bush administration, then populated the TV talk shows, such as Anderson Cooper's, to caution against Iranian treachery.

In fact, the Israeli lobby's efforts to torpedo any diplomatic rapprochement between the United States and Iran proved so powerful that the White House had to invite leaders of four major Jewish organizations to a meeting in late October 2013 to ask them to cease their lobbying efforts:

> ADL National Director Abe Foxman has confirmed that leaders of major Jewish organizations have agreed on a limited "time out" during which they will not push for stronger sanctions on Iran.

> "That means that we are not lobbying for additional sanctions and we are not lobbying for [fewer] sanctions," Foxman told *Haaretz* as well as other U.S. media outlets.

> Foxman was responding to a report in *Haaretz* on Friday that cited understandings reached among the leaders of four major Jewish organizations who participated in a Monday meeting at the White House with a group of senior White House officials led by National Security Adviser Susan Rice.

Immediately after the meeting, the newly established, ad hoc "quartet" of important Jewish organizations agreed to accede to the Administration's request and to refrain from campaigning on behalf of stronger sanctions at this time.[223]

Apparently, this effort by the White House has not yet succeeded, as Netanyahu continues his efforts to torpedo any chances of rapprochement between Iran and the United States and is joined in his efforts by the Saudis and pro-Israeli lobby. This sabotage has become so bad that the *New York Times* editorial page took on Netanyahu in a rare display of disaffection with Israeli leaders:

> Meanwhile, other reports blamed France for the failure to reach a deal after Foreign Minister Laurent Fabius complained that the proposed agreement was a "fool's game" just as negotiations were at a critical point. American and French diplomats have since said that France's area of concern—reportedly involving a heavy water reactor, which can produce plutonium—was easily resolved. Israelis and American lawmakers, however, have happily embraced Mr. Fabius's outburst in pushing the United States and its allies to take a tougher line against Iran. It would be alarming if his comments seriously impair chances of a deal.

> Unfortunately, the inconclusive negotiations have given an opening to the Israeli prime minister, Benjamin Netanyahu, who excoriated the proposed agreement as the "deal of the century" for Iran before it is made public, to generate more hysterical opposition. It would be nice if Iran could be persuaded to completely dismantle its nuclear program, as Mr. Netanyahu has demanded, but that is unlikely to ever happen. The administration of President George W. Bush made similar demands and refused to negotiate seriously and the result was an Iranian program that is more advanced than ever.[224]

This powerful lobby's major aim is to shape American foreign policy in the Middle East so that Israel's power and survival are guaranteed, and on many occasions this aim is in direct conflict with the national interests of the United States and what is best for the majority of Americans and, indeed, citizens of the world. In fact, one may argue that it is Israel that is the real threat to security and peace in the Middle East.[225]

This is no longer a controversial view. All one has to do is to look at a mainstream American government textbook: "Scholars often point to the American Israel Public Affairs Committee (AIPAC) as the preeminent example of an interest exercising powerful influence over U.S. foreign policy—in this case, policy towards Israel. ... AIPAC, critics point out, seeks to control the public conversation about policy towards Israel by influencing the media and minimizing debate in Congress."[226]

The result is that the Israeli lobby has largely succeeded in shaping American public opinion to support Israel. A just-released poll by the ADL shows that "personal attitudes were also strongly in Israel's favor, with three times as many Americans expressing sympathy for Israel rather than for the Palestinians—48 percent to 16 percent."[227]

The support for Israel is a reflection of the fact that in the United States, a largely uninformed general public—exposed to an all-encompassing, agenda-driven media campaign—can be swayed to view and interpret events in complete contrast to realities and facts. Thomas Patterson, a Harvard political scientist writes,

> Two decades ago, the "knowledge gap" was defined largely by the amount of attention that people paid to the news. Citizens who followed the news were much better informed than those who did not. That is less true today because of where people get their information. ... Most of [the media] outlets—whether on the left or right—have dropped all but the pretense of accuracy. They rarely tell flat-out lies, but they routinely slant the information to fit their purpose while burying contradictory facts. ... They are in the business of concocting versions of reality that will lure an audience and promote a cause.[228]

This "talk-show culture" of news and this mix of half-truths, facts, and untruths have real implications for how the American public views foreign policy. For instance, Patterson writes that after 2001, Americans who mistakenly thought that Iraq was allied with al-Qaeda and may have even helped plan and carry out the 9/11 attacks—a notion planted in the public's mind by neocons, particularly Dick Cheney[229]—were twice as likely to support the American invasion of Iraq compared to Americans who correctly did not see a connection between Iraq and al-Qaeda.[230] Similarly, the Israeli lobby has been successful in using the media effectively to shape a pro-Israeli public opinion by relying on the mix of propaganda, half-truths, and misleading statements by their allies in the media.

However, public opinion in a representative democracy still matters, despite what has been said before. When the issue of a possible US military strike against Syria came up, there was a clear outcry among the citizenry against yet another military entanglement in the Middle East. While our foreign policy establishment was pro-war, and while all the usual pundits in the media seemed to favor an attack, and despite the lobbying efforts of AIPAC, calls to many members of Congress were running overwhelmingly opposed to a war, sometimes 10 to 1 and, according to the conservative media, 499 to 1.[231]

Furthermore, when it comes to the current nuclear negotiations with Iran, it appears that the Israeli lobby's efforts are facing strong opposition:

> A CRISIS is brewing in America's relations with Israel. The American public—though strongly pro-Israel—seems either not have noticed or not care much. ...

> Israel's prime minister, Benjamin Netanyahu, has not held back [in attempts to sabotage a deal with Iran]. In a speech to thousands of Jewish-Americans in Jerusalem on November 10th he more or less called the American president and his envoys naïve to the point of imperiling Israel's survival. Mr. Netanyahu accused the negotiators in Geneva, including John Kerry, the secretary of state, of proposing "a bad and dangerous deal" that would start to unravel sanctions even as Iran retained its capacity to enrich enough fissile material to menace Israel's survival. America would be next, once Iran perfected long-range missiles, he warned. "Coming to a theatre near you." Mr. Kerry retorted that "we are not blind, and I don't think we are stupid." The ground might seem set for a familiar American political showdown in which Republicans denounce Democrats for coddling America's enemies while cold-shouldering its allies.

> Yet, with few exceptions, this is not happening. Instead some big-name Republicans, including likely contenders for the White House, have dodged invitations to whack the president with the cudgel proffered by Mr. Netanyahu. ... Bob Corker of Tennessee, the senior Republican on the Senate Foreign Relations Committee ... concedes that in the days after Mr. Kerry's abortive Geneva talks on Iranian nukes, his office did not receive a single call from a constituent. ...

> Most Jewish Americans vote Democratic. And they are divided in their views of Israel, too. A recent Pew poll of Jewish-American voters found them skeptical about Israeli government's commitment to making peace with the Palestinians.[232]

Therefore, despite the power of neocons and their outreach and influence in the media, when the public is provided with correct information about the costs of our adventurous foreign policy, grassroots movements can still put a check on the military industrial complex's desire to ever more involve us in the Middle East and squander national resources. In short, there is much hope that we can correct the current course of American foreign policy.

The American public has shown that it can evolve on civil rights issues. While racism, sexism, and discrimination still exist in America and affect many of us on a daily basis, they are much less severe than they were thirty years ago, when most of the public did not militantly oppose apartheid in South Africa and when discrimination against minorities was much more pervasive.

If we have evolved in the civil rights sphere, who is to say that we cannot evolve in our views about foreign policy? Who is to say that the day will not come when we solve our foreign policy disputes almost entirely through diplomacy, rather than through military force? Germany and France fought two world wars in the space of twenty-five years, yet they were among the six founding members of the European Union, which began with the Treaty of Rome in 1957, or, some might argue, as early as 1950 with the signing of the Schuman Plan, which merged German and French steel industry barely five years after the bloodiest war fought in human history.

Chapter Five

Conclusion

King Abdullah, upper left; F-15 fighter jet taking off from Hatzerim Air Force Base in Israel, below.

The Unholy Alliance:
Israel, Saudi Arabia, and US Foreign Policy in the Middle East

I have devoted much of this book to a discussion of the role of ideas, history, and domestic pressure groups in formulating American foreign policy toward the Middle East. Yet, as these words are written, the United States and European powers are negotiating with Iran in Geneva to sign an interim agreement that would pave the way toward resolving Iran's longstanding nuclear dispute with the West and ease sanctions on Iran.

This would be a great achievement for the Obama administration, and if it paves the way for the eventual normalization of relations with Iran, it would benefit both America and Iran tremendously. First, it would kill any ideas of a military confrontation and the shedding of blood of innocent Americans and Iranians. Second, it would benefit both economies tremendously. In 2010, Iran had the world's seventeenth-largest economy in GDP measured in purchasing power parity (PPP)[233] terms, and Mundi estimated that Iran's GDP in terms of PPP surpassed $1 trillion in 2011.[234] Despite sanctions, as late as 2012, the World Bank reported that Iran had the "the second largest economy in the Middle East and North Africa region in terms of [absolute] GDP—US$484 billion in 2012 (after Saudi Arabia) and in terms of population—78 million people (after Egypt)."[235]

Obviously, a normalization of relations with Iran that would open this large economy once again to the United States would tremendously benefit American companies and ordinary Americans who work for these countries. Just imagine if Iran was once again able to purchase aircraft from Boeing and replace its current aging civilian aircraft with 747s! How many jobs would that create for Washingtonians?

Of course, ordinary Iranians would benefit from the lifting of sanctions. Although Iran has made significant progress "in education, health, and income per capita, as measured in the annual Human Development Index and ranks as a high human development country," according to UN development chief Helen Clark, who visited Iran in October of 2013,[236] there is no question that sanctions have made life more difficult for ordinary folks. Higher inflation; difficulty in obtaining necessities, including medicine; and obstacles to trade and transferring of funds, which now plague Iran, would ease or disappear altogether with sanctions relief.

The irony of the sanctions is that they are hurting a people, the Iranians, who are the most pro-American population in the Middle East:

> With the recent election of Iranian President Hassan Rouhani by over 50 percent of the vote, it's clear the populace is seeking change—one in favor of the United States. In fact, aside from the Jewish Israeli population, the Iranian populace is the most pro-American public in the Middle East. After the Revolution, close to a million people from Iran immigrated to the United States. Millions of their relatives who would have loved to immigrate remain in Iran and are sympathetic towards the U.S. and appreciative that their relatives live a comfortable and accepting life here.[237]

Iran would also benefit tremendously by once again being able to export its petroleum products and other domestically manufactured goods to America and the West. More importantly, Iran would be able to once again use the advanced technology of giant oil companies to modernize its oil industry.

The flip side of this argument is that a better economy would enable the current regime—which still opposes US foreign policy aims in Lebanon, Syria, Iraq, and Central Asia, and which is theocratic—to last longer. One can hope that President Rouhani's election might make the human rights situation in Iran better, although so far, other than the release of a few political prisoners, major changes in policy have not yet taken place. It is unclear how much of this lack of substantial change is because of the fact that the judiciary in Iran operates independent of the presidency and how much of it is because of the lack of serious desire for change on the part of the president.[238]

Nonetheless, to those who want and desire a truly democratic Iran and would cry foul at any actions on the part of the United States that might strengthen the Islamic Republic, I would point out that modern Iranian intellectual thought, born in the nineteenth century in reaction to pressures of colonialism and the tyranny, incompetence, and corruption of the ruling Qajar dynasty, was "in fact produced by a very small band of expatriate intellectuals,"[239] who, while drawing on the rich tradition and history of Iran, were also exposed to reformist and radical European thought in Russia and the Ottoman Empire. Trade and interaction with the rest of the world would only strengthen reformist and democratic forces in Iran. Trade and engagement with the Western world might change the balance of power between the three major intellectual and ideological trends in Iran, "liberal democratic nationalism, social democratic socialism, and theocratic Islamism,"[240] that emerged from the nineteenth century and have ever since struggled for dominance in Iran.

To those who are champions of current US foreign policy goals in the region and would cry foul at the very thought of abandoning their imperial goals for fear that it might lower the standards of living in the United States—a frequent justification for neocolonial policies—I would point out the example of Japan, China, and Germany. None of these countries has invaded a country in decades, yet their economies thrive, and in two of the three countries, their citizens enjoy relatively high standards of living. War, bloodshed, and hegemonic policies might benefit the military industrial complex and their supporters in the foreign policy elite establishment, but they actually, as we have shown in chapter two of this work, impose a tremendous cost on ordinary Americans in terms of both physical and economic well-being.

Nonetheless, it is true that even if the nuclear issue is resolved, tremendous differences will remain between Iran and the United States. As stated earlier, many of the differences stem from competition among the two powers for supremacy in the Persian Gulf and Central Asia area. Some of the tension would center on the Israeli-Palestinian dispute and our blind, irrational, one-sided support of Israel and our support of repressive Persian Gulf monarchies. We need to reexamine our foreign policy goals in the region, and I would argue that the benefits to both Iran and United States, especially for ordinary citizens, are so tremendous that it should outweigh political disputes, even if neither side changes its foreign policy goals.

Yet America's erstwhile allies, Saudi Arabia and Israel, which are in competition with Iran for regional supremacy, are pulling out all the stops to sabotage these negotiations:

> ONCE they were sworn enemies. Now Israel's Mossad intelligence agency is working with Saudi officials on contingency plans for a possible attack on Iran if its nuclear programme is not significantly curbed in a deal that could be signed in Geneva this week.

> Both the Israeli and Saudi governments are convinced that the international talks to place limits on Tehran's military nuclear development amount to appeasement and will do little to slow its development of a nuclear warhead.

As part of the growing co-operation, Riyadh is understood already to have given the go-ahead for Israeli planes to use its airspace in the event of an attack on Iran.[241]

This brings home to me the fact that the making of American foreign policy toward the Middle East is even more complicated than the discussion that I have presented thus far. I have focused on the role of ideas, history, and domestic pressure groups. The influence of foreign actors on American foreign policy was discussed only insofar as these actors—for instance, Israel—work their desires through domestic pressure groups—AIPAC, to give an example.

Yet this case highlights the influence that a country's allies might have on foreign policy decision making, and those influences might be exerted through pressure directly on the decision makers or unilateral actions by foreign countries. It is not just in the matter of Iran that Saudi Arabia has hurt American interests. Saudi Arabia is actively supporting the radical Islamists in Iraq, where bombings are a daily occurrence, and in Syria, where jihadist rebels now dominate the opposition forces.

This case also highlights the consequences of foreign entanglement that George Washington warned us about. Furthermore, it once again points out the folly of alliances with repressive governments: governments such as Saudi Arabia, which denies half of its population (women) any chance at equal opportunity and mastery and control of their own lives, and Israel, which is an undemocratic state in terms of how it treats its Arab citizens and Palestinians.

While the Iranian theocratic regime imposes many of the same restrictions on minorities and women, these discriminatory practices pale in comparison to what is happening in Saudi Arabia, where women can't even drive, or Israel, where Palestinians have to go through more than ten checkpoints to go shopping or go to school.

In 1953, when the CIA, at the urging of the British, overthrew the democratically elected government of Mosaddegh, Iran had a vibrant civil society, multiple political parties, an established bureaucracy, and a constitutional government dating back to 1905, and hundreds of years of central government rule in the same geographic area—putting aside that the idea of Iran and an Iranian empire dating back to the sixth century BC or earlier. By contrast, in 1953 Saudi Arabia "had no constitution, no codes of governmental procedure, no political parties, and no institutionalized forms of consultation."[242]

While some five thousand Saudi princes have a monopoly of all political and decision-making positions, in Iran—both under the Shah and under the Ayatollahs—a person of humble origins who is loyal to the system can work up the ladder of power and even become the president (e.g., Ahmadinejad) or prime minister (when that position existed). The lack of upward mobility that is built into the political structure of Saudi Arabia makes that country inherently unstable, and unless the political system is modified, its collapse is inevitable.

Furthermore, Saudi Arabia is the main source of funding and support for radical jihadist Islam. The Saudis began the expansion of financial support of these radical fundamentalist groups with our blessings during the Soviet occupation of Afghanistan, when both the Pakistani intelligence services and the Central Intelligence Agency facilitated and encouraged these movements. In fact, the Taliban movement came into prominence with the encouragement of Pakistanis who were concerned about the difficulties that their truckers were facing in moving their goods through the lawless post–Soviet occupation Southern Afghanistan. The Taliban burst onto the scene with an attack at a warlord's checkpoint at the border of Pakistan at Spin Boldak that had prevented Pakistani truckers from moving their goods to Kandahar.[243] The Saudis then began to pump money into support of the Taliban. Iran, given its Shi'a nature, is fundamentally opposed to fundamentalist Sunni Wahhabis, such as the Taliban.

There are many more visible differences between Saudi Arabia and Iran other than political structure and support for Salafist movements that make trade and exchanges with Iran much more amenable to American values than trade and exchanges with Saudi Arabia. Hollywood is a big part of American culture, so consider the difference in simply being able to see a movie in Iran versus in Saudi Arabia. In Saudi Arabia, most people have to travel to a different country to go to a movie theater (movie theaters are allowed only in private places). Iran, even today, has a vibrant movie industry that has won worldwide recognition and even an Oscar (for *A Separation*).[244]

Women in Iran are prohibited from seeking their full potential and expressing themselves, but there is a vibrant and longstanding women's movement in Iran, and women can vote in local and national elections and assume governmental positions, including ministerial-level positions. Furthermore, the new Iranian president, Hassan Rouhani, has also come out in support of improving women's rights and situation in Iran. In a speech on April 20, 2014, on the occasion of Women's Day in Iran, Rouhani said, "Women must enjoy equal opportunity, equal protection, and equal social rights. ..." According to the Islamic rules, "man is not the stronger sex and woman is not the weaker one."[245]

But in Saudi Arabia, women can't even drive yet. Surprisingly, a May 2014 *Economist* report titled "Women in Saudi Arabia: Unshackling Themselves" states that the bans on driving and similar restrictions apparently have widespread support among Saudi women themselves. According to the report, 89 percent of Saudi women who were polled think that they should not be allowed to drive.[246] By contrast, in the same *Economist* issue, the article on Iran, "The Perils of Yoga," notes that although religious and stricter Iranians think of yoga as a corrupting influence, there are two hundred yoga centers in Iran, and Iranian women openly practice yoga in public parks.[247] To sum up, while Iranian women are discriminated against and are prevented from pursuing their full potential, their situation is light years ahead of that of Saudi women, and much of the difference is because of the Iranian women's own resistance to oppression and their highly advanced and developed social and political consciousness.

Iranian women (left) and a Saudi Arabian woman (right) out in public.

Source: Copyright © 2009 by Hamed Saber / CC by 2.0; Copyright © 2006 by Retlaw Snellac Photography / CC by 2.0.

So, if we can have alliances with Saudi Arabia and Israel, surely we can have trade with Iran. After all, if the character of the regime prevented trade, Nixon would have never "opened" China in the 1970s, and we would never have traded with many dictatorial regimes in Africa and Asia that we currently trade with.

Let me end this book by once again showing a portion of the long quotation from George Washington, our first president, which was presented in chapter three:

It is our true policy to steer clear of permanent alliances with any portion of the foreign world; so far, I mean, as we are now at liberty to do it; for let me not be understood as capable of patronizing infidelity to existing engagements. I hold the maxim no less applicable to public than to private affairs, that honesty is always the best policy. I repeat it, therefore, let those engagements be observed in their genuine sense. But, in my opinion, it is unnecessary and would be unwise to extend them.

Harmony, liberal intercourse with all nations, are recommended by policy, humanity, and interest. But even our commercial policy should hold an equal and impartial hand; neither seeking nor granting exclusive favors or preferences; consulting the natural course of things; diffusing and diversifying by gentle means the streams of commerce, but forcing nothing; establishing, with powers so disposed, in order to give trade a stable course, to define the rights of our merchants, and to enable the government to support them, conventional rules of intercourse, the best that present circumstances and mutual opinion will permit.[248]

Postscript: The "Historic Agreement"

I finished this manuscript and sent it out a few days before Iran and the Western powers reached what has been called a historic or landmark agreement on Iran's enrichment program.[249] According to the terms of the deal, Iran would receive some relief from the sanctions in return for promising to dilute its existing stockpile of 20 percent enriched uranium to 5 percent —a level appropriate for civilian use—and not to enrich beyond the 5 percent level. Iran can continue to operate its estimated eleven thousand centrifuges, but cannot add new ones. The agreement is viewed as an interim confidence-building measure, and the two sides have six months to work out a permanent solution to the issue.

While the Obama administration and the European powers hailed the agreement, as expected, Israel and its allies immediately began to attack the agreement, and the US Senate began working on further sanctions on Iran that would in effect torpedo the agreement.[250] Saudi Arabia also joined the forces critical of the agreement, although it appears now that an internal power realignment within Saudi Arabia might lessen its opposition to the agreement.[251]

The key point for Iran, aside from limited sanctions relief, is the implicit acknowledgement of its right to enrich uranium. Although according to Article IV of the Treaty on Non-Proliferation of Nuclear Weapons, Iran as a signatory state has the "inalienable right ... to develop research, production and use of nuclear energy for peaceful purposes."[252] However, it is important to note that despite the unquestionable right of Iran to enrich uranium, the United States has consistently opposed Iran's efforts to enrich uranium, and this opposition dates back to the shah's regime, when Iran's nuclear program was born.[253] Therefore, to argue that the opposition of the United States to Iran's mastery of the nuclear fuel cycle, which is clearly its right under NPT, is solely a function of Washington's fear of "irrational mullahs" is not backed by evidence. In fact, the reason that Iran in 1975 signed a contract with a West German firm, Kraftwerk Union Ag, to build the Bushehr nuclear reactors, and not an American firm, was the opposition of Washington to Iran's nuclear activity and its demand that all decisions regarding the nuclear program must be run through Washington. Iran continued to seek aid from Western powers in developing its nuclear energy after the Islamic Revolution and even took Kraftwerk to court to force it to complete the Bushehr plant. It was only the refusal of Western companies, under pressure from their governments, to cooperate with Iran that forced the Iranians to choose Russia as a partner.[254]

Iran's justification for wanting to have a nuclear program under the shah was similar to the reason stated by the Islamic Republic: to meet the increasing demand for electricity. Both the shah and the current regime viewed the use of fossil fuels to produce energy as inefficient and wasteful, and, at any rate, both regimes had difficulty meeting the demands of the electrical grid through conventional sources, which resulted in frequent power shortages. The choice of light-water reactors for Bushehr and the initial Iranian nuclear plans were also evidence of peaceful Iranian intentions, as heavy-water reactors are more suitable to developing nuclear weapons.

Although the later construction of a heavy-water reactor in Arak, which provides an easier path to weapons-grade fuel, has increased the suspicion of Iran's intentions, there is no denying that the initial Iranian plans were much more suited for production of nuclear fuel for civilian purposes.[255] As Patrikaros has argued, perhaps had the West cooperated with Iran, its nuclear activities might have been even more transparent and above ground than they are currently.

In sum, there is a history of American opposition to Iranian mastery of the nuclear fuel cycle that is independent of Iranian regime type and ideology. Iranians view this as a violation of their rights under NPT and consider their right to enrich to be a matter of national pride and sovereignty. Cooperation between Iran and the West on the nuclear issue can exist only if the West acknowledges Iran's right to enrich fuel domestically. Meanwhile, Iran must provide safeguards and assurances that it will not divert its nuclear program from its stated peaceful purposes. This November 23, 2013, accord seems to meet both of these conditions.

The Agreement's Implementation

Almost five months after the signing of the "historic agreement," it appeared that both sides were in compliance with the agreement, despite what skeptics in the US Congress, the Israelis, and the Saudis and their supporters had said.

These opponents to the agreement had persistently used the US Congress to express their skepticism and opposition. In March 2014, Senator Robert Menendez, who received more than $300,000 between 2007 and 2012 in contributions from AIPAC,[256] and eighty-three of his colleagues wrote to the White House and took [an] "aggressive stance, urging Obama to insist that any final agreement state that Iran "has no inherent right to enrichment under the Nuclear Non-Proliferation Treaty."[257] Obviously, if the White House had followed this advice, given Iranian insistence on Iran's right to enrich uranium, the agreement would be dead and this group of representatives would have achieved their real agenda, which is to forestall rapprochement between the United States and Iran.

Nonetheless, on April 17, 2014, the United Nations' nuclear watchdog agency released a report that indicated that Iran had lived up to the terms of its agreement, and the United States announced that it would release an additional $450 million in frozen Iranian assets.[258] However, the fourth round of talks in May failed to bridge the gap between both sides, with the Iranian side commenting unofficially that the demands of the Great Powers were unreasonable.[259] As the *Economist* reports, the differences are over three separate issues:

- The extent and scope of the Iranian enrichment program—that is, how many centrifuges Iran would be allowed to operate
- How and when the sanctions would be lifted
- How long the agreement should be enforced before the normalization of Iran's status[260]

To this specific difference we must add the domestic opposition that exists in both countries to reconciliation between Iran and the United States. The pro-Israeli US Congress and the so-called Iranian hardliners or conservatives ironically share agreement on this issue. This situation is the perfect example of the arguments of this book, among which is the fact that domestic interest and pressure groups have a tremendous influence on foreign policy.

While Iran and the United States as societies would benefit tremendously from reconciliation, neither domestic group wants to see Iranian-US reconciliation.

Chapter Six

Middle East Update, September 2014: Middle East in Flames

Source: This picture, apparently showing the gruesome mass execution of prisoners by the IS, was released by the IS and appeared on many websites, including CNN http://globalpublicsquare.blogs.cnn.com/category/terrorism.

Source: ISIL.

One of the main arguments of this book has been that our foreign policy towards the Middle East is flawed and will produce nothing other than suffering for the people of the area and long-term setbacks for the United States.

The best proof of my argument is the picture that we see today in the Middle East. Iraq, Syria, Palestine, and Libya are in flames and the *Islamic State* (**IS**) is on the march, presenting a threat to many countries in the region and American interests alike.

I argued that this flawed foreign policy was shaped by pressure from internal interest groups such as the Pro-Israeli lobby (AIPAC) and their *Neo-con* pundits, analysts, and foreign policy advisors, and their supporters in Congress. Furthermore, the implementation of our flawed policy was backed and encouraged by external allies such as Saudi Arabia who are advancing their own interests in the region.

In Chapter Two, I mentioned that the conflict in Syria was partly the result of our joint operations with Saudi Arabia to encourage and develop proxy forces that would oppose Iranian influence in the region. This policy, which served Israeli interests as well, has now come back to pose a serious threat to stability in the region.

The Saudis, just as they did in Afghanistan, supported extremist Wahhabi Sunni groups in Syria with our blessing and encouragement. The IS—originally named ISIS, The Islamic State of Iraq and Syria—was funded and nurtured by Saudi Arabia with our tacit approval to oppose the Syrian government. But just as with the Taliban in Afghanistan who harbored our enemies and allowed them to attack the United States on September 11, 2001, the IS has now attacked American interests and has begun killing Americans and has threatened to kill more Americans.

Because of our flawed policy, not only much of Northern and Western Iraq has been captured by the IS, but American forces have also had to redeploy to Iraq and our expenditure of blood and treasure will now have to continue.

We have begun to lunch airstrikes on IS targets in Iraq and have sent about a 1,000 special forces troops to Iraq to help a fledging Iraqi government, and the Iranian-backed Shi'a militias and Kurdish forces fight the very forces that the Saudi intelligence agencies and our support created in the first place. The Neo-cons and *Imperial Progressives* (see Chapter Four) should shoulder the blame for what is happening in Iraq today. Al Qaida and its offshoot, the IS, did not exist in Iraq before our invasion in 2003.

As indicated in Chapter Five, the United States and Iran have many common interests in the region, and despite the opposition of the Saudis, Israelis, and their Neo-con supporters, it is in the long-term interest of the United States to reach some sort of an accommodation with Iran. It is only now that we have begun to modify some of our policies and it appears that our military is coordinating some efforts with the Iranian military to combat the IS. A report by the BBC on September 5, 2014 indicates that the Iranian supreme leader has authorized an Iranian commander, who successfully organized a Syrian rollback of rebel forces, to work with American military to roll back the IS.[1] However, it remains uncertain if our domestic policies and our alliances with Israel and Saudi Arabia (discussed in chapters four and five) would allow our cooperation with Iran to expand.

The IS has also been able to expand its territory in Syria and as many observers feared, the conflict spilled over into Lebanon. In early August, the IS attacked Arsal, a border town in Lebanon, and engaged the Lebanese military. Tragically, many of the inhabitants of Arsal were Syrian refugees who had fled the IS and the civil war in Syria and once again had to flee for their lives. Yet, this time around, these suffering families had nowhere to go, as the Lebanese army apparently would not allow them to travel further in Lebanon.[2] Worse, their relationship with the town's residents, who blame them for bringing the IS to their doorsteps, may never be the same.

---

1   See BBC's report, "Iran 'Backs US Military Contacts' to Fight Islamic State" (2014, Sep 5). Retrieved from: <http://www.bbc.com/news/world-middle-east-29079052>.

2   See New York Times' article by Hwaida Saad and Rick Gladstone, (2014, Aug 4) "Border Fighting Intensifies Between ISIS and Lebanon." Retrieved from: NYTimes.com <http://www.nytimes.com/2014/08/05/world/middleeast/isis-lebanon-syria.html>.

While the IS eventually withdrew from the town, some 100 Lebanese soldiers were killed or wounded by the time the skirmish was over. Although a small battle by comparison to the IS's June 2014 capture of Iraq's second largest city Mosul, the Lebanese incident showed the danger that the IS poses to the entire region. Our policy created a monster in Syria, which might prove to be far more dangerous than the monster we created in Afghanistan in Taliban.

Similarly our intervention in Libya has proved to be a complete disaster. Libya is in a virtual civil war. Two factions, centered on tribal, ethnic, and ideological ties, "the tribes of Arab descent, like the Zintanis, against those of Berber, Circassian or Turkish ancestry, like the Misuratis"[3] have emerged and have engulfed the country in bloodshed and destruction. The international airport in Tripoli and some oil refineries have become battlefields and have been damaged and have been put out of operation. "Three years after the NATO-backed ouster of Col. Muammar el-Qaddafi, the violence threatens to turn Libya into a pocket of chaos destabilizing North Africa for years to come."[4]

We had to pull out our personnel out of our embassy in July and now reportedly our residential compounds in the embassy have been overrun by militias. Surely, this is not an outcome that serves American national interests.

In Chapter Four I talked about how pro-Israeli lobbying groups, particularly AIPAC, have hijacked American foreign policy towards the Middle East and how their influence is rampant in the media and Congress. Nothing better proves my point than the recent Gaza conflict that showed how ineffective our policies are.

Over 2,000 Palestinians, a count that by all accounts included mostly civilians and hundreds of children, were killed: "More than 2,100 Palestinians were killed in the 50 days of fighting, most of them civilians, according to UN and Palestinian estimates. Thousands of buildings were destroyed and tens of thousands of people were left homeless. Seventy-two people were killed on the Israeli side, including six civilians."[5] Meanwhile, we resupplied Israel with bombs and ammunition after Israel apparently ran out of bombs to drop on Gaza. Our Congress, who does not seem to be able to agree on any of crucial issues affecting American society and welfare, such as immigration, healthcare, gun control, veterans, and the like, was able to quickly and almost unanimously (100 to 0 vote in the Senate) approve additional funds for Israel.

---

3   Kirkpatrick, D. D. (2014, 8 24). "Strife in Libya Could Presage Long Civil War." Retrieved from: NYTimes.com: <http://www.nytimes.com/2014/08/25/world/africa/libyan-unrest.html?_r=0>.

4   See Ibid.

5   See Josef Federman's report for the Associated Press, reprinted in the Canadian newspaper, The Globe and Mail. Retrieved from: *The Globe and Mail.* "Israeli Military Gears up for UN War-crimes Investigation. (2014, Sep 5) <http://www.theglobeandmail.com/news/world/israeli-military-gears-up-for-un-war-crimes-investigation/article20357024/>.

While in Latin America, Asia, and Europe, opposition to support for Israel and its brutal actions in Gaza was so strong that a British minister (Sayeeda Warsi) resigned in protest of the UK's support for Israel, our networks, politicians, the pundits, and a virtual who's who of American politicians could not wait to come out and express their support for Israel's right to defend itself. None of these leaders ever spoke of the fact that Israel might have withdrawn from Gaza, but has imposed a blockade from air, land, and sea on Gaza that has turned this narrow strip of land into a virtual prison for several million people. None of these leaders ever accused Israel of war crimes (as the United Nations has) but were quick to condemn Hamas's actions. By not addressing the core issue—Israeli occupation of Palestinian land, and its suffocation of Gaza and the West Bank—our politicians and leaders only guarantee the return of the conflict.

In sum, the current chaos and mayhem in the Middle East only proves the arguments of this book that the current foreign policies of the United States towards the area, shaped to a large degree by Neo-con influence and advice from agenda-driven pundits, only harm our national interests.

We need to rethink our priorities and goals in the region and reevaluate our alliances. In particular, we need to rethink our obsession with having an empire. Japan, China, and Germany do not have empires and none have been involved in a major war in a significant manner in decades. Yet these countries' economies are doing rather well.

Finally, we need to better understand the dynamics of the region by advancing advisors who are schooled in the language, culture, and history of the region and are not part of an agenda-driven foreign policy establishment.

Chapter Seven

Middle East Update II, May 2015: Upheaval and Promise of Peace: Nuclear Negotiations, Yemen, and ISIS

The ministers of foreign affairs and other officials from the P5+1 countries, the European Union, and Iran while announcing the framework of a comprehensive agreement on the Iranian nuclear programme, 2 April 2015.

Source: U.S. Department of State / Copyright in the Public Domain.

The Nuclear Accords: Parameters Agreement

On April 2, 2015, Federica Mogherini, the European Union's Foreign Policy Chief, along with Iranian Foreign Minister, Javad Zarif, held a joint news conference to announce the details of the parameters of a nuclear accord agreement between Iran and the P5+1 powers (The United States, China, Russia, Germany, France, and the United Kingdom).[261]

The agreement addressed the issues of enrichment, number and kind of centrifuges, the Ferdo, Arak, and Natanz facilities' allowed use, and inspections.

In return for the lifting of sanctions, Iran agreed to reduce its stock pile of low enriched uranium by 97 percent (from the current 10,000 kg to 300), and reduce its centrifuges from the current 19,000 to 6,104 and operate only 5,060 of these for 10 years.

Iran further agreed to give unprecedented access to the International Atomic Agency's (IAEA) inspectors by signing the Additional Protocols of IAEA, and giving full access to all its nuclear facilities and, just as importantly, its entire supply chain of nuclear material.

Iran also agreed to convert the Arak's heavy water research reactor so that it cannot be used as an avenue to create plutonium which can then be used for military purposes.[262]

In return, the P5+1 powers agreed to produce a new United Nations resolution which ends the UN sanctions on Iran, and to lift EU sanctions and those American sanctions which do not require an act of Congress to lift.

The agreement took 18 months to negotiate and was the result of hard negotiations among technical experts, foreign ministers, and heads of atomic agencies of various countries involved in the deal.

The parameters agreement seems like a win-win situation to most reasonable observers; including the American public who, by a margin of 2 to 1, expressed support for the agreement in a Washington Post poll.[263] Writing in Foreign Policy, Kori Schake, a republican and a fellow at the conservative Hoover Institution, supported the agreement based on the strength of the inspection regime and other factors.[264] The West does not have to worry about an Iran with nuclear weapons for anywhere from 10 to 25 years, and Iran can get relief from sanctions which have severely hurt ordinary Iranians. This agreement wasn't just approved by the Obama administration, which is accused of wanting the deal to secure a presidential legacy for President Obama, but also by the governments of Germany, France, Russia, China, and the United Kingdom.

Most of the experts whose opinions I have read and/or have given lengthy interviews on programs devoted to news, such as Charlie Rose,[1] agree that Iran has not decided to build a nuclear weapon, and that even if she had one, she would not use it out of fear of the catastrophic retaliatory attacks she would face. Yet, due to the power of the Israeli Lobby, and the Saudi and Persian Gulf states' worries about the rising regional influence of Iran; attacks on the agreement began before the parameters deal was even reached and intensified thereafter.

Benjamin Netanyahu, the Israeli Premier, accepted an invitation from the Speaker of the House, John Boehner and gave an unprecedented speech to a joint session of the United States Congress on March 4, 2015 to criticize the foreign policy of a sitting American president while that president was in the midst of negotiations with a foreign power; an event without parallel in American History. As if this outrage was not enough, a few days later some of his supporters, the 47 Republican Senators, headed by Freshman Senator, Tom Cotton, signed a letter which essentially told Iran that a deal was no deal and that a future administration (supposedly run by Republicans) could void it.[265]

Netanyahu's speech had been arranged without the knowledge of the executive branch of the United States government, and was unprecedented in that it was the

---

1   The most comprehensive work on the myth of Iran's nuclear danger is by highly respected historian and journalist, Gareth Porter, Manufactured Crisis: The Untold Story of Iran Nuclear Scare. (2014). Some of the most in-depth TV interviews on Iran are Charlie Rose's, particularly Charlie Rose episodes on April 2, April 7, April 28, April 29, May 5, and May 8 2015. These can be seen at <http://www.charlierose.com/search>. The April 28 and 29 interviews were with Iran's foreign minister Zarif. Regarding the decision not to build a bomb, Zarif said that Iran had the fissile material to build 8 bombs in 2012, but decided not to build one.

first time a foreign leader was allowed to criticize the United States' foreign policy in our own Congress. Yet, Netanyahu received a hero's welcome from the majority of both Republican and Democratic senators, which goes to show the extent of Israel's support in our Congress. As mentioned above, the speech was then followed by the letter of the 47 Republicans to Iran's Supreme Leader, which was even more unprecedented. However, this time, the opponents of the nuclear deal might have gone a step too far. General outrage forced some republican senators to backtrack. Senator John McCain, for instance, claimed that he had not read the report carefully. Nonetheless, several hundred thousands of Americans were so outraged that they signed a petition to try the senators for treason and the Vice President, Joe Biden, and the Secretary of State, John Kerry, were uncharacteristically harsh in their denunciation of the letter.[266]

The White House then began an intense lobbying effort to assure both the domestic and international opponents of the nuclear deal that the possible accord would not jeopardize American allies and that it was a good accord for the United States. Subsequently, the Senate passed a compromise oversight bill on May 7, 2015 which gives the Congress 30 days to review an accord before the president can lift any congressionally imposed sanctions. The Senate vote was 98 to 1 and Senator Cotton, the author of the controversial letter to Iran's supreme leader, cast the only opposing vote. On the same day, 151 House Democrat members wrote a letter to President Obama and supported his efforts.

Internationally, Israel continues to do everything she can to torpedo any chances of rapprochement between Iran and the United States. The Obama administration has decided that it cannot change the Israeli position on the nuclear accord and, instead, has focused its efforts on soothing the fears of the Arab countries in the region. Some news sources reported that the United States might even be willing to form an informal defense treaty with these Persian Gulf states to assure them that Iran would not be in a position to threaten their sovereignty.

The Administration took these diplomatic efforts to new heights when it hosted a meeting of the Gulf Cooperation Council at Camp David where President Obama met with Persian Gulf Arab leaders on Thursday May 14. However, it is not certain if these efforts will pay off for the Administration. The Saudi King Salman and Hamd Al Khalifa (Bahrain) chose not to attend the meeting, which is interpreted by many to show the distrust, or at least the disapproval of these monarchs of current U.S. foreign policy initiatives.[267] Nonetheless, the Arab opposition has been muted. Although the sincerity of the Saudis—given their regional rivalry with Iran and their earlier efforts to torpedo an agreement between Iran and the United States, and the current absence of their King from Camp David talks—is questionable; both Saudi Arabia and Turkey have expressed public support for the agreement and Egypt seems to be on board as well.

In Iran, the reaction to the original framework agreement in 2014 was mixed. A Guardian newspapers' article shows that reactions varied. Responses to the Guardian interviewer's questions ranged from joyous remarks made by a third grade girls' civic class who viewed Zarif as a savior, to cautious optimism of businessmen and the cynicism of taxi drivers. While reformist newspapers were very supportive of the accord, conservative papers thought that Iran had been too soft on P5+1.[268] However, the overwhelming majority of Iranians support the new April 2, 2015 framework agreement and are optimistic that relations between Iran and the p5+1 will improve:

> On Thursday night, jubilant Iranians took to the streets within hours of the news breaking in Lausanne. Drivers in Tehran honked their car horns even after midnight as men and women waved flags and showed victory signs from open windows. In an unprecedented move, Iran's national TV also broadcast Obama's Thursday speech on the agreement live. "Everyone is happy," an Iranian journalist based in Tehran told the Guardian. "You can see it in people's faces. This agreement is lifting up their heart." The deal was announced as Iranians were celebrating the last day of the Nowruz new year holiday. On Saturday, when the exchange market opens, many experts predict that the country's currency, the rial, will benefit from the breakthrough almost immediately.[269]

The Supreme Leader, Ayatollah Khamenei, has given his lukewarm endorsement by saying that he is neither for nor opposed to the parameters agreement. However, all Iran observers know that without his approval, even a preliminary agreement would have been impossible.

Given both Khamenei and Obama's desire to reach an accord, as of this writing, the likelihood of reaching an agreement by June 30 deadline is strong.

ISIS

Saddam's Legacy

It is now commonplace for pundits and analysts on various TV programs and newspapers to refer to the crisis in the Middle East and the rise of ISIS as a product of Sunni-Shi'a conflict which, according to the pundits, has been raging for over a millennia. Even political comedy shows, such as Bill Maher's and his frequent bigoted attacks on Islam, seem to advance this view.[2]

---

2   Bill Maher, whose show I watch on a regular basis and like, other than his bigoted attacks on Islam, has a history of criticizing Muslims and Islam as violent and fundamentally opposed to decent values which we cherish. See the Guardian article, October 7, "A history of the Bill Maher's

This is a gross oversimplification. The Middle East conflicts operate an intricate web of alliances that at times cross sectarian divisions and at times work along sectarian lines. Take ISIS for example. The top command of ISIS has many former secular, socialist Saddam Baathists officers in its ranks. Amniat or ISIS's intelligence service is headed by a former member of Saddam's Mukhabarat (General Directorate of Intelligence), Abu Ali al-Anbari.[270]

More importantly, as Weiss and Hassan point out in ISIS: Inside the Army of Terror, the relationship between ISIS and the secular Baathists goes back to before ISIS separated itself from Al-Qaida in 2014. Weiss and Hassan state that the 2003 bombing of the UN compound was carried out by a follower of Abu Musab al-Zarqawi, the founder of an Al-Qaida branch that morphed into ISIS, in a VBIED (*vehicle-borne improvised explosive device*) provided by officers in charge of the former Special Security Organization who supervised the Special Republican Guards and Special Forces.

In fact, the current leader of ISIS, Al-Badari, better known by his surname Abu-Bakr al-Baghdadi (the second ISIS leader with the surname al-Baghdadi) is a graduate of a PhD program in Islamic studies from Saddam's era when, according to Weiss and Hassan, all admissions were vetted by the Baath party. Weiss and Hassan also point out that the career of al-Baghdadi was helped along by Adnan Ismael Najam, a former Capitan in Saddam's army, and al-Baghdadi's chief of ISIS's general military council, known previously as Abu-al Anbari.[271] The influence of Saddam's former army officers in ISIS is such that Liz Sly of Washington Post writes:

> Even with the influx of thousands of foreign fighters, almost all of the leaders of the Islamic State are former Iraqi officers, including the members of its shadowy military and security committees, and the majority of its emirs and princes, according to Iraqis, Syrians and analysts who study the group.[272]

Hence, one argument against simplification of the conflict in the Middle East is to point out the role of secular Baathists in ISIS.

A second argument against the Sunni-Shi'a simplification centers on the role of tribes in Iraqi al-Anbar and the Syrian desert. These tribes, exclusively Sunni in Deir Ezzor, Raqqa and Derra (Syria) and al-Anbar (Iraq) from the time of general Petraeus and his sponsorship of the Son's of Iraq, have at times allied with ISIS but at other times fought Al-Qaida and ISIS. Their actions are based on tribal rivalries and politics, genuine disgust with ISIS or the Iraqi government, and economic incentives and not based on religion.

'not bigoted' remarks on Islam" at <http://www.theguardian.com/tv-and-radio/tvandradioblog/2014/oct/06/bill-maher-islam-ben-affleck>.

It is true that al-Zarqawi, the founder of Al-Qaida in Iraq—which later morphed to Islamic State of Iraq (ISL) and then Islamic State of Iraq and Syria ISIS (now officially IS-Islamic State)—targeted Shi'a population centers to create sectarian tensions. But this was not because Shi'a and Sunni communities were at war with each other; rather, it was to create that communal war. ISIS actions were aided, as previously discussed, by the unintended consequences of Saudi and American actions to stop the growing Iranian influence through her Shi'a proxies. Hence, if there is a Sunni-Shi'a war, it is only a facet of the overall conflict and can end by adopting more inclusive political actions. The party that now seems to emphasize the sectarian nature of the Middle East conflict, other than pundits on American TV, is the government of Saudi Arabia which simplifies even the complicated Yemen conflict incorrectly (see below) as Shi'a Iran's attempt to expand her influence at the cost of Sunnis.

The third argument against an over simplification of the conflict to Shi'a versus Sunni is the conduct of war in Syria. The Alawite Assad regime has refrained from attacking ISIS for much of the conflict in Syria. It has instead focused on combating the Free Syrian Army and the Saudi, and Qatari backed Al-Qaida official branch Al-Nusra front.

The Ebb and Flow of War against ISIS

Prior to May 17, 2015 when Ramadi, the capital of Anbar province, fell to ISIS after a protracted battle, some of the headlines in an Iraqi newspaper from May 2015 read as follows: Iraqi forces repel ISIS attack on Ajil oilfield, kill 73 ISIS elements, announces Dijla Operations; Security forces kill large number of terrorists in al-Karma area; and Iraqi federal police shells ISIS sites in northern Tikrit, 13 militants killed.[3] These headlines are a far cry from what they would have read just a few months ago when Mosul, Iraq's second largest city, fell in June of 2014. Back then, Iraqinews.com headlines reported the failures of Iraqi and Kurdish security forces and the atrocities of ISIS.[273]

Back in June of 2014, ISIS looked unstoppable and Baghdad itself was in danger of falling into ISIS hands. Had it not been for the immediate and rapid response of Iranian-backed militias, who formed a defensive ring around Baghdad, and Kurdish Peshmarga forces, who attacked ISIS from the north after receiving Iranian Arms and equipment, Baghdad could have collapsed. The United States and the coalition's aerial bombardment of ISIS forces has certainly been effective, but it was not the main factor which saved Baghdad in the summer of 2014, or recaptured Tikrit. A

---

3   See Iraqinews.com, for instance the May 10 2015 article titled: "Iraqi forces repel ISIS attack on Ajil oilfield, kill 73 ISIS elements, announces Dijla Operations." <http://www.iraqinews.com/iraq-war/iraqi-forces-repel-isis-attack-ajil-oilfield-kill-73-isis-elements-announces-dijla-operation>.

September 2014 article in the Los Angeles Times captured the significance of Iranian aid:

> At his office here, Mala Bakhtiar, military supervisor of the Kurdish *peshmerga* forces and a local politician, spoke openly of comprehensive Iranian involvement in logistics, intelligence-sharing and provision of military equipment to Kurdish troops.
>
> "They gave us rockets, cannons, maps," a grateful Bakhtiar said of the Iranians, gesturing at the large-scale maps competing for wall space. "We needed these things badly."[274]

Since the fall of Mosul in June of 2014, ISIS lost about 30 percent of the territory she had captured, almost all in Iraq. The biggest loss for ISIS was the fall of Tikrit. A Wall Street Journal article's subtitle captured the significance of this event in late March 2015: "The development is the biggest setback to the militants since they began to seize large swaths of land in Iraq and Syria last year."[275]

However, the United States put pressure on the Iraqi government to restrict the role of Shi'ite militias in the fight against ISIS. These militias were formed after the fall of Mosul in 2014 when Ayatollah Sistani, the Iranian born religious leader of Iraqi Shia's, had issued a fatwa and had urged Shias to fight against ISIS which was threatening Baghdad. They are called al-Hashd al-Sha'bi Forces (Popular Mobilization Forces).[276]

The U.S. claims that their opposition to the involvement of Shia militias in Al-Anbar province is to reduce sectarian tensions between Sunni's and Shi'ites as the majority of Anbar inhabitants are Sunni. However, the real reason behind American opposition to the involvement of Al-Hashad Al Sha'bi forces might be more sinister; to check the growing Iranian influence in the region. These militias receive military and financial aid from Iran and consider Iran their patron. So a victory for Al-Hashad Al Sha'bi can be considered a victory for Iran, something that the United States and its Arab allies do not want to see.

In fact, former Secretary of Defense, Robert Gates, explicitly stated that he did not want to see Iran's influence grow when Rose pondered why the United States does not rely on Shi'a militias who have proven effective in pushing ISIS back.[277] This way of thinking about Iraq precisely proves my point in chapter three about the need for people who are familiar with the history and culture of the region to advise American presidents. Gates, who is a distinguished academic and public servant and has served many years in high positions with access to classified intelligence, should know better than anyone that the cultural, historical, and religious ties between Iran and Iraq mean that Iran will always be influential in Iraq. Perhaps it would be best for American policy makers to see a win-win situation as opposed to a zero-sum game with Iran when it comes to Iraq. Even if you set aside the current financial support of the Iranian government for Iraq, a historically and culturally aware and knowledgeable observer could not help but notice that the name of the Iraqi capital, Baghdad, is a Persian word meaning God-given. The city was founded near the Iranian Ctesiphon, the capital of the Iranian Parthian and the Persian Sassanid empires who fought with Rome for hegemony over the Middle East and ruled Eastern Iraq for almost a 1000 years. Hundreds of thousands of Iranians go to Iraq each year and Iraq's leading religious authority, Al-Sistani, was born in Iran.

To sum up, the policy goals of America in combating ISIS are sometimes modified if an ISIS defeat means an Iranian victory. The U.S. put pressure on the Iraqi government not to allow Iranian-backed forces into Ramadi and, as a result, Ramadi fell on May 17 and the headlines changed once again. However, apparently the Anbar population and Iraqi government are no longer willing to completely succumb to sectarian politics and American pressure and have reconsidered Shia militias' participation in the campaign to liberate Ramadi and Al-Anbar from the clutches of ISIS. On May 17, Iraqinews.com included a news item that Anbar Provincial Council had voted to allow the Shi'ite forces to enter Ramadi:

> "Anbar provincial council voted on the participation of al-Hashd al-Sha'bi in the liberation of the province from the ISIS group."

> On Sunday, Anbar tribes demanded the Prime Minister Haider al-Abadi to send urgent reinforcements and the entry of Hashd al-Sha'bi militia to the city of Ramadi, while the government called for closing the Syrian border with Iraq.[278]

The confusion over U.S. policy goals in Iraq, particularly as it concerns combating ISIS, is not just limited to U.S. pressure to limit Shia militia participation in campaigns against ISIS. It is obvious to everyone after almost a year of aerial bombardment of ISIS that military success requires fighting ISIS with ground forces.

The Kurdish Peshmarga and the Iranian-backed militias are the only forces who have proven their mettle and who have beaten ISIS. Yet the U.S. wants to limit the role of the Shia militia, but might consider arming the Kurds and Sunni tribes directly.

The Administration apparently wants the Iraqi government to arm the Sunni tribes, yet the Congress is inclined to arm the Kurds directly. Hill.Com reported on May 6 that a bipartisan Senate bill proposed by Senators Joni Ernst (R-Iowa) and Barbara Boxer (D-Calif.), if passed by both houses and signed by the president, would "provide three-year, emergency authority for the president to provide weapons and training directly to Iraqi Kurdish peshmerga forces ... [and] is meant to reduce delays in arming Kurdish fighters, who are widely regarded as highly trained and have often led the charge in retaking territory seized last year by the terrorist group."[279] The Hill.Com report also notes that the House has already passed a bill that grants up to 715 million dollars to Kurds, but it might discard that provision.

Hence, there is disagreement among various branches of the U.S. government on who to arm to fight ISIS, while all ignore the most effective fighting force on the ground, the Iranian backed Shia militias.

Furthermore, the biggest difficulty in fighting ISIS in Iraq might actually have nothing to do with Iraq and it might be the support that the U.S. and her allies provide for Syrian rebels; many of whom are foreign and extremists and are in Syria to support ISIS. As these forces gain ground in Syria, they can shift resources at will across the nonexistent Iraq-Syria border and put pressure on Iraqi troops.

On March 28, 2015, the Ahrar al-Sham, Jund al-Aqsa and Nusra Front, all Islamic extremists groups—in fact Al Nusra is the official branch of Al-Qaeda—captured Idlib. Idlib is the provincial capital of Idlib Governorate which is a gateway to Assad regime's heartland, Latakia province by the Mediterranean.[280]

Meanwhile, ISIS has taken advantage of the Syrian government's recent setbacks and has captured a good part of the Yarmouk refugee camp, which is at the outskirts of Damascus, the Syrian capital. Not only the rebel advances in the north had weakened the government forces elsewhere, but Al Nusra, according to news reports, actually aided ISIS's takeover of the Yarmouk camp.[281]

Some analysts including CNN's Lina Khatib, argued that the Assad government, which already did not control good parts of the camp, actually benefited from the fall of Yarmouk to ISIS. The capture, nonetheless, puts ISIS at the door steps of the Syrian capital where they can occasionally lob mortar at even the best protected parts of the capital.[282]

To sum up, the contradictory policy goals of the United States and her allies in Iraq and Syria, have allowed ISIS to remain as a strong and dangerous force. This is despite the fact that we have bombed ISIS since August of 2014, and have hit over 6,200 targets.[283]

To destroy ISIS, we need to work with Iran and her Shia militias in Iraq and put the goal of a transition in the Syrian government behind the goal of destroying ISIS. This is not just the advice put forward here, but is similar to the opinion of Iraqi Prime Minister, Haider Al-Abadi, who has urged cooperation between the United States and Iran in Iraq.[284] The idea of the need for cooperation with Iran is also supported by a number of former CIA and State Department officials, among whom is Robert Baer. In *The Devil We Know: Dealing with the New Iranian Superpower*, Baer writes:

> What America needs to do is to ask for a truce with Iran, deal with it as an equal, reach a settlement one issue at a time, and continue along the same course until Iran is ready for détente … and may be more.[285]

As well as working a détente with Iran, we also need to face the ugly truth that our ally Saudi Arabia has been, and still is, a supporter of radical Islam by means which range from allowing private donation to go to Al-Nusra and other radical groups, to outright government funding and support. Therefore, we need to put pressure on Saudi Arabia to cut their financial and military ties to extremist groups in Syria.

Unfortunately, the lobbying by the Israelis and the web of Saudi money, funneled through defense and non-defense-related major civilian contracts, and the activities of the Carlyle group, have proven to be very difficult obstacles in a U.S.-Iran rapprochement. We have said quite a bit about Israeli influence in American politics; it is time to say a few words about the Saudi influence.

The Saudis influence our politics through our need for their oil and their massive military and civilian purchases which keep our companies happy and supportive. Our political leaders serve on the board of directors of many of these companies and are well compensated for doing so. A prime example of these companies is the Carlyle group which, according to Robert Baer's book, *Sleeping with the Devil: How Washington Sold our Soul for Saudi Crude,* has had "a long and profitable relationship with the Al Sa'ud family."[286] The Carlyle group's General Council in 2001 was our former Secretary of State James Baker and its Chairman our former Defense Secretary Frank Carlucci. Baer mentions that Carlyle has also employed a former head of our Securities and Exchange Commission (Arthur Levitt) a former head of Federal Communication Commission (William Kennard) and a former President George Herbert Walker Bush who acts as an advisor for Carlyle. Bush reportedly earned $80,000 to $100,000 for each speech which he gave from Carlyle. Of course, the list of recipients of generous support and speech honorarium is not limited to republicans. Conservatives critics allege that the Clintons took millions from Saudi Arabia either directly or through contributions to the Clinton Foundation and even mainstream media have recently written quite a few articles on foreign donations to the Clintons.[287]

Therefore, while it would be very difficult to overcome the Saudi and Israeli opposition to a rapprochement with Iran, particularly when it comes to fighting ISIS, we can't end our efforts there. We also need to pressure Turkey to seal her border with Syria and Qatar to end her meddling in Syria and Iraq. Assad might lie about many things, but he is not lying when he claims that a lot of the opposition fighters are foreign terrorists who are allowed to cross the Turkish border into Syria on a regular basis.

Yemen: The Fallacy of Sectarianism

Nowhere is the fallacy of simplifying current Middle Eastern conflicts to a millennia-long Sunni-Shi'a struggle more obvious than in Yemen. The Houthi rebel group who has captured Sana'a, the capital, and much of Aden, the most important port in

Yemen, is now allied with parts of the military and former president Saleh who was ousted from power in 2011 largely due to the demands of Houthis.

Saleh and parts of the Yemen military are now allied and fighting the Saudi-backed President Abed Mansour Hadi who fled to Saudi Arabia after Houthi advances in Aden. What makes the sectarian conflict thesis even more nonsensical is that both Hadi and Houthis belong to the Zaidi sect, an offshoot of Shi'a Islam.

Moreover, Saleh, Hadi, and Houthis have all fought the Sunni Salafi Al-Qaida in the Arabian Peninsula (AQAP) at one time or the other. In fact, Saleh who was Yemen's president for almost 38 years, received quite a bit of money and support from the United States in return for his policy of allowing drone strikes against Al-Qaida. Saleh was even able to garner American support for his war against the Hirak movement, a Southern secessionist movement which first began as a protest against marginalization of the South by President Saleh, but then morphed into armed opposition which received the backing of AQAP[288].

The Middle East Editor of the Guardian, Ian Black, summarizes the fallacy of simplifying Yemen's conflict to a sectarian conflict as follows:

> The conflict is fundamentally a political and tribal one rather than sectarian—in a country which has no tradition of Sunni-Shia animosity.

> The Zaidis emerged from Shia Islam but of all the Shia they are the most similar to Sunnis in terms of religious practice ... The Houthis subsequently gained power because the Saudis lost influence with the Yemeni tribes and because the ruling elite in Sana'a had been fragmented by the fall of Saleh.[289]

While estimates of the tribal population of Yemen vary, a figure of 35% seems to be reasonable and the majority of the tribal population are settled and integrated in the urban settings. Caton states that two third of "the parliament is composed of elected tribal sheikhs" and "almost the entire army is composed of tribesmen."[290] Tribes, such as the Houthis, therefore constitute an important factor in Yemeni politics and their shifting alliances go a long way in explaining the changing landscape of Yemeni politics.

The Saudis, who are now in their second month of bombing the Zaidi Houthis, used to support the same tribes in the 1950s against the Republicans backed by Egypt. The Houthi tribes, who are now allied with Saleh, used to fight Saleh for years after Yemeni troops killed Hussein Badr-al-Din al-Houthi in 2004. Saleh, who spent years fighting AQAP and other Islamists, used Arab–Afghans and other Islamists in his attack on separatists in the South in 1994 and it is said that without their support he would have had difficulty winning the civil war. When Aden was sacked on July 7, 1994, Jihadists entered Aden "in a caravan of battered Land Cruisers and bullet-scarred pickups."[291]

Therefore, despite the pundits on TV, and Saudi protestations of a Shi'a/Iranian takeover of Yemen, the picture that emerges from a study of the country is that tribal and personal politics and loyalties are more important than sectarian issues and beliefs. If the conflict in Yemen—which since the start of Saudi aerial bombardments two months ago has claimed over a 1,000 civilians, displaced over half a million people, and destroyed much of the infrastructure of the poorest country in the Middle East—is to come to an end; these tribal and personal loyalties must be understood and incorporated into a political solution.[292]

The Promise of Peace?

Historians typically date the beginning of History as opposed to pre-history to the invention of writing around 3300 BC in the Sumerian city of Uruk in Southwestern Iraq. It was in Sumer, in the Early Dynastic period (2900–2334 BC) that the world's first armies clashed over resources and power[4]. More than five thousand years later, the region we now call the Middle East is once again at the center of a historic struggle for power. Conflict rages from Yemen in the Southern tip of the Arabian Peninsula to the shores of the Mediterranean cities of Syria and the African cities of Libya.

Some have called this, erroneously, a clash of civilizations. Others, equally mistaken, have attributed the conflict to a struggle within Islam akin to the Protestant and Catholic wars of the 16th and 17th centuries. However, the truth is much more complex and one must take into account superpower rivalry, regional power rivalries, tribal rivalries, the role of authoritarianism, along with individual ambitions for power. Sectarian issues are but a small part of the origins of many of the wars raging in the area.

In 1976, before the Iranian Revolution and the Soviet Invasion of Afghanistan, the only simmering conflicts in the region were the Arab-Israeli conflict and Kurdish rebellion in Turkey and Iraq. The Taliban came into existence in Afghanistan only after we and the Saudis responded to the Soviet invasion of the country by supporting Islamic fundamentalists who fought the Soviets. Al-Qaida came into existence only after we stationed troops in Saudi Arabia and Osama Bin Laden's efforts to oust unbelievers from the Arabian Peninsula began. ISIS emerged from the ashes of Al-Qaida in Iraq after our invasion in 2003.

---

4   Some elements of writing were in place even before 3300 BC. See the concise account of ancient civilizations by John Haywood, 2013. *The Ancient World*. New York: Metro Books.

So to insure a lasting peace, if that is truly our aim, we need a three-pronged policy which sets our actions in motion simultaneously in all three areas.

First, the oldest conflict in the region, the Arab-Israeli conflict, must be solved by putting pressure on Israel to accept a two-state solution and give Palestinians dignity and their own state. Solving this conflict will remove a long-standing source of radicalization and tension in the region.

Second, support for democratic movements and aspirations of people in the region must be more than rhetoric. We need to apply pressure to authoritarian governments in the Persian Gulf and elsewhere in the region, to allow the development of civil society and viable democratic opposition. Authoritarianism breeds terrorism and terrorism justifies authoritarianism. Terrorists emerge after the collapse of the authoritarian governments only because these governments have destroyed all other viable alternatives to their rule. The Saudi royal family has been funding radical Islam outside Saudi Arabia, out of its fear of radicalized youth inside her borders. In Syria, Assad relies on the brutality of ISIS to justify his refusal to move to a transitional government. In Iran, the hardliners oppose a U.S.-Iran rapprochement out of a fear that renewed ties between the two countries will jeopardize their economic and political interests by strengthening democratic forces.

Third, we must build on the nuclear agreement and reach a comprehensive deal with Iran that safeguards our access to resources, supports the civil society in Iran, and reduces tension in the region. With Iran's help we can stabilize Afghanistan, Iraq and Syria and remove ISIS from the scene. Engagement with Iran does not mean that we approve of the domestic policies of the Iranian government which have resulted in discrimination against minorities and women and arrests of journalists and reformist figures. Instead, engagement will allow us to better support reform and improvement in social and political freedoms in Iran.

Of course, achieving any of these goals, given the complexity of domestic forces in the U.S. and the region, is very difficult, but such a three-pronged policy approach at least carries a promise for peace.

Endnotes

1. See G. N. Curzon, *Curzon's Persia*, ed. P. King (London: Sidgwick & Jackson Limited, 1986), 10.

2. See page 15 in King's edition of *Curzon's Persia*. King states that Curzon's view of the Persians wasn't all negative and that Curzon gave credit to Persians for their vitality and freedom from deep prejudice and bigotry. Better yet, if Persians served the British, they could be considered "courageous and resourceful," as was the case of Ramzan Ali Khan, the boss of Curzon's Iranian, Armenian, and Turcoman attendants. Ramzan Ali Khan was "an Afghan of Persian extraction" (ibid., 27).

3. Professor Khalidi argues that American inexperience in the area and the dynamics of superpower rivalry played a role in the influence of the British on American thinking: "American policymakers, less experienced in international affairs than their British counterparts, often tended to be influenced by the latter's deep concern about the spread of communism in the Middle East (which they often conflated with nationalism and anticolonialism)." See Rashid Khalidi, *Sowing Crisis: The Cold War and American Dominance in the Middle East* (Boston: Beacon Press, 2009), 3.

4. Ibid., 20–21.

5. See Kenneth Waltz, *Theory of International Politics* (New York: McGraw-Hill, 1979), 36.

6. See Kenneth Waltz's discussion of Marxist and neocolonial theories of international relations in chapter two of his book, ibid.

7. See Gregory G. Dess, G. T. Lumpkin, Alan B. Eisner, and Gerry McNamara, *Strategic Management: Creating Competitive Advantages* (New York: McGraw-Hill, 2014), 5.

8. See the end of chapter four, where I cite data about the proportions of calls against as opposed to for an attack on Syria.

9. Richard Becker of the ANSWER coalition (a pacifist, antiracist national organization) thinks that "the real aim of the U.S. 'is to remove all the independent governments in the Middle East, to destroy the popular movements in order to secure the domination of this key strategic and oil rich region.'", "U.S. Aims to Overthrow All Independent Governments in the Middle East," RT.Com, September 2, 2013, http://rt.com/op-edge/us-overthrow-middle-east-328/.

10. See http://www.chomsky.info/books.htm. His latest book—Noam Chomsky, *Power Systems: Conversations on Global Democratic Uprisings and the New Challenges to U.S. Empire (Interviews with David Barsamian)* (New York: Metropolitan Books, 2013)—makes a particularly strong connection between the imperialistic goals of US foreign policy and the beneficiary few privileged members of the elite.

11. See Andrew J. Bacevich, *The Limits of Power: The End of American Exceptionalism* (New York: Metropolitan Books, 2008), 2–4.

12. See Michael E. Porter and Scott Stern, with Michael Green, *Social Progress Index 2014* (2014), http://www.socialprogressimperative.org/publications.

13. On official thresholds for poverty, see table 3.E1, US Social Security Administration, *Annual Statistical Supplement, 2013*, http://www.ssa.gov/policy/docs/statcomps/supplement/2013/3e.html#table3.e1. On the number of poor people in America, see table 3.E2 from the same source, http://www.ssa.gov/policy/docs/statcomps/supplement/2013/3e.html#table3.e2. On the cost of housing in New York, see "Erectile Resumption: Could the Miami Skyline One Day Resemble Manhattan's?" *Economist*, http://www.economist.com/news/united-states/21600172-could-miami-skyline-one-day-resemble-manhattans-erectile-resumption?zid=311&ah=308cac674cccf554ce65cf926868bbc2.

Insane City, reasonable prices

Urban apartment prices per square foot
2012–13 average, $'000

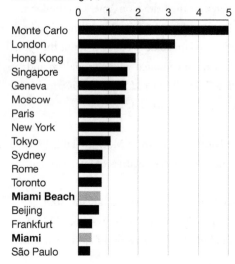

Miami-Dade County, new sales of:
'000

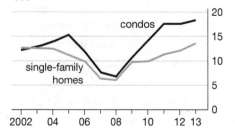

For rental costs in California, see USC's report on multifamily housing at USC Casden Multifamily Forecast 2013, http://lusk.usc.edu/casden/multifamily/forecast and data provided in Numbeo.com at http://www.numbeo.com/cost-of-living/compare_cities.jsp?country1=United+States&country2=United+States&city1=New+York%2C+NY&city2=Los+Angeles%2C+CA.

14. See the article by David Leonhardt and Kevin Quealy, "The American Middle Class Is No Longer the World's Richest," *New York Times*, April 22, 2014, http://www.nytimes.com/2014/04/23/upshot/the-american-middle-class-is-no-longer-the-worlds-richest.html?hp&_r=0.

15. See the article by David Leonhardt, "Inequality Has Been Going On Forever … but That Doesn't Mean It's Inevitable," *New York Times*, May 4, 2014, http://www.nytimes.com/2014/05/04/magazine/inequality-has-been-going-on-forever-but-that-doesnt-mean-its-inevitable.html?hpw&rref=magazine, which is based on the thirty-five-year-long data collection and analysis of Leonhardt's organization, The Upshot.

16. See the article by Dylan Matthews, "Defense Spending in the U.S., in Four Charts," *Washington Post*, August 28, 2012, http://www.washingtonpost.com/blogs/wonkblog/wp/2012/08/28/defense-spending-in-the-u-s-in-four-charts/.

17. See New America Foundation, "Federal Education Budget Project," April 30, 2014, http://febp.newamerica.net/background-analysis/education-federal-budget.

18. See James A. Morone and Rogan Kersh, *By the People: Debating American Government* (Oxford: Oxford University Press, 2013), 653.

19. See Center on Budget and Policy Priorities, *Policy Basics: Where Do Our Federal Tax Dollars Go?* March 31, 2014, http://www.cbpp.org/cms/?fa=view&id=1258.

20. See Edith Hall *Inventing the Barbarian: Greek Self Definition Through Tragedy* (Cambridge: Clarendon Press, 2006), 99.

21. Jacobsen, who passed away in 1989, is among the best-known authorities on early Mesopotamia, particularly Assyria and Sumer. Among his early major works was *The Sumerian King List, Assyriological Studies 11* (Chicago: Oriental Institute, 1939). Cf. A. L. Oppenheim in ANET 265. You can see a later interpretation of the work in R. K. Harrison, *Reinvestigating the Antediluvian Sumerian King List*, 1993). The work referred to here is Thorkild Jacobsen, "Primitive Democracy in Ancient Mesopotamia," in *Toward the Image of Tammuz and Other Essays on Mesopotamian History and Culture*, ed. W. L. Moran (Harvard University Press, 1970).

22. See B. Isakhan, "Engaging 'Primitive Democracy': Mideast Roots of Collective Governance," *Middle East Policy* XIV (Fall 2007): 104.

23. See Michael J. Sadaro, *Comparative Politics: A Global Introduction*, 3rd ed. (New York: McGraw-Hill, 2008), 171.

24. See J. S. Goldstein and J. C. Pevehouse, *International Relations: 2013–2014 Update*, brief 6th ed. (Upper Saddle River, NJ: Pearson, 2014), 96.

25. Although we are taught that democracy started from Greece, many modern scholars dispute that assertion. Raul S. Manglapus, in his book *Will of the People: Original Democracy in Non-Western Societies*, cites the following examples as non-Greek cultures who had a more inclusive form of participatory democracy:

> Agrarian communities in Mesopotamia that were autonomous and self-sufficient and used an assembly to direct their "communal affairs," and coexisted with the temple-palace system.

In Assyria, "the highest judicial authority was a general assembly of all the colonist; Karum sahir rabi—the colony young and old." Manglapus states that Karum had the power to "grant kingship and take it back."

The Babylonian "assembly," Puhrum, which, according to Jacobsen, was open to all citizens and in the "days of the Kings of Akkad," could choose a king. Gilgamesh, the fifth king of the first Uruk dynasty around 2500 BC, is said to have consulted on matters of war and peace with both with an assembly of "the elders of Uruk," and then "the assembly of the men of the town, perhaps comparable to our bicameral parliamentary structure." Manglapus argues that the inclusion of female gods among spirits who were represented in these assemblies implies that they might have been open to female participation.

Ebla, a city about fifty-five miles from Aleppo in Syria, elected its king, and Indian "open assemblies, Santhagaras or Mote-halls, where the young and old, the rich and the poor alike were present, conducted legislative and executive functions." In Rigveda, which Manglapus calls the "earliest literary production of the Aryans," he places much emphasis on a bicameral assembly structure, the samitti, for the common people and Sabha for the nobles.

Teutonic assemblies included "all men fit to fight." Manglapus argues that as Romans advanced among the Germanic tribes, they destroyed these participatory forms of government.

Raul S. Manglapus, *Will of the People: Original Democracy in Non-Western Societies*. Praeger (May 14, 1987), Westport CT, USA.

26. Benjamin Isakhan, "Engaging 'Primitive Democracy': Mid East Roots of Collective Governance," *Mid East Policy* XIV (Fall 2007): 97–117.

27. The reference to Toynbee's quote is from Louise Fawcett, *International Relations of the Middle East*, 3rd ed. (Oxford: Oxford University Press, 2012). Here is the passage quoted by Fawcett, which is taken from another work (Hourani, 1961):

They have gone wrong because they are egocentric, in diverse ways: because they deal only with Western history, or because they consider other histories only in so far as they are relevant to Western history, or because they look at other histories through categories applicable only to Western history, or because they think of themselves as somehow standing outside history and able to judge it. See pages 6 and 7 in Fawcett, *International Relations of the Middle East.*

28. See Peter von Sivers, Charles A. Desnoyers, and George B. Stow, *Patterns of World History* (Oxford: Oxford University Press, 2012), 204. Von Sivers et al. state that "what has been idealized by people in modern era [the Greek Democracy] as a forerunner of our own institutions was in fact not very different from the urban assemblies in Mesopotamian cities or those of the early Indian city-states in the Ganges Valley. ... In retrospect Greece was thus not the only pioneer of constitutional rule. It shared this role with other societies" (204).

29. "Erythrae or Erythrai (Greek: Ἐρυθραί), later Litri, was one of the twelve Ionian cities of Asia Minor, situated 22 km north-east of the port of Cyssus (modern name: Çeşme), on a small peninsula stretching into the Bay of Erythrae, at an equal distance from the mountains Mimas and Corycus, and directly opposite the island of Chios. ... About 453 BC Erythrae, refusing to pay tribute, seceded from the Delian League. A garrison and a new government restored the union, but late in the Peloponnesian War (412 BC) it revolted again with Chios and Clazomenae.

Later it was allied alternately with Athens and Persia" (http://en.wikipedia.org/wiki/Erythrae.

30. Hall, *Inventing the Barbarian*, p. 60.

31. A recent op-ed by the new Iranian president in the *Washington Post* argued against a zero-sum view of the world:

> In a world where global politics is no longer a zero-sum game, it is—or should be—counterintuitive to pursue one's interests without considering the interests of others. A constructive approach to diplomacy doesn't mean relinquishing one's rights. It means engaging with one's counterparts, on the basis of equal footing and mutual respect, to address shared concerns and achieve shared objectives. In other words, win-win outcomes are not just favorable but also achievable. A zero-sum, Cold War mentality leads to everyone's loss.
>
> Sadly, unilateralism often continues to overshadow constructive approaches. Security is pursued at the expense of the insecurity of others, with disastrous consequences.
>
> Hassan Rohani, "See Why Iran Seeks Constructive Engagement," *Washington Post*, September 19, 2013, http://www.washingtonpost.com/opinions/president-of-iran-hassan-rouhani-time-to-engage/2013/09/19/4d2da564-213e-11e3-966c-9c4293c47ebe_story_1.html.

32. For a chronology of pre-Islamic Iranian history, see Dr. Kaveh Farrokh, *Shadows in the Desert: Ancient Persia at War* (Oxford: Osprey Publishing, 2007), 9–11. The dates listed here are taken from his work. I should also point out that the spelling of Iranian names, even dynastic names, varies. Dr. Farrokh spells the second Persian dynasty's name the Sasanids with two "s's," whereas most others, including Parvaneh Pourshariati's work (listed in citation cxviii) on the Sasanian Empire, spell the name with one "s."

33. Ibid., 10.

34. On the production of oil and its impact on Middle East political economy, see Giacomo Luciani, "Oil and Political Economy in the International Relations of the Middle East," in *International Relations of the Middle East*, 3rd. ed., ed. Louise Fawcett (Oxford: Oxford University Press, 2012). Furthermore, while some may argue that American involvement in the Middle East began with oil concession granted to ARAMCO in 1933 by Saudi Arabia, the US government did not become actively and directly involved until its participation in the invasion and occupation of Iran in 1942. It was only in 1943 when Americans became interested in basing rights in Saudi Arabia, and the first high-level contact between Americans and Saudis—a meeting between FDR and Saudi King Abd al Aziz ibn Saud—did not take place until 1945. See Khalidi, *Sowing Crisis*, chapters one and two on the history of American involvement in the Middle East.

35. See Eugene Rogan, "The Emergence of the Middle East into the Modern State System," in *International Relations of the Middle East*, 3rd. ed., ed. Louise Fawcett (Oxford: Oxford University Press, 2012).

36. See Human Rights Watch, *Syria: Groups Call for ICC Referral*, May 15, 2014, http://www.hrw.org/news/2014/05/15/syria-groups-call-icc-referral.

37. Ibid.

38. See "The Syrian Rebel Groups Pulling in Foreign Fighters," BBC.com, December 24, 2013, http://www.bbc.com/news/world-middle-east-25460397.

39. Ibid.

40. See Peter Sluglett, "The Cold War in the Middle East," in *International Relations of the Middle East*, 3rd. ed., ed. Louise Fawcett (Oxford: Oxford University Press, 2012), 71.

41. Nancy A. Youssef, "Syrian Rebels Describe U.S.-Backed Training in Qatar," *http://www.pbs.org/wgbh/pages/frontline/foreign-affairs-defense/syria-arming-the-rebels/syrian-rebels-describe-u-s-backed-training-in-qatar/*, May 26, 2014.

42. This argument is made by Dr. Erlich. See R. Erlich, *The Iran Agenda: The Real Story of U.S. Policy and the Middle East Crisis* (Sausalito, CA: Polipoint Press, 2007), 174.

43. See the analysis of the poll by Telhami at http://www.brookings.edu/research/reports/2011/11/21-arab-public-opinion-telhami. Telhami looks at the fact that 18 percent of respondents viewed Iran as a threat, as a major negative for Iran, ignoring the 71 and 59 percentages attached to Israel and the United States.

44. See the PDF of the poll at http://www.google.com/url?sa=t&rct=j&q=&esrc=s&source=web&cd=3&ved=0CDUQFjAC&url=http%3A%2F%2Fwww.brookings.edu%2F~%2Fmedia%2Fresearch%2Ffiles%2Freports%2F2011%2F11%2F21-arab-public-opinion-telhami%2F1121_arab_public_opinion.pdf&ei=gPV-U_HBPMH8oATOz4K4Dg&usg=AFQjCNHy2I-jtLDqZPVj84A9snQMnx_b3A&sig2=tazeroRtJ4QOB-tyn2sRcA&bvm=bv.67720277,d.cGU. See also the analysis of the poll at http://www.brookings.edu/research/reports/2011/11/21-arab-public-opinion-telhami. Telhami looks at the fact that 18 percent of respondents viewed Iran as a threat, as a major negative for Iran, ignoring the 71 and 59 percentages attached to Israel and the United States.

45. See "The ACRPS Announces the Results of the 2012/2013 Arab Opinion Index," June 2013, http://english.dohainstitute.org/content/af5000b3-46c7-45bb-b431-28b2de8b33c7.

46. See Raymond Hinnebusch, "The Politics of Identity in Middle East International Relations," in *International Relations of the Middle East*, 3rd. ed., ed. Louise Fawcett (Oxford: Oxford University Press, 2012), 152.

47. See James Carafano, "Top 5 Reasons Not to Use Missile Strikes in Syria," August 25, 2013, http://blog.heritage.org/2013/08/25/top-5-reasons-not-to-use-missile-strikes-in-syria/.

48. Clark, N. (2013, 08 30). "Britain's Parliament Finally Turns Against the Neo-Cons and Serial Warmongers." Retrieved from: RT.Com: http://rt.com/op-edge/uk-parliament-vote-syria-warmongers-209/.

49. See "Exclusive: CIA Files Prove America Helped Saddam as He Gassed Iran," *Foreign Policy*, August 16, 2013, http://www.foreignpolicy.com/articles/2013/08/25/secret_cia_files_prove_america_helped_saddam_as_he_gassed_iran. Also see http://en.wikipedia.org/wiki/Halabja_poison_gas_attack.

50. See Fawaz Gerges, "Aljazeera, Syria: The Odds Are against the Opposition," May 13, 2014, http://www.aljazeera.com/indepth/opinion/2014/05/syria-odds-are-against-oppositi-201451165115169429.html.

51. However, the current chairman of the Joint Chiefs of Staff, General Martin Dempsey, on July 22, 2013, estimated the cost of just imposing a no-fly zone would be $1 billion per month. See "Syria's war: The new normal; territorial divisions are deepening, regardless of regime and rebel advances," *The Economist*, July 27, 2013, 42.

52. See the advance, unedited *Report of the International Commission of Inquiry on Libya* released on March 2, 2012, by the Human Rights Council, Nineteenth Session, agenda item 4, "Human Rights Situations that Require the Council's Attention," March 2, 2012, 100, http://www.nytimes.com/interactive/2012/03/03/world/africa/united-nations-report-on-libya.html?_r=0. You can also download the document from http://www.refworld.org/docid/4ffd19532.html.

53. Ibid., 130 The finding on torture by both Qadhafi and Thuwar starts on page 97, and the discussion of brutal treatment of black Libyans starts on page 112 and continues to page 131.

54. See "Libya in Crisis: Rival Militias Position Themselves for Civil War as Country Disintegrates," *The Independent*, May 19, 2014, http://www.independent.co.uk/news/world/africa/libya-in-crisis-rival-militias-position-themselves-for-civil-war-as-country-teeters-on-brink-9399311.html.

55. See the Congressional Budget Office's page at http://www.cbo.gov/topics/national-security/iraq-and-afghanistan. Also see the Final Sequestration Report for Fiscal Year 2013 at http://www.cbo.gov/sites/default/files/cbofiles/attachments/44021-Sequestration_1column.pdf. Note that "c" in the table indicates that "Overseas Contingency" is basically Afghanistan.

Here is the table on caps for discretionary budget spending:

Table 1. Return to Reference 1, 2

Limits on Discretionary Budget Authority for Fiscal Year 2013

(Millions of dollars)

	Security[a]	Nonsecurity[a]	Total
Caps Set in the Deficit Control Act[b]	684,000	359,000	1,043,000
Adjustments			
Overseas contingency operations[c]	98,683	0	98,683
Emergency requirements[d]	7,042	34,627	41,669
Disaster relief[e]	11,779	0	11,779
Program integrity initiatives[f]	0	483	483
Total	117,504	35,110	152,614
CBO's Estimate of Adjusted Caps for 2013	801,504	394,110	1,195,614
Budget Authority as Estimated by CBO When Legislation Was Enacted	801,504	394,109	1,195,613
Amount by Which Budget Authority Is Above or Below (-) Caps	0	-1	-1

Source: Congressional Budget Office.

(Office S. o., 2013) (Office S. o., 2010)

56. Here is the summary of the findings as published on March 14, 2013, by Brown University in a press release:

> More than 70 percent of those who died of direct war violence in Iraq have been civilians—an estimated 134,000. This number does not account for indirect deaths due to increased vulnerability to disease or injury as a result of war-degraded conditions. That number is estimated to be several times higher.

> The Iraq War will ultimately cost U.S. taxpayers at least $2.2 trillion. Because the Iraq war appropriations were funded by borrowing, cumulative interest through 2053 could amount to more than $3.9 trillion.

57. See C. Coelho, "'Costs of War' Project," March 14, 2013, http://news.brown.edu/pressreleases/2013/03/warcosts.

58. Linda J. Bilmes, "The Financial Legacy of Iraq and Afghanistan: How Wartime Spending Decisions Will Constrain Future National Security Budgets Faculty Research Working Paper Series" Joseph Stiglitz and Linda Bilmes, "No U.S. Peace Dividend after Afghanistan," *Financial Times*, January 3, 2013, http://www.ft.com/cms/s/0/da88f8fe-63e9-11e2-84d8-00144feab49a.html#axzz2TFIhx4wr.

59. See L. J. Bilmes, , "Harvard Kennedy School," March 28, 2013, https://research.hks.harvard.edu/publications/workingpapers/citation.aspx?PubId=8956&type=WPN.

60. Ibid.

61. See "Construction Cost Estimates for Hospital, 2–3 Story in National, US," http://www.reedconstructiondata.com/rsmeans/models/hospital/.

62. See "Construction Cost Estimates for High School in National, US," http://www.reedconstructiondata.com/rsmeans/models/high-school/. Also see "National Center for Education Statistics," http://nces.ed.gov/surveys/sass/tables/sass0708_2009321_s1s_01.asp. In 2008, there were 90,760 public schools in the United States.

63. "Timeline: The story behind the VA scandal," *USA Today*, May 22, 2014.

64. The 2,700 figure and corresponding death rates are taken from J. D. Lehren, "Baffling Rise in Suicides Plagues the U.S. Military," *New York Times*, May 15, 2013, http://www.nytimes.com/2013/05/16/us/baffling-rise-in-suicides-plagues-us-military.html?pagewanted=all&_r=0. The *Guardian*'s data indicate much higher numbers in military compared to civilian populations. In 2009, 21.74 deaths by suicide occurred among the members of armed forces, whereas the comparable rates in the civilian population were twelve per one hundred thousand. See http://www.theguardian.com/news/datablog/2013/feb/01/us-military-suicides-trend-charts.

65. See Lehren, "Baffling Rise in Suicides."

66. This is one of the main arguments that Lehren makes. See ibid.

67. See S. Bannerman, "Husbands Who Bring the War Home," *The Daily Beast*, September 25, 2010, http://www.thedailybeast.com/contributors/stacy-bannerman.html.

68. See N. Montgomery, "Reports of Family Violence, Abuse Within Military Rise," *Stars and Stripes*, July 10, 2011, http://www.stripes.com/reports-of-family-violence-abuse-within-military-rise-1.148815.

69. A 2011 *USA Today* survey reports that "the Army divorce rate of 3.7% and the Navy's 3.6% are the highest for either service since 2004. The Air Force rate of 3.9% is the highest in more than two decades. Nearly 5% of marriages among Air Force enlisted personnel ended in divorce this year." Overall military divorce rates averaged 3.7 versus a civilian rate of 3.5. See Gregg Zoroya's article at http://usatoday30.usatoday.com/news/military/story/2011-12-13/military-divorce-rate-increases/51888872/1.

70. George Washington University, "Face the Facts USA: A Project of George Washington University," (2013, 01 18). "U.S. Spends More Rebuilding Iraq, Afghanistan than Post-WWII Germany"—See more at: http://www.facethefactsusa.org/facts us-spends-more-rebuilding-iraqafghanistan-than-post-wwii-germany. Retrieved from: Face the Facts USA: A Project of George Washington University: http://www.facethefactsusa.org/facts/us-spends-more-rebuilding-iraq-afghanistan-than-post-wwii-germany, 2013.

71. See B. Dreyfuss, "Al Qaeda and the Iraq-Syria Civil War," *The Nation*, July 30, 2013, http://www.thenation.com/blog/175498/al-qaeda-and-iraq-syria-civil-war#.

72. See "Exploding Violence Threatens to Renew Civil War in Iraq," *USA Today*, September 8, 2013, http://www.usatoday.com/story/news/world/2013/09/17/iraq-violence/2789107/.

73. See C. Otten, "Exploding Violence Threatens to Renew Civil War in Iraq," *USA Today*, September 18, 2013, http://www.usatoday.com/story/news/world/2013/09/17/iraq-violence/2789107/.

74. See E. Gordts, "Iraq War Anniversary: Birth Defects and Cancer Rates at Devastating High in Basra and Fallujah," *Huffington Post*, March 20, 2013, http://www.huffingtonpost.com/2013/03/20/iraq-war-anniversary-birth-defects-cancer_n_2917701.html.

75. Ibid.

76. See M. Levine, "Syria, Iraq, and Moral Obscenities Big and Small: Other Governments Should Be Held to the Same Standard as Syria When It Comes to Use of Chemical Weapons," *Aljazeera*, August 27, 2013, http://www.aljazeera.com/indepth/opinion/2013/08/201382710851628525.html.

77. See Ahmed Rashid, *Taliban*, 2nd ed. (New Haven: Yale University Press, 2010), 46–47.

78. Ibid., 235–246. Rashid's book provides a fascinating account of the rise of the Taliban that began in 1994 with support from Pakistan's ISA and, at times, the Central Intelligence Agency.

79. *Afghanistan Annual Report, 2013: Protection of Civilians in Armed Conflict*. Kabul, Afghanistan. February 2014, United Nations. Unama.unmissions.org/.

80. Pew Research Center, "Mistrust of America in Europe Ever Higher, Muslim Anger Persists." http://www.people-press.org/2004/03/16/a-year-after-iraq-war/, 2004.

81. Pew Research Center, "Arab Spring Fails to Improve U.S. Image: Obama's Challenge in the Muslim World. http://www.pewglobal.org/2011/05/17/arab-spring-fails-to-improve-us-image/]," May 17, 2011.

82. See R. Wike, "Obama's Israel Challenge," Pew Research Center, March 19, 2013, http://www.pewglobal.org/2013/03/19/obamas-israel-challenge/.

83. See B. Stokes, "Middle Eastern and Western Publics Wary on Syrian Intervention," Pew Research Center, May 2, 2013, http://www.pewresearch.org/fact-tank/2013/05/02/middle-eastern-and-western-publics-wary-on-syrian-intervention/.

84. See J. Goldstein and Jon Pevehouse, *International Relations: 2013–2014 Update*, 10th ed. (Boston: Pearson, 2014), 195–200.

85. See the discussion of the six principles of realism in Hans J. Morgenthau, *Politics Among Nations: The Struggle for Power and Peace*, 4th ed. (New York: Alfred A Knopf, 1967), 6–7.

86. For a more detailed discussion and summary of these schools of thought, see ibid.

87. See Brigid Harrison, Jean Harris, and Michelle Deardorf, *American Democracy Now* (NY: McGraw-Hill, 2013); Joseph Losco and Ralph Baker, *Am Gov 2013–2014* (New York: McGraw-Hill, 2014); Anthony Maltese, Joseph A. Pika, and W. Phillips Shively *Government Matters: American Democracy in Context* (New York: McGraw-Hill, 2013); Thomas. E. Patterson *We the People: A Concise Introduction to American Politics*, 10th ed. (New York: McGraw-Hill, 2013); and James A. Morone and Rogan Kersh, *By the People: Debating American Government* (Oxford: Oxford University Press, 2013).

88. See the picture on the first page of chapter three, from "DoD Has Problems Locating Damascus in New Map Quiz," RT.com, http://rt.com/news/dod-locate-damascus-syria-230/.

89. See Kyle Dropp, Joshua D. Kertzer and Thomas Zeitzoff, "The Less Americans Know about Ukraine's Location, the More They Want U.S. to Intervene, *Washington Post*, April 7, 2014, http://www.washingtonpost.com/blogs/monkey-cage/wp/2014/04/07/the-less-americans-know-about-ukraines-location-the-more-they-want-u-s-to-intervene/.

90. "The further our respondents thought that Ukraine was from its actual location, the more they wanted the U.S. to intervene militarily. Even controlling for a series of demographic characteristics and participants' general foreign policy attitudes, we found that the less accurate our participants were, the more they wanted the U.S. to use force, the greater the threat they saw Russia as posing to U.S. interests, and the more they thought that using force would advance U.S. national security interests; all of these effects are statistically significant at a 95 percent confidence level. Our results are clear, but also somewhat disconcerting: The less people know about where Ukraine is located on a map, the more they want the U.S. to intervene militarily" (ibid.).

91. See Morone and Kersh, *By the People*, 667.

92. Ibid., 668.

93. One can easily find the full text of the farewell speech on the Internet today. These passages are from the US government information page on about.com, http://usgovinfo.about.com/library/blgwfarewell.htm.

94. See James Madison, "Political Observations, Apr. 20, 1795," in *Letters and Other Writings of James Madison*, vol. 4 (1865), 491–492, http://archive.org/stream/lettersandotherw04madiiala#page/492/mode/2up.

95. See Robert W. Tucker and David C. Hendrickson, "Thomas Jefferson and American Foreign Policy," *Foreign Affairs* (Spring 1990), http://www.foreignaffairs.com/articles/45445/robert-w-tucker-and-david-c-hendrickson/thomas-jefferson-and-american-foreign-policy.

96. For a detailed discussion of the Louisiana Purchase, its timeline, and parties involved, see "The Louisiana Purchase" at Monticello.org, http://www.monticello.org/site/jefferson/louisiana-purchase.

97. See "The Lewis and Clark Expedition" at Monticello.org, http://www.monticello.org/site/jefferson/lewis-and-clark-expedition.

98. See William O. Kellogg, *American History the Easy Way*, 2nd ed. (New York: Barron's, 1995), 79.

99. See Tucker and Hendrickson, "Thomas Jefferson and American Foreign Policy."

100. See Robert C. Gray and Stanley J. Michael, Jr., *American Foreign Policy Since Détente* (New York: Harper and Row, 1984), 6. Of course, we have continued to very selectively apply human rights issues where it benefits our foreign policy and turn a blind eye to abuses by our allies, such as Saudi Arabia and Israel.

101. See the video clip of the March 19 speech at http://www.georgewbushlibrary.smu.edu/en/Photos-and-Videos/Video-Clips/Video-Clips.aspx.

102. See Maltese et al., *Government Matters*, 638, for a discussion of idealism, realism, and isolationism.

103. See Jeff Bloodworth, "Humanitarian Intervention: The American Experience from William McKinley to Barack Obama," *Ohio State's Origins* 5 (June 2012), http://origins.osu.edu/article/humanitarian-intervention-american-experience-william-mckinley-barack-obama.

104. See "Commodore Perry and the Opening of Japan" in the National Museum of the US Navy, http://www.history.navy.mil/branches/teach/ends/opening.htm.

105. See John M. Blum, Edmund S. Morgan, Willie Lee Rose, Arthur M. Schlesinger, Jr., Kenneth M. Stampp, and C. Vann Woodward, *The National Experience*, 4th ed. (New York: Harcourt Brace Jovanovich, Inc., 1977), 287.

106. See "Commodore Perry Sails into Tokyo Bay," http://www.history.com/this-day-in-history/commodore-perry-sails-into-tokyo-bay.

107. See "Matthew C. Perry,." http://en.wikipedia.org/wiki/Matthew_C._Perry.

108. See Manglapus, *Will of the People*, xviii.

109. A good, quick, and concise summary is found at http://en.wikipedia.org/wiki/Banana_Wars.

110. Democratic Peace Theory argues that democracies do not go to war with each other. Therefore, wars would end if all countries of the world were democratic countries. Of course, the reality is that representative democracies such as ours are constantly involved in wars, provoked or unprovoked. See Goldstein and Pevenhouse, *International Relations*, for a more detailed discussion of democratic peace.

111. See Tucker and Hendrickson, "Thomas Jefferson and American Foreign Policy."

112. See Michael Roskin's definition of behavioralism in *Encyclopedia Britannica*, http://www.britannica.com/EBchecked/topic/467721/political-science/247910/Behavioralism.

113. See the discussion of behavioralism in Robert Jackson and Greg Sorensen, *Introduction to International Relations: Theories and Approaches*, 3rd ed. (Oxford: Oxford University Press, 2007), 40.

114. See Fred H. Lawson, "International Relations Theory and the Middle East," in *International Relations of the Middle East*, 3rd. ed., ed. Louise Fawcett (Oxford: Oxford University Press, 2012), 31–33.

115. Ibid., 31–32. Note that I am not criticizing Lawson's work. He has done an admirable job of reviewing these articles. I am simply pointing out the futility of this research.

116. Ibid., 32.

117. Ibid., 130–131.

118. See "Julian Assange: UK 'Threat' to Arrest Wikileaks Founder," BBC, http://www.bbc.com/news/world-19259623.

119. See Ed Payne and Catherine E. Shoichet, "Morales Challenges U.S. after Snowden Rumor Holds Up Plane in Europe," CNN, http://www.cnn.com/2013/07/04/world/americas/bolivia-morales-snowden/.

120. See the discussion of constructivism in Lawson, "International Relations Theory," 29.

121. The quote is from the description of Nye's thinking in Eric Shirav and Vladislav Zubok, *International Relations*, brief ed. (Oxford: Oxford University Press, 2015, 52.

122. Ibid., 81; also see Lawson, "International Relations Theory."

123. See the interview with Kevin Dunn at *Theory Talks*, http://www.theory-talks.org/2008/10/theory-talk-22.html.

124. Ibid.

125. See Jackson and Sorensen, *Introduction to International Relations*, 45. Kenneth Waltz's theory was set in his book *Theory of International Politics*, first printed in 1979 by McGraw-Hill. Hans Morgenthau's book *Politics Among Nations: The Struggle for Power and Peace* was first printed in 1948 and then reprinted by McGraw-Hill in 1993.

126. See Graham Allison and Philip Zelikow, *Essence of Decision: Explaining the Cuban Missile Crisis* (New York: Longman, 1999), 27.

127. Ibid., 30.

128. Robert Owen Keohane, ed., *Neo Realism and Its Critics* (New York. Colombia University Press, 1986), 167.

129. These three principles are the framework for Joshua Goldstein and Jon Pevehouse's 2014 book on international relations (Goldstein and Pevehouse, *International Relations*).

130. See Allison and Zelikow, *Essence of Decision*, 144.

131. See Lucien Vandenbroucke, "Anatomy of a Failure: The Decision to Land at the Bay of Pigs," *Political Science Quarterly* 99 (Fall 1984): 471–491, http://www.latinamericanstudies.org/bay-of-pigs/failure.pdf.

132. See Allison and Zelikow, *Essence of Decision*, 255.

133. Ibid., 295.

134. Ibid., 296.

135. See Bari Weiss' interview with Lewis in O. Fiona Yap, ed., "The Weekend Interview with Bernard Lewis: The Tyrannies Are Doomed," *Annual Editions* (New York: McGraw-Hill, 2013), 208–210. This article was originally published in the *Wall Street Journal*.

136. Ibid., 208–210.

137. See Matthew Kroenig, "Time to Attack Iran: Why a Strike Is the Least Bad Option," *Foreign Affairs* (January/February 2012).

138. See Alexander Debs and Nuno P. Monteiro, "The Flawed Logic of Striking Iran: Handle it Like North Korea Instead," *Foreign Affairs*, January 17, 2012, www.foreignaffairs.com/articles/137036/alexandre-debs-and-nuno-p-monteiro/the-flawed-logic-of-striking-iran. Here is an excerpt from the article published in *Foreign Affairs*:

> Kroenig's view of the way Iranian leaders are willing to take on risks is deeply incongruous. In his view, a nuclear bomb will push Tehran to block U.S. initiatives in the Middle East, unleash conventional and terrorist aggression on U.S. forces and allies, and possibly engage in a nuclear exchange with Israel. This would mean Iranian leaders are reckless: given the United States' conventional and nuclear superiority, any of these actions would provoke considerable retaliation from Washington. And, of course, a nuclear exchange with Israel would invite annihilation. At the same time, Kroenig suggests that Tehran would remain remarkably timid after a preventive strike from the United States. Presented with clear redlines, Iran would not retaliate against U.S. troops and allies or attempt to close the Strait of Hormuz. Kroenig's inconsistency is clear: If Iranian leaders are as reckless as he seems to believe, a preventive strike would likely escalate to a full-blown war. If they are not, then there is no reason to think that a nuclear Iran would be uncontainable. In short, a preventive attack on Iran can hardly be both limited and necessary.

139. See Kenneth Waltz, "Why Iran Should Get the Bomb: Nuclear Balancing Would Mean Stability," *Foreign Affairs* (July/August 2012), http://www.foreignaffairs.com/articles/137731/kenneth-n-waltz/why-iran-should-get-the-bomb. Here is an excerpt that was published online:

> Although the United States, the EU, and Iran have recently returned to the negotiating table, a palpable sense of crisis still looms. It should not. Most U.S., European, and Israeli commentators and policymakers warn that a nuclear-armed Iran would be the worst possible outcome of the current standoff. In fact, it would probably be the best possible result: the one most likely to restore stability to the Middle East

140. That is my term for these propagandists and agenda-driven analysts. They are not real analysts; rather, they serve an agenda, in this case, Israel's lobby.

141. This is what Lewis wrote in Bernard Lewis, *What Went Wrong? The Clash Between Islam & Modernity in the Middle East* (New York: Harper Perennial, 2002). 7: "This disease [syphilis] … is indeed is still known in Arabic, Persian, Turkish, and other languages as the 'Frankish disease.'" I was born and raised in Iran and never heard anyone refer to syphilis as the Frankish disease, either from my generation or my parents' generation. Syphilis was called syphilis. I suppose that it is possible that at some point syphilis might have been called the Frankish disease in some languages, but it certainly is not a contemporary usage in Persian.

142. By "imperial progressives," I refer to people such as Chris Matthews of MSNBC, who, while pushing progressive ideas for Americans, is a supporter of the empire and has repeatedly advocated an attack on Iran. Apparently Chris's progressivism stops at the border, and while

human beings in America are entitled to many rights and privileges, it is OK in his view if we bomb and kill the human beings in Iran, simply because they pose a theoretical threat to our hegemony in the Middle East.

The networks and mainstream news media are populated with these pundits and commentators who support the tyranny of the empire, yet proclaim themselves as champions of human rights. Christiane Amanpour and Anderson Cooper of CNN expressed their justified outrage at Assad's purported use of chemical weapons with strong statements and repeated showing of the videos of dead children, yet remained largely silent when Israeli and American troops used depleted uranium and white phosphorus. Again, it appears that human rights belong only to the citizens of the empire and its allies.

The use of chemical weapons by both the United States (2004) and Israel (2009) is documented in Washingtonsblog.com at http://www.washingtonsblog.com/2013/08/the-u-s-and-israel-have-used-chemical-weapons-within-the-last-8-years.html.

143. Kelly, C. (2010). The End of Empire: Attila the Hun and the Fall of Rome. New York: W.W. Norton & Company Ltd.

144. The quote here is from Wikipedia's discussion of Virgil. See http://en.wikipedia.org/wiki/Aeneid.

145. See the discussion of Ammianus Marcellinus, a Roman historian who wrote extensively about the Huns in 380 AD, in Christopher Kelly, *The End of Empire: Attila the Hun & the Fall of Rome* New York: W.W. Norton & Company Ltd. 2010, 25–28.

146. Matthews actually frequently favored a military attack on Iran on his show while saying that he was not a hawk!

147. I recall that once I was watching Anderson Cooper, and he actually seemed to be outraged that someone had dared criticize American foreign policy. Although I don't recall the episode or even the context, his tone and implication have stuck in my memory.

148. American exceptionalism is an outgrowth of this feeling of superiority. When Vladimir Putin dared to criticize this idea of exceptionalism in his opinion in the *New York Times*, the whole American political elite was offended. Here is a synopsis on MSNBC:

"It is extremely dangerous to encourage people to see themselves as exceptional, whatever the motivation," Putin wrote.

That was enough to unleash a torrent of criticism from both sides of the aisle on Capitol Hill.

"I was insulted," House Speaker John Boehner said flatly.

Senate Foreign Relations Chair Bob Menendez, D-N.J., told MSNBC that the op-ed "turned my stomach."

The complete text of Putin's opinion is at http://www.nytimes.com/2013/09/12/opinion/putin-plea-for-caution-from-russia-on-syria.html?pagewanted=all&_r=0.

149. Samuel P. Huntington, *The Clash of Civilizations and the Remaking of the World Order* (N.Y Simon & Schuster, 2011).

150. Edward Said, *Orientalism* (New York: Random House, 1978), 2–3.

151. Ibid., 4.

152. Ibid., 7–11.

153. McNutt, M. (2013, 04 13). "Oklahoma Governor Urged to Sign Revised Sharia Law Measure." Retrieved from: NEWSOK: http://newsok.com/oklahoma-governor-urged-to-sign-revised-sharia-law-measure/article/3785689.

154. See Andrew C. McCarthy, "The Huma Unmentionable," *National Review Online*, http://www.nationalreview.com/corner/354351/huma-unmentionables-andrew-c-mccarthy.

155. See Reza Aslan's interview with Chris Hayes in "All In with Chris Hayes" on MSNBC on July 31, 2013.

156. Rachel Newcomb, "Reza Aslan: Speaking Truth to Power," *Huffington Post*, **July 3**, 2013.

157. The program's site is on http://www.hbo.com/real-time-with-bill-maher#/. See episode 317 at http://www.hbo.com/real-time-with-bill-maher#/real-time-with-bill-maher/episodes/12/317-episode/index.html. I am actually a fan of Bill Maher, but I find his criticism of Islam based on actions of fanatics to be harmful and bigoted.

158. See Frank Gardner, "Have Boko Haram Over-reached Themselves?" BBC, http://www.bbc.com/news/world-africa-27334894.

159. See "Joseph Kony: US Military Planes to Hunt LRA Leader," BBC, http://www.bbc.com/news/world-africa-26712774, and "Joseph Kony: Profile of the LRA Leader," BBC, http://www.bbc.com/news/world-africa-17299084.

160. (Herodotus, 1987, p. 455) As translated by David Green.

161. The movie *300* portrayed the Persians as wild beasts and savages who fought against the democratic and noble Greeks. The idea of this battle's saving democracy and by implication saving Western civilization has now been popularized even on the Internet. For instance, consider the following: "If the Spartans hadn't fought so well, if the Greek navy hadn't fought so well, and Persia remained in Greece, democracy would have died" (http://planetpov.com/2011/03/16/the-battle-of-thermopylae-how-democracy-was-saved/).

162. Herodotus, *The History*, 34.

163. http://en.wikipedia.org/wiki/Miletus.

164. For a detailed discussion of the painting, see Francis and Vickers (1985). Here is a quote:

> 'Imagine yourselves at the Stoa Poikile', Aeschines declared, 'for the monuments of all your glories are in the Agora' (3. 186). The Tyrannicide monument stood nearby, and in the Stoa itself the bronze shields of the Scionians and their allies were still displayed in Pausanias' day, together with spoils taken from the Spartans at Sphacteria (i. 15. 4).1 Among the paintings of the Stoa, the Battle of Marathon was especially famous. Not only was it a great monument of past glory, but 'probably the most celebrated picture in the city'. 2 Our fullest description of the paintings in the Stoa is that of Pausanias (I1.15). According to him the Battle of Marathon was the 'last' in a series of four murals. Besides the Marathon, Pausanias describes 'in the middle of the walls' (p. 107, below) a battle of Athenians fighting with Theseus against Amazons, and 'next to this "Amazonomachy"' () Polygnotus' scene of Troy Taken, which included a joint council called by the Greek leaders to discuss Locrian Ajax's Rape of Cassandra. The first scene, so Pausanias tells us (LEV … , I. 15. I), depicted 'Athenian forces marshalled in Argive Oenoe against Spartans'. The

conflict, however, has not yet reached its crisis. On the contrary, the battle is only just beginning and the combatants are said still to be in the process of engaging.

165. Hall, *Inventing the Barbarian* 68–69.

166. See Robin Waterfield, *Xenophon's Retreat: Greece, Persia, and the End of the Golden Age* (Cambridge: Harvard University Press, 2006).

167. Ibid., 20–21.

168. See Said, *Orientalism*, 21. On page 56, Said changes his interpretation of the play and uses the word "hostile" to describe the view of Europeans about Asians or Persians. See pages 56–57 and 243. The interpretation of the play is, of course, controversial, as others view it as celebratory and xenophobic:

> Interpretations of Persians either read the play as sympathetic toward the defeated Persians or else as a celebration of Greek victory within the context of an ongoing war. The sympathetic school has the considerable weight of Aristotelian criticism behind it; indeed, every other extant Greek tragedy arguably invites an audience's sympathy for one or more characters on stage. The celebratory school argues that the play is part of a xenophobic culture that would find it difficult to sympathize with its hated barbarian enemy during a time of war. (http://en.wikipedia.org/wiki/The_Persians)

169. Hassan Pirnia, *Iran e Bastan*, 71. The first printing of the book that I received when I was but ten years old has the title as *Iran e Bastan: Or Ancient Iran*, and it was published by the printing arm of Majlis (Iranian parliament). I have seen the title translated as the *History of Ancient Iran*, but that title is not correct, at least not for the printing that I have. My printing also has a subtitle that translates to *Comprehensive History of Ancient Iran*. The book does not have a publication date, but my copy is signed in the Iranian year of 1336, which is 1957, although Pirnia died in 1935, and I am not sure if the Majlis published his work posthumously or my print is actually from before 1935. Pirnia was also prominent in politics and served four brief terms as prime minister. He last served as prime minster in 1923, and his replacement was none other than Reza Shah Pahlavi.

170. Edith Hall, *Inventing the Barbarian: Greek Self-Definition Through Tragedy*. Oxford: Clarendon Press, 1989.

171. Ibid.

172. *Babaricum* means the "the world of barbarians." A cohort had about five hundred soldiers. This Roman army was composed of a legion and five additional cohorts, so it had somewhere between seven and eight thousand soldiers. See Peter Heather, *The Fall of the Roman Empire: A New History of Rome and the Barbarians* (New York: Oxford University Press, 2006).

173. Shayegan, M. R. (2011). *Arsacids and Sasanians: Political Ideology in Post-Hellenistic and Late Antique Persia*. Cambridge: Cambridge University Press. 369–372.

174. http://en.wikipedia.org/wiki/Valerian_(emperor)

175. Heather, *Fall of the Roman Empire*, 69.

176. Ibid., 12, 68.

177. Ibid., 71.

178. Ibid., 62–64.

179. Ibid., 65.

180. Ibid., 58.

181. Ibid., 58.

182. Ibid., 123–125.

183. The rest of the areas are Segan (Makhelonia = Mingrelia), Arran (Albania), Balasakan, up to the Caucasus Mountains and the Gates of Albania, and all of the mountain chain of Pareshwar, Media, Gurgan, Merv, Herat (and all of Aparshahr), Kerman, Seistan, Turan, Makuran, Paradene, Hindustan (= Sind), the Kushanshahr up to Peshawar, and up to Kashgar, Sogdiana, and to the mountains of Tashkent, and on the other side of the sea, Oman.

184. The rest of Roman lands mentioned are Noricum, Dacia, Pannonia, Moesia, Istria, Spain, Africa, Thrace, Bithynia, Asia, Pamphylia, Isauria, Lycaonia, Galatia, Lycia, Cilicia, Cappadocia, Phrygia, Syria, Phoenicia, Judaea, Arabia, Mauritania, Germania, Rhodes (Lydia), Osrhoene, and Mesopotamia.

185. This is from a translation by R. N. Frye, *The History of Ancient Iran: Handbuch der Altertumswissenschaft*; 3. Abt., T. 7 (1984), posted on Wikipedia by the Classics Department of the University of Colorado. Source: http://www.colorado.edu/classics/clas4091/Text/Shapur.htm. Another important conclusion from the inscription is the high regard that the Persian king had for his daughter, which indicated the importance of royal women in ancient Iran:

> And here by this inscription, we founded a fire. Khosro-Shapur by name for our soul and to perpetuate our name, a fire called Khosro-Aduranahid by name for the soul of our daughter Aduranahid, queen of queens, to perpetuate her name, a fire called Khosro-Hormizd-Ardashir by name for the soul of our son, Hormizd-Ardashir, great king of Armenia, to perpetuate his name, another fire called Khosro Shapur by name, for the soul of our son Shapur king of Mesene.

> The Sasanids actually did select two female kings toward the end of their dynasty and admittedly in chaotic circumstances. However, Shapur's passage might be a precursor for these later events. The daughter is mentioned before the son.

186. Also of note is that in the passage, the king first refers to his daughter and then to his sons, which indicates the high status of Iranian women in Sasanid Iran.

187. Mehdi Estakhr, *The Place of Zoroaster in History.* Lewiston, NY: The Edwin Mellen Press, 2012, 4.

188. See Parvaneh Pourshariati, *Decline and Fall of the Sasanian Empire: The Sasanian-Parthian Confederacy and the Arab Conquest of Iran.* London: I.B. Tauris, 2008.

189. See Karen Armstrong, *Holy War: The Crusaders and their Impact on Today's World* (New York: Anchor Books, 2001), 1.

190. Ibid., 68–75.

191. Ibid., ix.

192. Ibid., xii.

193. See Julian Glover, "We Still View the East from the Crusaders' Battlements," *Guardian*, May 24, 2009, http://www.guardian.co.uk/commentisfree/2009/may/24/miliband-islam-tony-blair.

194. See Richard T. Cooper, "General Casts War in Religious Terms: The Top Soldier Assigned to Track Down bin Laden and Hussein Is an Evangelical Christian Who Speaks Publicly of 'The Army of God,'" *Common Dreams*, Oct. 16, 2003, http://www.commondreams.org/headlines03/1016-01.htm. (Note: This article was originally published in the *Los Angeles Times*.)

195. See Dan Elliott, "41% of Non-Christian Air Force Cadets Cite Proselytizing," Associated Press, October 29, 2010. Note: This article was reprinted in the *Huffington Post* on November 22, 2013.Rachel Maddow's show on MSNBC on November 21, 2013, also devoted considerable attention to this issue: http://www.huffingtonpost.com/2010/10/29/air-force-proselytizing-christianity-evangelicals_n_775859.html.

196. Flynt Leverett and Hillary Mann Leverett, 2013.

197. Wikipedia.

198. See "AIPAC to Deploy Hundreds of Lobbyists to Push for Syria Action," *Haaretz*, Sep 7, 2013, http://www.haaretz.com/news/diplomacy-defense/1.545661: the "Pro-Israel lobby says 250 activists will meet with their senators and representatives in Washington in a bid to win support Congressional support for military action in Syria."

199. Shalev, Shemi, 2013.

200. John J. Mearsheimer and Stephen M. Walt, *The Israel Lobby and U.S. Foreign Policy*. New York: Farrar, Straus and Giroux., 2007, 3.

201. Ibid., 4.

202. Jimmy Carter, "Speaking Frankly about Israel and Palestine, *Los Angeles Times*, December 8, 2006, http://www.latimes.com/news/la-oe-carter8dec08,0,7161592.story. Jimmy Carter says that his recent book is drawing knee-jerk accusations of anti-Israel bias.

203. John J. Mearsheimer and Stephen M. Walt, *The Israel Lobby and U.S. Foreign Policy*. New York: Farrar, Straus and Giroux., 2007, 8.

204. Ibid., 10.

205. This is according to Leverett and Leverett, 310.

206. See Robert Dreyfuss, "Is AIPAC Still the Chosen One?" 2009, http://www.motherjones.com/politics/2009/09/aipac-still-chosen-one.

207. See "Under the Influence: AIPAC Americas' Pro Israeli Lobby," USC's News 21, , http://usc.news21.com/madeline-story/aipac-money-0.

208. See Barbara Plett Usher and Suzanne Kianpour, "Iran Hostage Crisis Wounds Linger for US Government," BBC, April 25, 2014, http://www.bbc.com/news/world-us-canada-27161268.

209. The reference is to Jimmy Carter, *Palestine: Peace Not Apartheid* (New York: Simon and Schuster, 2006). Carter writes, "The ultimate purpose of my book is to present facts about the Middle East that are largely unknown in America, to precipitate discussion and to help restart peace talks (now absent for six years) that can lead to permanent peace for Israel and its neighbors. Another hope is that Jews and other Americans who share this same goal might be motivated to express their views, even publicly, and perhaps in concert. I would be glad to help with that effort."

210. You have to go to Israeli media to see this criticism of Dershowitz. You won't see it on CNN or MSNBC. See Dylan Williams, *Haaretz*, November 15, 2013, Haaretz.com. *J Street* responds: "Don't undermine chance for 'good deal' on Iran. Alan Dershowitz is wrong: The

only way to ensure Iran doesn't go nuclear is the verifiable, negotiated settlement that the U.S. administration is seeking."

211. See "'Economist' Magazine Cartoon Sparks Anti-Semitism Row," *The Jerusalem Post*, January 22, 2014, http://www.jpost.com/Jewish-World/Jewish-Features/ Economist-magazine-cartoon-sparks-anti-Semitism-row-338962.

212. See Philip Weiss, "'*Economist*' Pulls Cartoon Showing Obama Shackled to Congress Bearing Star of David," *Mondoweiss*, January 21, 2014, http://mondoweiss.net/2014/01/economist-shackled-congress.html. The cartoon is also in that article.

213. See Maltese et al., *Government Matters*, 648.

214. See Morone and Kersh, *By the People*, 317.

215. Ibid., 318–319.

216. Of course, I can't claim that I saw all the shows and read all analysis of Kerry's wording. What I personally saw on "progressive" shows such as those of Chris Matthews and Chris Hayes and CNN was the appearance of guests who are pro-Israel and who basically said that Kerry used the wrong words. In almost all the shows, with the exception of Chris Hayes's, the program host did not challenge the assertion of the guests that Israel is not an apartheid state.

217. See Erlich, *The Iran Agenda*.

218. In an interview with Mohammad Khazaee on March 4, 2013, when Khazaee talked about how US foreign policy has victimized Iran, Zakaria came to the defense of the United States by pointing out that Iran had taken hostages in 1979. The first six minutes of Zakaria's interview with Ahmadinejad in September 2012 were devoted to the questioning of his comments about Israel while Zakaria was putting forward the standard administration's arguments. Zakaria, during another conversation with an Iranian envoy on *GPS* in 2012, commented that the United States aided Saddam only by sending agricultural products.

219. See Erlich, *The Iran Agenda*.

220. A prime example of these experts is Kenneth Pollack, who worked at the Brookings Institution, and is the author of *The Persian Puzzle: The Conflict Between Iran and America*, which was published in 2004. By the time he wrote that book, Pollack had never been to Iran and neither wrote nor understood Farsi. In 2002 Pollack published another book, *The Threatening Storm: The Case for Invading Iraq*. Pollack was the director of Bill Clinton's National Security Council, Persian Gulf Affairs.

221. See Leverett and Leverett, *Going to Tehran*, 300.

222. Rohani blasts U.S. sanctions, says 'peace is within reach' Haaretz, Sep. 25, 2013 | 2:20 AM. http://www.haaretz.com/news/diplomacy-defense/1.548815

223. See Shemi Shalev, "Foxman Confirms: Jewish Groups to Take 'Time Out' in Iran Sanctions Campaign," *Haaretz*, November 2, 2013, http://www.haaretz.com/blogs/west-of-eden/1.555822. Also see Barak Ravids, "Netanyahu: Rohani's UN Speech Cynical, Full of Hypocrisy," *Haaretz*, September 24, 2013, http://www.haaretz.com/news/diplomacy-defense/. premium-1.548957.

224. See "Iran Nuclear Talks: Unfinished, but Alive," *New York Times*, November 11, 2013, http://www.nytimes.com/2013/11/12/opinion/iran-nuclear-talks-unfinished-but-alive. html?partner=rssnyt&emc=rss&_r=0.

225. See Akbar Ganji, "Who Is the Real Threat: Iran or Israel?" *Aljazeera*, http://www.aljazeera. com/indepth/opinion/2013/10/who-real-threat-iran-israel-2013101791830213883.html. Here is an extensive quotation from the article.

> After a meeting in July 2009 with then U.S. Secretary of Defense Robert Gates, Ehud Barak, Israel's Defence Minister, said that attacking Iran's nuclear facilities is an option, adding, "We clearly believe that no option should be removed from the table. This is our policy; we mean it. We recommend to others to take the same position. ... "

> Barak and Netanyahu were determined to attack Iran in 2010, but were thwarted by the military and intelligence establishments within Israel. In November 2012, Netanyahu again threatened Iran with military attacks, even if the U.S. does not go along.

> *1992: Israeli Foreign Minister Peres tells French TV that Iran was set to have nuclear warheads by 1999. "Iran is the greatest threat and greatest problem in the Middle East," Peres warned, "because it seeks the nuclear option while holding a highly dangerous stance of extreme religious militancy."*

226. See Maltese et al., *Government Matters*, 651, and Morone and Kersh, *By the People*, 411: When the Washington insider's magazine, *National Journal*, quizzes members of Congress and their staffers about the most powerful US lobbying groups, the American Israel Public Affairs Committee (AIPAC) routinely lands in the top three (Morone and Kersh, *By the People*, 411).

227. See Poll: *Americans Strongly Support Israel, But Don't Want to Get Involved in Middle East, Haaretz*, November 5, 2013, http://www.haaretz.com/news/diplomacy-defense/. premium-1.556493.

228. See Thomas. E. Patterson, *We the People: A Concise Introduction to American Politics*, 10th ed. (New York: McGraw-Hill, 2013), 3–4.

229. A typical example of how Cheney spun the Iraq war and made the connection with al-Qaeda is seen in his interview with Bill O'Reilly on October 23, 2013, ten years after we invaded Iraq. In this interview Cheney was still trying to use the al-Qaeda connection as justification for invasion of Iraq:

> Cheney responded by saying, essentially, that Saddam Hussein was a threat with access to weapons of mass destruction. Cheney said, "But remember what we were faced with in the immediate aftermath of 9/11. We had a lot of evidence, they indicate, that in fact al-Qaeda was trying to get their hands on weapons of mass destruction. We had in Saddam Hussein a guy who had produced and used weapons of mass destruction."

> O'Reilly interrupted. "OK ... I don't blame you—you, Vice President Cheney, or President Bush for doing what you did. I'm not Monday morning quarterbacking," he assured Cheney again. "But right now, what did we get out of Iraq for all that blood and treasure? What did we get out of it?"

Cheney replied by going back to WMDs. He said, "What we gained—and my concern was then and it remains today—is that the biggest threat we face is the possibility of terrorist groups, like al-Qaeda, equipped with weapons of mass destruction. With nukes, bugs, or gas. That was the threat after 9/11, and when we took down Saddam Hussein, we eliminated Iraq as a potential source of that."

O'Reilly pushed back somewhat by saying, "But they're back! Al-Qaeda in Mesopotamia is back!" But that was more of an opening for Cheney to attack President Obama's handling of the Middle East than any real challenge to Cheney's WMD spin. Even though he was supposedly in the No-Spin Zone,

Cheney seized the opening. He said, "That's right. But they wouldn't be if they'd followed our policies that we they laid out for 'em when we left."

See "O'Reilly Lets Dick Cheney Spin the Iraq War, Saddam Hussein and Those Weapons of Mass Destruction." *Newshounds*, October 28, 2013, http://www.newshounds.us/o_reilly_lets_dick_cheney_spin_the_iraq_war_saddam_hussein_and_those_weapons_of_mass_destruction_10282013.

230. Ibid., 2.

231. See, for instance, "Calls to Congress 499 to 1 Against Syria War," Conservativebyte.com, September 5, 2013, http://conservativebyte.com/2013/09/calls-congress-499-1-syria-war/ or Before It's News at http://beforeitsnews.com/home/featuredlist/top_politics.html.

232. See Lexington, "Barack, Bibi and Iran," *Economist*, November 16–22, 2013, 38.

233. See "GDP, Purchasing Power Parity (Top 50)," IndexMundi, http://www.indexmundi.com/g/r.aspx?t=50&v=65.

234. See IndexMundi, http://www.indexmundi.com/iran/economy_profile.html.

235. See the World Bank's Iran Overview report, September 2013, http://www.worldbank.org/en/country/iran/overview.

236. See "UN Development Chief Visits Iran; Addresses United Nations Day Celebration in Tehran," UNDP, October 24, 2013, http://www.undp.org/content/undp/en/home/presscenter/pressreleases/2013/10/24/un-development-chief-visits-iran-addresses-united-nations-day-celebration-in-teheran.html.

237. See Fariborz Ghadar, "Is It Time to Reassess Our Long-Term Alliances in the Middle East?", November 11, 2013, http://www.defenseone.com/ideas/2013/11/it-time-reassess-our-long-term-alliances-middle-east/73565/?oref=d-interstitial-continue.

238. See Amir Paivar, "Iran: Rouhani's First 100 Days," *BBC Persian*, November 12, 2013, http://www.bbc.co.uk/news/world-middle-east-24908733.

239. See Hamid Dabashi, *Iran: A People Interrupted* (New York: The New Press, 2007), 60. A great source on the history of Iran is Ervand Abrahamian, an American professor of history who was born in Iran, and his many books, particularly *Iran Between the Two Revolutions* (Princeton: Princeton University Press, 1982), which is one of the first books that I read on Iran in America. It provides a comprehensive introduction to Iran and is truly timeless.

240. Ibid., 72.

241. See Uzi Mahnaimi, "Two Old Foes Unite Against Tehran: Convinced That Iran Is Tricking the World over Nuclear Weapons, Israel and Saudi Arabia May Work Together to Curb Its Ambitions, November 17, 2013, http://www.thesundaytimes.co.uk/sto/news/world_news/Middle_East/article1341561.ece.

242. See William L. Cleveland and Martin Bunton, *A History of the Modern Middle East*, 5th ed. (Boulder, CO: Westview Press, 2013), 394.

243. See Rashid, *Taliban*, and his discussion of the rise of Taliban.

244. The Iranian movie *A Separation*, released on December 30, 2011, won the Academy Award for Best Foreign-Language Film. Cinema, literature, and poetry have long been avenues for expressing political dissent in Iran. You might want to consult Hamid Naficy, "Cinema as a Political Instrument," in *Continuity and Change in Modern Iran*, ed. Michael E. Bonnie and Nikki Keddi (Albany: State University of New York, 1980), 265–284. On Saudi restrictions on movie theatres, see "Top 10 Everyday Things You Can't Do in Saudi Arabia," http://thetop-10site.com/politics-and-religion/top-10-everyday-things-you-cant-do-in-saudi-arabia/.

245. See "Iran President Rouhani Urges Equal Rights for Women," BBC, April 20, 2014, http://www.bbc.com/news/world-middle-east-27099151. Of course, many Iranian officials do not go as far as Rouhani has gone. The same BBC article also discusses the supreme leader's comments a day earlier that while he did not oppose women's employment, he thought women's focus should be on the family.

246. "Women in Saudi Arabia: Unshackling Themselves," *Economist*, May 17, 2014.

247. "The Perils of Yoga," *Economist*, May, 2014.

248. http://usgovinfo.about.com/library/blgwfarewell.htm.

249. See the article on the agreement, which was signed on Sunday, November 23, in the Palace of Nations in Geneva, written by Michael Gordon, "Accord Reached with Iran to Halt Nuclear Program," *New York Times*, November 23, 2013, http://www.nytimes.com/2013/11/24/world/middleeast/talks-with-iran-on-nuclear-deal-hang-in-balance.html. Also see the explanatory article by Sergio Pecanha, "Understanding the Deal with Iran: Iran Retains the Technology and Material to Produce Fuel for a Weapon for Now," *New York Times*, http://www.nytimes.com/interactive/2013/11/24/world/middleeast/Understanding-the-Deal-With-Iran.html?action=click&contentCollection=Middle%20East&module=RelatedCoverage&region=Marginalia&pgtype=article.

250. The opposition to the agreement also exists among Iranian hardliners who do not trust the United States and/or see the agreement as strengthening the hand of the reformist faction that seeks closer relations with the West: "The agreement faced opposition from Iranian hard-liners and Israeli leaders, as well as heavy criticism from some American lawmakers, who have threatened to approve further sanctions despite President Obama's promise of a veto." See Michael Gordon and Erik Schmitt, "Negotiators Put Final Touches on Iran Accord," *New York Times*, January 12, 2014, http://www.nytimes.com/2014/01/13/world/middleeast/iran-nuclear-deal.html.

251. See Awad Mustafa, "Saudis Invite Iran Foreign Minister to Talks," DefenseNews, May 13, 2014.

252. See the comprehensive account of the Iranian nuclear program by David Patrikarkos, *Nuclear Iran: The Birth of an Atomic State* (London: I. B. Tauris & Co. Ltd., 2012), 52.

253. Henry Kissinger went to Iran in 1976 to meet with Etemad, the head of Iran's nuclear agency, to pressure Iran on giving up its attempts to enrich uranium and accused Iran of noncooperation. Etemad thought that American attempts to prevent Iran from enrichment were "an infringement of Iranian sovereignty." See ibid., 76.

254. All of these issues are discussed in detail in ibid.

255. See ibid., 240–242.

256. See Map Light, "Revealing Money's Influence on Politics: Senators Urge Obama to Stand Firm over Iran Nuclear Talks," 2014, http://maplight.org/us-congress/interest/J5100/view/all.

257. On the US Congress's skepticism and opposition to the agreement, see "Senators Urge Obama to Stand Firm over Iran Nuclear Talk: Twenty-Three Lawmakers Ask U.S. President to Insist on a Final Deal That Would Prevent Iran from Acquiring Nuclear Weapons," *Haaretz*, March 22, 2014, http://www.haaretz.com/news/middle-east/1.581404. Also see Amos Harel, "U.S. Knows Iran Is Lying, but Chooses Diplomacy over Force," *Haaretz,* March 14, 2014, http://www.haaretz.com/news/diplomacy-defense/.premium-1.579881.

258. See "U.S. to Release $450 Million of Frozen Iranian Funds: U.S. Gesture Follows IAEA Report That Iran Has Lived Up to Its End of Landmark Nuclear Pact," *Haaretz*, April 18, 2014, http://www.haaretz.com/news/middle-east/1.586259.

259. See Barak Ravid, "Nuclear Talks between Iran, World Powers End with No Progress," *Haaretz*, May 16, 2014, http://www.haaretz.com/news/middle-east/1.591141.

260. See "Iran: Nuclear Talks," *Economist*, May 17–23, 2014, 48.

261. See a video of the joint announcement at New York Times Video published on April 2, 2015 at http://www.nytimes.com/video/world/middleeast/100000003608354/details-given-of-iran-nuclear-agreement.html.

262. See U.S. Department of State, Parameters for a Joint Comprehensive Plan of Action Regarding the Islamic Republic of Iran's Nuclear Program, Retrieved from: http://www.state.gov/r/pa/prs/ps/2015/04/240170.htm.

263. Scott Clement and Peyton M. Craighill, Poll: Clear majority supports nuclear deal with Iran. Retrieved from: http://www.washingtonpost.com/world/national-security/poll-2-to-1-support-for-nuclear-deal-with-iran/2015/03/30/9a5a5ac8-d720-11e4-ba28-f2a685dc7f89_story.html.

264. See Kopri Schake's article on April 2, 2015. I am a republican and I support the Iran Deal. http://foreignpolicy.com/2015/04/02/im-a-republican-and-i-support-the-iran-nuclear-deal.

265. See the Washington Post's article by Jose DelReal, Here is the List of the GOP Senators who signed the Iran Letter. March 10, 2015. Retrieved from: http://www.washingtonpost.com/blogs/post-politics/wp/2015/03/10/heres-a-list-of-the-gop-senators-who-signed-the-iran-letter.

266. See Heather Cox Richardson's article on March 15, 2015 in Salon.com, Tom Cotton's unpatriotic forefathers: Treasonous Iran letter not the first time GOP has crossed the line: The ideology of movement conservatives is not simply partisanship. It is an attack on American democracy itself. Retrieved from: http://www.salon.com/2015/03/15/tom_cottons_unpatriotic_forefathers_treasonous_iran_letter_not_the_first_time_gop_has_crossed_the_line.

267. See Julie Hirschfeld Davis's May 14, 2015 article in New York Times, Obama Faces Skepticism as He Tries to Reassure Wary Persian Gulf Allies. Retrieved from: http://www.nytimes.com/2015/05/15/world/middleeast/obama-saudi-arabia-iran-persian-gulf-security.html?ref=middleeast&_r=0.

268. See the November 25, 2014 article in the Guardian, Tehran reacts to Iran nuclear deal while many continue to hope for new economic opportunities, some say a final agreement will only benefit the ruling elite. Retrieved from: http://www.theguardian.com/world/iran-blog/2014/nov/25/-sp-iranian-nuclear-talks-tehran-reactions.

269. See Saeed Kemali's April 3, 2015 article in the Guardian, Iran's chief nuclear negotiator receives hero's welcome in Tehran. Jubilant crowd greets Mohammad Javad Zarif amid hopes that nuclear pact will end years of international isolation. Retrieved from: http://www.theguardian.com/world/2015/apr/03/iran-nuclear-mohammad-javad-zarif.

270. See Michael Weiss and Hassan Hassan. 2015. ISIS: Inside the Army of Terror. New York: Regan Arts. p. 211.

271. See Michael Weiss and Hassan Hassan. 2015. ISIS: Inside the Army of Terror. New York: Regan Arts. pp. 116–117, 124–125.

272. See Liz Sly, April 4, 2015, The hidden hand behind the Islamic State militants? Saddam Hussein's. The Washington Post. Retrieved from: http://www.washingtonpost.com/world/middle_east/the-hidden-hand-behind-the-islamic-state-militants-saddam-husseins/2015/04/04/aa97676c-cc32-11e4-8730-4f473416e759_story.html.

273. For instance see the December 10, 2014 headline, Over 700 Peshmerga killed, 3,564 wounded since June, Iraqinews.com. Retrieved from: http://www.iraqinews.com/iraq-war/700-peshmerga-killed-3564-wounded-since-june.

274. See the September 15, 2015 Los Angeles Times' article, Iran fills key role in battling Islamic State in Iraq, by Nabih Bulos, Patrick J. McDonnell. Retrieved from: http://www.latimes.com/world/middleeast/la-fg-iraq-iran-20140915-story.html.

275. Matt Bradely and Julian Barnes. March 31, 2015. See Iraq Recaptures Tikrit From Islamic State. The development is the biggest setback to the militants since they began to seize large swaths of land in Iraq and Syria last year. Wall Street Journal (wjs.com) Retrieved from: http://www.wsj.com/articles/iraqi-security-forces-recapture-tikrit-from-islamic-state-1427812777.

276. See the very interesting article on Shi'a militias by Janine Di Giovanni, November 26, 2014. The Militias of Baghdad. Newsweek. Retrieved from: http://www.newsweek.com/2014/12/05/militias-baghdad-287142.html.

277. See Robert Gates' interview on Charlie Rose on May 17, 2015 at http://www.charlierose.com/watch/60563239.

278. Anbar Council votes on al-Hashd al-Sha'bi participation in liberating Anbar. May 17, 2014. Iraqinews.com. Retrieved from: http://www.iraqinews.com/features/anbar-council-votes-al-hashd-al-shabi-participation-liberating-anbar.

279. See Martin Matishak—05/06/15, a Hill.com article, Bipartisan Senate bill urges arms, support for Kurds. Retrieved from: http://thehill.com/policy/defense/241206-bipartisan-senate-bill-urges-arms-support-for-kurds.

280. See the May 19, 2015 article by Caleb Weiss, Al Nusrah Front and allies claim victory at Al Mastoumah, Idlib in the Long War Journal, A Project of the Foundations for Defense of Democracy. Retrieved from: http://www.longwarjournal.org/archives/2015/05/al-nusrah-and-allies-claim-victory-at-al-mastoumah-idlib.php.

281. See NBCNews.com article on March 11, 2015, ISIS Seizes Yarmouk Refugee Camp in Damascus, Syria: Witnesses Retrieved from: http://www.nbcnews.com/storyline/isis-terror/isis-seizes-yarmouk-refugee-camp-damascus-syria-witnesses-n333981.

282. See Lina Khatib's article on April 11, 2015, Why Yarmouk's takeover by ISIS is good news for Bashar al-Assad. CNN.com. Retrieved from: http://www.cnn.com/2015/04/07/opinions/isis-yarmouk-assad.

283. See Kedar Pavgi's article on the air campaign: How the Air Campaign Against ISIS Is Changing, in Three Charts: Coalition forces are going after smaller targets in missions designed to support Iraqi forces, in Defenseone, May 14, 2015. Retrieved from: http://www.defenseone.com/threats/2015/05/how-air-campaign-against-isis-changing-three-charts/112861.

284. See Gassan Charbel's article in Almonitor: The Pulse of the Middle East on January 21, 2015 Iraqi PM talks Iran, IS and Saudi Arabia. Retrieved from: http://www.al-monitor.com/pulse/politics/2015/01/iraq-abadi-iran-relations-islamic-state.html#ixzz3bBEMM4Yk.

285. See Robert Baer. 2008. The Devil We Know: dealing with the New Iranian Superpower. NY: The Three Rivers Press. p. 234.

286. See Robert Baer. Sleeping with the Devil: How Washington Sold our Soul for Saudi Crude. NY: Three Rivers Press. p. 48.

287. See the February 17, 2015 Wall Street journal article by James V. Grimaldi and Rebecca Ballhaus, Foreign Government Gifts to Clinton Foundation on the Rise. Retrieved from: http://www.wsj.com/articles/foreign-government-gifts-to-clinton-foundation-on-the-rise-1424223031.

288. See Steven Caton (editor). 2013. Yemen. Santa Barbara. ABC-CLIO. p 272.

289. See Ian Black, Yemen: understanding Houthi motives is complicated but essential. The Guardian, January 19, 2015. Retrieved from: http://www.theguardian.com/world/2015/jan/19/understanding-houthi-motives-complicated-essential-yemen-future.

290. See Charles Schemitz's chapter on Yemen's geography and population in Steven Caton (editor). 2013. Yemen. Santa Barbara. ABC-CLIO. p. 18 and Caton's chapter five. p 175.

291. See Gregory D. Johnsen. 2014. The Last Refuge: Yemen, Al-Qaeda, and America's War in Arabia. NY: W.W Norton & Company p. 44.

292. The casualty figures are from the United Nations. See BBC's article (no author) on May 26, 2015, Yemen conflict: Rebels 'driven out of southern city.' Retrieved from: http://www.bbc.com/news/world-middle-east-32890057.

References

Abrahamian, E. (1982). *Iran: Between the Two Revolutions*. Princeton: Princeton University Press.

"ACRPS Announces the Results of the 2012/2013 Arab Opinion Index." (2013, 6 13). Retrieved from: Arab Center For Research & Policy Studies (dohainstitute.org): http://english.dohainstitute.org/content/af5000b3-46c7-45bb-b431-28b2de8b33c7

Aeneid. (n.d.). Retrieved from: Wikipedia: http://en.wikipedia.org/wiki/Aeneid

Aid, S. H. (2013, 08 26). "Exclusive: CIA Files Prove America helped Saddam as He Gassed Iran." Retrieved from: *Foreign Policy*: http://www.foreignpolicy.com/articles/2013/08/25/secret_cia_files_prove_america_helped_saddam_as_he_gassed_iran

Allison, G., & Zelikow, P. (1999). *Essence of Decision: Explaining the Cuban Missile Crisis*. New York: Longman.

Al-Tamimi, A. J. (2013, 12 24). "The Syrian rebel groups pulling in foreign fighters." Retrieved from: BBC.com: http://www.bbc.com/news/world-middle-east-25460397

"Americans Strongly Support Israel, But Don't Want to Get Involved in Middle East." (2013, 11 5). Retrieved from: Haaretz.com: http://www.haaretz.com/news/diplomacy-defense/.premium-1.556493

"Anbar Council votes on al-Hashd al-Sha'bi participation in liberating Anbar." (2015, 05 17). Retrieved from: Iraqinews.com: http://www.iraqinews.com/features/anbar-council-votes-al-hashd-al-shabi-participation-liberating-anbar

Annual Statistical Supplement, 2013. "Number and percentage of poor persons, by age, at end of selected years 1959–2012." (2014). Retrieved from: U.S. Social Security Administration: http://www.ssa.gov/policy/docs/statcomps/supplement/2013/3e.html#table3.e2

Annual Statistical Supplement, 2013. "Weighted average poverty thresholds for non-farm families, by size, 1959–2012." (2014). Retrieved from: U.S. Social Security Administration: http://www.ssa.gov/policy/docs/statcomps/supplement/2013/3e.html#table3.e1

Armstrong, K. (2001). *Holy War: The Crusades and Their Impact on Today's World*. New York: Anchor Books.

Bacevich, A. J. (2008). *The Limits of Power: The End of American Exceptionalism*. New York: Metropolitan Books.

Baer, R. (2004). *Sleeping with the devil: How Washington Sold our Soul For Saudi Crude*. New York: Three Rivers Press.

Baer, R. (2008). *The Devil We Know: Dealing with the New Iranian Superpower*. New York: Three Rivers Press.

"Banana Wars." (n.d.). Retrieved from: Wikipedia.com: http://en.wikipedia.org/wiki/
   Banana_Wars

Bannerman, S. (2010, 09 25). "Husbands Who Bring the War Home." Retrieved from: The
   Daily Beast: http://www.thedailybeast.com/contributors/stacy-bannerman.html

Battle, J. (2003, 02 25). "Shaking Hands with Saddam Hussein: The U.S. Tilts Toward
   Iraq, 1980–1984." Retrieved from: The National Security Archive: http://www2.gwu.
   edu/~nsarchiv/NSAEBB/NSAEBB82/

Bilmes, L. J. (2013, 03 28). "Harvard Kennedy School." Retrieved May 13, 2013, from
   Harvard University: https://research.hks.harvard.edu/publications/workingpapers/cita-
   tion.aspx?PubId=8956&type=WPN

Bilmes, L. J. (2013, 03). "The Financial Legacy of Iraq and Afghanistan: How Wartime
   Spending Decisions Will Constrain Future National Security Budgets." Retrieved from:
   https://www.google.com/url?sa=t&rct=j&q=&esrc=s&source=web&cd=1&ved=0CB8
   QFjAA&url=https%3A%2F%2Fresearch.hks.harvard.edu%2Fpublications%2FgetFile.
   aspx%3FId%3D923&ei=p0VnVYswhcCCBKyQgcgD&usg=AFQjCNGd46Ux3YFWe9
   lZ4zClQI4SXALjJw

Bloodworth, J. (2012, 06). "Humanitarian Intervention: The American Experience from William
   McKinley to Barack Obama." Retrieved from: Origins: http://origins.osu.edu/article/
   humanitarian-intervention-american-experience-william-mckinley-barack-obama

Blum, J. M., Morgan, E. S., Rose, W. L., Schlesinger, A. M., Stampp, K. C., & Woodward, C.
   V. (1977). *The National Experience: A History of the United States to 1877.* New York:
   Harcourt Brace Jovanovich, Inc.

Bradely, M., & Barnes, J. (2015, 03 31). "Iraq Recaptures Tikrit From Islamic State: The development is the biggest setback to the militants since they began to seize large swaths of
   land in Iraq and Syria last year." Retrieved from: WJS.com: http://www.wsj.com/articles/
   iraqi-security-forces-recapture-tikrit-from-islamic-state-1427812777

Bulos, N., & McDonnel, P. (2015, 09 15). "Iran fills key role in battling Islamic State in Iraq."
   Retrieved from: LAtimes.com: http://www.latimes.com/world/middleeast/la-fg-iraq-iran-
   20140915-story.html

"Calls to Congress 499 to 1." (2013, 09 5). Retrieved from: Conservativebyte.com: http://
   conservativebyte.com/2013/09/calls-congress-499-1-syria-war/

Carafano, J. (2013, 08 25). "Top 5 Reasons Not to Use Missile Strikes in Syria." Retrieved
   from: The Foundry: Conservative Policy News Blog from the Heritage Foundation:
   http://blog.heritage.org/2013/08/25/top-5-reasons-not-to-use-missile-strikes-in-syria/

Carter, J. (2006). *Palestine: Peace Not Apartheid.* New York: Simon and Schuster.

Carter, J. (2006, 12 08). "Speaking Frankly About Israel and Palestine." Retrieved from: Los
   Angeles Times: http://www.latimes.com/news/la-oe-carter8dec08,0,7161592.story

Caton, S. C. (Ed.). (2013). *Yemen.* Santa Barbara: ABC-CLIO.

Center on Budget & Policy Priorities. (2014, 3 31). "Policy Basics: Where Do Our Federal Tax
   Dollars Go?" Retrieved from: cbpp.org: http://www.cbpp.org/cms/?fa=view&id=1258

Charbel, G. (2015, 1 21). "Iraqi PM talks Iran, IS and Saudi Arabia." Retrieved from: Almonitor: The Pulse of the Middle East: http://www.al-monitor.com/pulse/politics/2015/01/iraq-abadi-iran-relations-islamic-state.html#

Chomsky, N. (2013). *Power Systems: Conversations on Global Democratic Uprisings and the New Challenges to U.S. Empire (Interviews with David Barsamian).* New York: Metropolitan Books.

Chowdhury, A. (2013, 1 9). "Top 10 Everyday Things You Can't Do in Saudi Arabia." Retrieved from: TheTop10site.com: http://thetop10site.com/politics-and-religion/top-10-everyday-things-you-cant-do-in-saudi-arabia/

Clark, N. (2013, 08 30). "Britain's Parliament Finally Turns Against the Neo-Cons and Serial Warmongers." Retrieved from: RT.Com: http://rt.com/op-edge/uk-parliament-vote-syria-warmongers-209

Clemens, S., & Craighill, P. (2015, 3 30). "Poll: Clear majority supports nuclear deal with Iran." Retrieved from: The Washington Post: http://www.washingtonpost.com/world/national-security/poll-2-to-1-support-for-nuclear-deal-with-iran/2015/03/30/9a5a5ac8-d720-11e4-ba28-f2a685dc7f89_story.html

Cleveland, W. L. & Bunton, M. (2013). *A History of the Modern Middle East.* Boulder, CO: Westview Press.

Coelho, C. (2013, 03 14). "'Costs of War' Project." Retrieved 05 13, 2013 from news.brown.edu: http://news.brown.edu/pressreleases/2013/03/warcosts

"Commodore Perry and the Opening of Japan." (n.d.). Retrieved from: National Museum of the U.S. Navy: http://www.history.navy.mil/branches/teach/ends/opening.htm

"Commodore Perry Sails into Tokyo Bay." (n.d.). Retrieved from: History.com: http://www.history.com/this-day-in-history/commodore-perry-sails-into-tokyo-bay

Cookson, J. (2011, 08 23). "How Much Does the Libya Intervention Cost the U.S.?" Retrieved from: CNN.com: http://globalpublicsquare.blogs.cnn.com/2011/08/23/question-how-much-does-the-intervention-in-libya-cost-the-u-s/

Cooper, R. T. (2003, 10 16). "General Casts War in Religious Terms." Retrieved from: Common Dreams: General Casts War in Religious Terms

"Cost of Living Comparison Between New York, NY and Los Angeles, CA." (n.d.) Retrieved from: Numbeo.com: http://www.numbeo.com/cost-of-living/compare_cities.jsp?country1=United+States&country2=United+States&city1=New+York%2C+NY&city2=Los+Angeles%2C+CA

"Countries and Economies." (n.d.) Retrieved from: Worldbank.org: http://data.worldbank.org/country

Curzon, G. N. (1986). Curzon's Persia. (P. King, Ed.) London: Sidgwick & Jackson Limited.

Dann, C. (2013, 09 12). "Putin Op-Ed Slammed by Hill Leaders." Retrieved from: MSNBC.Com: http://firstread.nbcnews.com/_news/2013/09/12/20460216-putin-op-ed-slammed-by-hill-leaders?lite

David, J. (2015, 5 14). "Obama Faces Skepticism as He Tries to Reassure Wary Persian Gulf Allies." Retrieved from: NYtimes.com: http://www.nytimes.com/2015/05/15/world/middleeast/obama-saudi-arabia-iran-persian-gulf-security.html?ref=middleeast&_r=0

Debs, A. and Monteiro, N. P. (2012, January 17). "The Flawed Logic of Striking Iran." Retrieved from: Foreign Affairs: http://www.foreignaffairs.com/articles/137036/alexandre-debs-and-nuno-p-monteiro/the-flawed-logic-of-striking-iran

"Defense Data Portal." (n.d.). Retrieved from: European Defense Agency (eda.europa.edu): http://www.eda.europa.eu/info-hub/defence-data-portal

"Defense Spending in Denmark." (2014, 5 17). Retrieved from: FriedINet: http://www.friedlnet.com/product/defense_spending_in_denmark

Dehghan, S. K. (2015, 4 3). "Iran's chief nuclear negotiator receives hero's welcome in Tehran." Retrieved from: The Guardian: http://www.theguardian.com/world/2015/apr/03/iran-nuclear-mohammad-javad-zarif

DelReal, J. A. (2015, 3 10). "Here's a list of the GOP senators who signed the Iran letter." Retrieved from: The Washington Post: http://www.washingtonpost.com/blogs/post-politics/wp/2015/03/10/heres-a-list-of-the-gop-senators-who-sig

"Departing Norwegian Government Boosts Defense Spending for 2014." (2013, 10 14). Retrieved from: DefenseNews.com: http://www.defensenews.com/article/20131014/DEFREG01/310140010Departing-Norwegian-Government-Boosts-Defense-Spending-2014

Dess, G. G., Lumpkin, G. T., Eisner, A. B., & McNamara, G. (2014). *Strategic Management: Creating Competitive Advantage*. New York: Mcgraw-Hill.

"DoD has problems locating Damascus in new map quiz." (2013, 08 11). Retrieved from: Rt.Com: http://rt.com/news/dod-locate-damascus-syria-230/

"DoD has problem locating Damascus in new map quiz." (2013, 09 13). Retrieved from: RT.Com: http://rt.com/news/dod-locate-damascus-syria-230/

Dreyfuss, B. (2013, 07 30). "Al Qaeda and the Iraq-Syria Civil War." Retrieved from: The Nation: http://www.thenation.com/blog/175498/al-qaeda-and-iraq-syria-civil-war#

Elliott, D. (2013, 11 22). "41% of Non-Christian Air Force Cadets Cite Proselytizing." Retrieved from: Huffingtonpost.com: http://www.huffingtonpost.com/2010/10/29/air-force-proselytizing-christianity-evangelicals_n_775859.html

"Erectile resumption: Could the Miami skyline one day resemble Manhattan's?" (2014, 4 15). Retrieved from: Economist.com: http://www.economist.com/news/united-states/21600172-could-miami-skyline-one-day-resemble-manhattans-erectile-resumption?zid=311&ah=308cac674cccf554ce65cf926868bbc2

Erlich, R. (2007). *The Iran Agenda: The Real Story of U.S. Policy and the Middle East Crisis*. Sausalito, CA: Polipoint Press.

Estakhr, M. (2012). *The Place of Zoroaster in History:Using the Cult of Personality as a Literary Source of Authority in the Western Tradition*. Lewiston, NY: The Edwin Mellen Press.

Face the Facts USA: A Project of George Washington University. (2013, 01 18). "U.S. Spends More Rebuilding Iraq, Afghanistan than Post-WWII Germany"—See more at: http://www.facethefactsusa.org/facts/us-spends-more-rebuilding-iraq-afghanistan-than-post-wwii-germany. Retrieved from: Face the Facts USA: A Project of George Washington University: http://www.facethefactsusa.org/facts/us-spends-more-rebuilding-iraq-afghanistan-than-post-wwii-germany

Farrokh, K. (2007). *Shadows in the Desert: Ancient Persia at War.* Oxford: Osprey Publishing.

Farrokh, K. (n.d.). "The *300* Movie: Separating Fact from Fiction." Retrieved from: KavehFarrokh.com: http://www.kavehfarrokh.com/articles/nordicism/the-300-movie-separating-fact-from-fiction-1/

Fawcett, L. (Ed.). (2012). *International Relations of the Middle East.* (3 ed.). Oxford: Oxford University Press.

"Federal Education Budget Project." (2014, 4 30). Retrieved from: febp.newamerica.net: http://febp.newamerica.net/background-analysis/education-federal-budget

Francis, E. D. &Vickers, M. (1985). "The Oenoe Painting in the Stoa Poikile, and Herodotus' Account of Marathon." Retrieved from: The Annual of the British School at Athens: http://www.jstor.org/stable/30102822?seq=3

"FY 2014 Budget Proposal." (n.d.). Retrieved from: U.S. Department of Defense: www.defense.gov/home/features/2013/0413_budget

Gardner, F. (2014, 05 8). "Have Boko Haram over-reached themselves?" Retrieved from: BBC.com: http://www.bbc.com/news/world-africa-27334894

"GDP, Purchasing Power Parity (Top 50)." (n.d.). Retrieved from: IndexMundi: http://www.indexmundi.com/g/r.aspx?t=50&v=65

George W. Bush Presidential Library and Museum:Video Clips. (n.d.). Retrieved from: George W. Bush Presidential Library and Museum: http://www.georgewbushlibrary.smu.edu/en/Photos-and-Videos/Video-Clips/Video-Clips.aspx

"George Washington's Farewell Address." (n.d.). Retrieved from: About.com: http://usgov-info.about.com/library/blgwfarewell.htm

"Getting to Yes with Iran." (2013, 11 24). Retrieved from: nytimes.com: http://www.nytimes.com/interactive/2013/11/25/world/middleeast/iran-nuclear-deal-document.html?hp

Ghadar, F. (2013, 11 11). "Is It Time to Reassess Our Long-Term Alliances in the Middle East?" Retrieved from: Defenseone.com: http://www.defenseone.com/ideas/2013/11/it-time-reassess-our-long-term-alliances-middle-east/73565/?oref=d-interstitial-continue

Giovanni, J. D. (2014, 11 26). "The Militias of Baghdad." Retrieved from: Newsweek.com: http://www.newsweek.com/2014/12/05/militias-baghdad-287142.html

Goldstein, J. S. & Pevehouse, J. C. (2014). *International Relations: 2013–2014 Update. Brief Sixth Edition.* Upper Saddle River, NJ: Pearson.

Goldstein, J. & Pevehouse, J. C. (2014). International Relations (10 ed.). Boston: Pearson.

Goldstone, J., Gurr, T., & Moshiri, F. (Eds.). (1991). *Revolutions of the Late Twentieth Century*. Boulder: Westview.

Gordon, M. (2013, 11 23). "Accord Reached with Iran to Halt Nuclear Program." Retrieved from: NYTimes.com: http://www.nytimes.com/2013/11/24/world/middleeast/talks-with-iran-on-nuclear-deal-hang-in-balance.html

Gordon, M. & Schmitt, E. (2014, 1 13). "Negotiators Put Final Touches on Iran Accord." Retrieved from: NYtimes.com: http://www.nytimes.com/2014/01/13/world/middleeast/iran-nuclear-deal.html

Gordts, E. (2013, 03 20). "Iraq War Anniversary: Birth Defects and Cancer Rates at Devastating High in Basra and Fallujah." Retrieved from: Huffington Post: http://www.huffingtonpost.com/2013/03/20/iraq-war-anniversary-birth-defects-cancer_n_2917701.html

Gray, R. C. & Michalak, S. (1984). *American Foreign Policy Since Détente*. New York: Harper & Row.

Grimaldi, J. V., & Ballhaus, R. (2015, 2 17). "Foreign Government Gifts to Clinton Foundation on the Rise." Retrieved from: WJS.com: http://www.wsj.com/articles/foreign-government-gifts-to-clinton-foundation-on-the-rise-1424223031

Hall, E. (1989). *Inventing the Barbarian: Greek Self-Definition Through Tragedy*. Oxford: Clarendon Press.

Harel, A. (2014, 3 14). "U.S. knows Iran is lying, but chooses diplomacy over force." Retrieved from: Haaretz.org: http://www.haaretz.com/news/diplomacy-defense/.premium-1.579881

Harrison, B., Harris, J. W., & Deardorf, M. D. (2013). *American Democracy Now*. New York: McGraw-Hill.

Harrison, R. K. (1993, March 1). "Reinvestigating the Antediluvian: Sumerian King List." *Journal of the Evangelical Theological Society*, 3–8.

Hayes, C. (Performer). (2013, July 30). *All In with Chris Hayes*.

Haywood, J. (2013). *The Ancient World*. New York: Metro Books

Heather, P. (2006). *The Fall of the Roman Empire: A New History of Rome and the Barbarians*. New York: Oxford University Press.

Herodotus. (1987). *The History*. (D. Green, Trans.) Chicago: The University of Chicago Press.

Hinnebusch, R. (2013). "The Politics of Identity in Middle East International Relations." In L. Fawcett (Ed.), *International Relations of the Middle East* (pp. 148–166). Oxford: Oxford University Press.

http://www.bbc.com/news/world-19259623. (2012, 8 16). Retrieved from: BBC.com: http://www.bbc.com/news/world-19259623

Huntington, S. (2011). *The Clash of Civilizations and the Remaking of the World Order*. New York: Simon & Schuster Paperbacks.

"Iran." (2013, 09). Retrieved from: WorldBank.org: http://www.worldbank.org/en/country/iran/overview

"Iran Economy Profile 2013." (n.d.). Retrieved from: IndexMundi: http://www.indexmundi.com/iran/economy_profile.html

"Iran President Rouhani urges equal rights for women." (2014, 4 20). Retrieved from: BBC.com: http://www.bbc.com/news/world-middle-east-27099151

"Iran Strongly Rejects Text of Geneva Agreement Released by White House." (2013, 11 26). Retrieved from: FarsNews.com: http://english.farsnews.com/newstext.aspx?nn=13920905001087

"Iraq Body Count: Documented Civilian Deaths from Violence." (n.d.). Retrieved from: Iraqbodycount.org: https://www.iraqbodycount.org/database

Iraqinews. (2015, 5 10). "Iraqi federal police shells ISIS sites in northern Tikrit, 13 militants killed." Retrieved from: Iraqinews.com: http://www.Iraqinews.com

Iraqinews. (2015, 5 10). "Iraqi forces repel ISIS attack on Ajil oilfield, kill 73 ISIS elements, announces Dijla Operations." Retrieved from: Iraqinews: http://www.iraqinews.com/iraq-war/iraqi-forces-repel-isis-attack-ajil-oilfield-kill-73-isis-elements-announces-dijla-operations

Isakhan, B. (2007, Fall). "Engaging 'Primitive Democracy': Mideast Roots of Collective Governance." *Middle East Policy,* Vol. XIV No. 3, 97–117.

Jackson, R. & Sorensen, G. (2007). *Introduction to International Relations: Theories and Approaches.* Oxford: Oxford University Press.

Jacobsen, T. (1970). "Primitive Democracy in Ancient Mesopotamia." In W. L. Moran (Ed.), *Toward the Image of Tammuz and Other Essays on Mesopotamian History and Culture.* Boston: Harvard University Press.

Jalabi, R. (2014, October 7). "A history of the Bill Maher's 'not bigoted' remarks on Islam." Retrieved from: TheGuardian.com: http://www.theguardian.com/tv-and-radio/tvandradioblog/2014/oct/06/bill-maher-islam-ben-affleck

Johnsen, G. D. (2014). *The Last Refuge: Yemen, A-Qaeda and America's War in Arabia.* New York: W.W Norton & Company.

"Joseph Kony: Profile of the LRA leader." (2012, 3 8). Retrieved from: BBC.com: http://www.bbc.com/news/world-africa-17299084

"Joseph Kony: US military planes to hunt LRA leader." (2014, 3 24). Retrieved from: BBC.com: http://www.bbc.com/news/world-africa-26712774

Kellogg, W. O. (1995). *American History the Easy Way.* New York: Barron's.

Kelly, C. (2010). *The End of Empire: Attila the Hun and the Fall of Rome.* New York: W.W Norton & Company Ltd.

Keohane, R. O. (1986). *Neorealism and Its Critics.* New York: Colombia University Press.

Khalidi, R. (2009). *Sowing Crisis: The Cold War and American Dominance in the Middle East.* Boston: Beacon Press.

Khatib, L. (2015, 4 11). "Why Yarmouk's takeover by ISIS is good news for Bashar al-Assad." Retrieved from: CNN.com: http://www.cnn.com/2015/04/07/opinions/isis-yarmouk-assad

Kroenig, M. (2012, 01-02). "Time to Attack Iran." Retrieved from: Foreign Affairs: http://www.foreignaffairs.com/articles/136917/matthew-kroenig/time-to-attack-iran

Kyle Dropp, J. D. (2014, 4 7). "The less Americans know about Ukraine's location, the more they want U.S. to intervene." Retrieved from: washingtonpost.com: http://www.washingtonpost.com/blogs/monkey-cage/wp/2014/04/07/the-less-americans-know-about-ukraines-location-the-more-they-want-u-s-to-intervene/

Lawson, F. H. (2013). "Internation Relations Theory And The Middle East." In L. Fawcett (Ed.), *International Relations of the Middle East* (pp. 19–36). Oxford: Oxford University Press.

Lehren, J. D. (2013, 05 15). *Baffling Rise in Suicides Plagues the U.S. Military*. Retrieved from: the New York Times: http://www.nytimes.com/2013/05/16/us/baffling-rise-in-suicides-plagues-us-military.html?pagewanted=all&_r=0

Leonhardt, D. (2014, 5 2). "Inequality Has Been Going On Forever … but That Doesn't Mean It's Inevitable." Retrieved from: nytimes.com: http://www.nytimes.com/2014/05/04/magazine/inequality-has-been-going-on-forever-but-that-doesnt-mean-its-inevitable.html?hpw&rref=magazine

Leonhardt, D., & Quealy, K. (2014, 4 22). "he American Middle Class Is No Longer the World's Richest." Retrieved from: nytimes.com: http://www.nytimes.com/2014/04/23/upshot/the-american-middle-class-is-no-longer-the-worlds-richest.html?hp&_r=0

Leverett, F. & Leverett, H. M. (2013). *Going to Tehran: Why the United States Must Come to Terms with the Islamic Republic of Iran*. New York: Metropolitan Books.

Levine, M. (2013, 08 27). "Syria, Iraq, and Moral Obscenities Big and Small: Other Governments Should Be Held to the Same Standard as Syria When It Comes to Use of Chemical Weapons." Retrieved from: Aljazeera: http://www.aljazeera.com/indepth/opinion/2013/08/201382710851628525.html

Lewis, B. (2002). *What Went Wrong? The Clash Between Islam and Modernity in the Middle East*. New York: Harper Perennial.

Lexington. (2013, 11 16). "Barack, Bibi and Iran: Binyamin Netanyahu Thinks Barack Obama a Feckless Ally, But He Has No Better One." *Economist*, p. 38.

"Libya in crisis: Rival militias position themselves for civil war as country disintegrates." (2014, 5 19). Retrieved from: independent.co.uk: http://www.independent.co.uk/news/world/africa/libya-in-crisis-rival-militias-position-themselves-for-civil-war-as-country-teeters-on-brink-9399311.html

Losco, J. & Baker, R. (2013). *Am Gov 2013–2014*. New York: McGraw-Hill.

Madison, J. (n.d.). "James Madison, Political Observations, Apr. 20, 1795" in: *Letters and Other Writings of James Madison, vol. 4*. Retrieved from: archive.org: http://archive.org/stream/lettersandotherw04madiiala#page/222/mode/2up

Mahnaimi, U. (2013, 11 17). "Two Old Foes Unite Against Tehran." Retrieved from: Thesundaytimes.com.uk: http://www.thesundaytimes.co.uk/sto/news/world_news/Middle_East/article1341561.ece

Maltese, J. A., Pika, J. A., and Shively, P. W. (2013). *Government Matters: American Democracy in Context*. New York: McGraw-Hill.

Manglapus, R. S. (1987). *Will of the People: Original Democracy in Non-Western Societies.* New York: Greenwood Press.

Matishak, M. (2015, 05 06). "Bipartisan Senate bill urges arms, support for Kurds." Retrieved from: TheHill.com: http://thehill.com/policy/defense/241206-bipartisan-senate-bill-urges-arms-support-for-kurds

"Matthew C. Perry." (n.d.). Retrieved from: Wikipedia: http://en.wikipedia.org/wiki/Matthew_C._Perry

Matthews, D. (2012, 4 28). "Defense spending in the U.S., in four charts." Retrieved from: Washingtonpost.com: http://www.washingtonpost.com/blogs/wonkblog/wp/2012/08/28/defense-spending-in-the-u-s-in-four-charts/

McCarthy, A. (2013, 07 24). "The Corner: The Huma Unmentionables." Retrieved from: National Review Online: http://www.nationalreview.com/corner/354351/huma-unmentionables-andrew-c-mccarthy

McNutt, M. (2013, 04 13). "Oklahoma Governor Urged to Sign Revised Sharia Law Measure." Retrieved from: NEWSOK: http://newsok.com/oklahoma-governor-urged-to-sign-revised-sharia-law-measure/article/3785689

Mearsheimer, J. J. and Walt, S. M. (2007). *The Israel Lobby and U.S. Foreign Policy.* New York: Farrar, Straus and Giroux.

"Military Expenditure as % of GDP." (n.d.). Retrieved from: UN.org: http://data.un.org/Data.aspx?d=WDI&f=Indicator_Code%3AMS.MIL.XPND.GD.ZS

"Miltary Expenditure % of GDP." (n.d.). Retrieved from: World Bank: http://search.worldbank.org/data?qterm=military+spending&language=EN&op=

Montgomery, N. (2011, 07 10). "Reports of Family Violence, Abuse Within Military Rise." Retrieved from: Stars and Stripes: http://www.stripes.com/reports-of-family-violence-abuse-within-military-rise-1.148815

Morgenthau, H. (1993). *Politics Among Nations: The Struggle for Power and Peace.* New York: McGraw-Hill.

Morone, J. A., & Kersh, R. (2013). *By The People: Debating American Government.* Oxford: Oxford University Press.

Moshiri, F. (1985). *State and Social Revolution in Iran: A Theoretical Perspective.* New York: Peter Lang.

Moshiri, F. (Ed.). (2012). *Management Communication: An Anthology.* San Diego: Cognella.

Murray, C. T. (2014). *Approaches to Reducing Federal Spending on National Defense.* Washington D.C.: Congressional Budget Office.

Naficy, H. (1980). "Cinema as a Political Instrument." In M. E. Bonine and N. Keddie, *Continuity and Change in Modern Iran* (pp. 265–284). Albany: New York State University Press.

NBC NEWS. (2015, 3 11). "ISIS Seizes Yarmouk Refugee Camp in Damascus, Syria: Witnesses." Retrieved from: NBCNEWS.com: http://www.nbcnews.com/storyline/isis-terror/isis-seizes-yarmouk-refugee-camp-damascus-syria-witnesses-n333981

Newcomb, R. (2013, July 30). "Huff Post Media." Retrieved from: Huffington Post: http://www.huffingtonpost.com/rachel-newcomb/reza-aslan-islam_b_3675507.html

"No Syrian War." (2013, 09 5). Retrieved from: Before It's News: http://beforeitsnews.com/war-and-conflict/2013/09/calls-to-congress-499-to-1-no-syrian-war-2448396.html

"O'Reilly Lets Dick Cheney Spin the Iraq War, Saddam Hussein and Those Weapons of Mass Destruction." (2013, 10 28). Retrieved from: NewsHounds: We watch Fox so you don't have to!: http://www.newshounds.us/o_reilly_lets_dick_cheney_spin_the_iraq_war_saddam_hussein_and_those_weapons_of_mass_destruction_10282013

Office, S. O. (2010, 1 21). Congressional Budget Office. Retrieved from: Congressional Budget Office: http://www.cbo.gov/topics/national-security/iraq-and-afghanistan

Office, S. O. (2013, 3 27). Congressional Budget Office. Retrieved from: Congressional Budget Office: http://www.cbo.gov/publication/44021

"Opinion." (2013, 11 13). Retrieved from: NYtimes.com: http://www.nytimes.com/2013/11/12/opinion/iran-nuclear-talks-unfinished-but-alive.html?partner=rssnyt&emc=rss&_r=0

Otten, C. (2013, 09 18). "Exploding Violence Threatens to Renew Civil War in Iraq." Retrieved from: USA Today: http://www.usatoday.com/story/news/world/2013/09/17/iraq-violence/2789107/

Paivar, A. (2013, 11 12). "Iran: Rouhani's First 100 Days." Retrieved from: bbc.co.uk: http://www.bbc.co.uk/news/world-middle-east-24908733

Patrikarakos, D. (2012). *Nuclear Iran: The Birth of an Atomic State.* London: I.B. Tauris & Co. Ltd.

Patterson, T. E. (2013). *We the People: A Concise Introduction to American Government.* New York: McGraw-Hill.

Paul, J. & Weinthal, B. J. (2014, 1 22). Economist' magazine cartoon sparks anti-Semitism row. Retrieved from: Jpost.com (The Jerusalempost): http://www.jpost.com/Jewish-World/Jewish-Features/Economist-magazine-cartoon-sparks-anti-Semitism-row-338962

Pavgi, K. (2015, 5 14). How the Air Campaign Against ISIS Is Changing, in Three Charts. Retrieved from: Defenseone.com: http://www.defenseone.com/threats/2015/05/how-air-campaign-against-isis-changing-three-charts/112861

Payne, E. & Shoichet, C. E. (2013, 7 5). Morales challenges U.S. after Snowden rumor holds up plane in Europe. Retrieved from: CNN.Com: http://www.cnn.com/2013/07/04/world/americas/bolivia-morales-snowden/

Pecanha, S. (2013, 11 24). "Understanding the Deal with Iran." Retrieved from: NYtimes.com: http://www.nytimes.com/interactive/2013/11/24/world/middleeast/Understanding-the-Deal-With-Iran.html?action=click&contentCollection=Middle%20East&module=RelatedCoverage&region=Marginalia&pgtype=article

Pew Research Center. (2011, 05 17). "Arab Spring Fails to Improve U.S. Image." Retrieved from: PewResearchCenter: http://www.pewglobal.org/2011/05/17/arab-spring-fails-to-improve-us-image

Pew Research Center. (2004, 03 16). "A Year After Iraq War: Mistrust of America in Europe Ever Higher, Muslim Anger Persists." Retrieved from: PewResearchCenter: http://www.pewglobal.org/2004/03/16/a-year-after-iraq-war/

Pirnia, H. (1957). *Iran e Basetan*. Tehran: Majlis.

Pollack, K. (2004). *The Persian Puzzle: The Conflict Between Iran and America*. New York: Random House.

Porter, G. (2014). *Manufactured Crisis: The Untold Story of the Iran Nuclear Scare*. Charlottesville, VA: Just World Books.

Porter, M., Stern, S., & Green, M. (2014, 4 15). Social Progress Index 2014. Retrieved from: Socialprogressimperative.org: http://www.socialprogressimperative.org/data/spi/findings

Pourshariati, P. (2008). *Decline and Fall of the Sasanian Empire: The Sasanian-Parthian Confederacy and the Arab Conquest of Iran*. London: I.B. Tauris.

Putin, V. (2013, 09 11). "A Plea for Caution." Retrieved from: New York Times: http://www.nytimes.com/2013/09/12/opinion/putin-plea-for-caution-from-russia-on-syria.html?pagewanted=all&_r=0

Rashid, A. (2010). *Taliban*. New Haven: Yale University Press.

Ravid, B. (2013, 09 24). "Netanyahu: Rohani's UN Speech Cynical, Full of Hypocrisy." Retrieved from: Haaretz: http://www.haaretz.com/news/diplomacy-defense/.premium-1.548957

Ravid, B. (2014, 5 16). "Nuclear talks between Iran, world powers end with no progress." Retrieved from: Haaretz.com: http://www.haaretz.com/news/middle-east/1.591141

"Real Time with Bill Maher." (2014, May 9). Retrieved from: Hbo.com: http://www.hbo.com/real-time-with-bill-maher#/real-time-with-bill-maher/episodes/12/317-episode/index.html

Reed. (2013). "Construction Cost Estimates for Hospital, 2–3 Story in National, U.S." Retrieved from: Reed Construction Data: http://www.reedconstructiondata.com/rsmeans/models/hospital/

Reuters. (2013, 09 08). "AIPAC to Deploy Hundreds of Lobbyists to Push for Syria Action." Retrieved from: Haaretz.com: http://www.haaretz.com/news/diplomacy-defense/1.545661

Reuters. (2014, 4 18). "U.S. to release $450 million of frozen Iranian funds." Retrieved from: Haaretz.com: http://www.haaretz.com/news/middle-east/1.586259

"Revealing Money's Influence on Politics." (n.d.). Retrieved from: maplight.org: http://maplight.org/us-congress/interest/J5100/view/all

Richardson, H. C. (2015, 3 15). "Tom Cotton's unpatriotic forefathers: Treasonous Iran letter not the first time GOP has crossed the line." Retrieved from: Salon: http://www.salon.com/2015/03/15/tom_cottons_unpatriotic_forefathers_treasonous_iran_letter_not_the_first_time_gop_has_crossed_the_line

Rogan, E. L. (2013). "The Emergence of the Middle East into the Modern State System." In L. Fawcett (Ed.), *International Relations of the Middle East* (pp. 37–55). Oxford: Oxford University Press.

Roskin, M. G. (n.d.). "Behavioralism." Retrieved from: Britannica.com: http://www.britannica.com/EBchecked/topic/467721/political-science/247910/Behavioralism

RT. (2013, 9 02). "U.S. Aims to Overthrow All Independent Governments in the Middle East." Retrieved from: RT.com: http://rt.com/op-edge/us-overthrow-middle-east-328/

Sadaro, M. J. (2008). *Comparative Politics: A Global Introduction* (third ed.). New York: McGraw-Hill.

Said, E. W. (1978). *Orientalism.* New York: Random House.

Schake, K. (2015, 4 2). "I'm a Republican and I Support the Iran Nuclear Deal." Retrieved from: Foreign Policy: http://foreignpolicy.com/2015/04/02/im-a-republican-and-i-support-the-iran-nuclear-deal

"Senators urge Obama to stand firm over Iran nuclear talks." (2014, 3 22). Retrieved from: Haaretz.com: http://www.haaretz.com/news/middle-east/1.581404

Shalev, C. (2013, 09 11). "From Zionist Grandfather to Chemical Cannibal: Bashar Assad, Syria and More." Retrieved from: haaretz.com: http://www.haaretz.com/blogs/west-of-eden/.premium-1.544046

Shalev, S. (2013, 11 2). "West of Eden." Retrieved from: Haaretz.com: http://www.haaretz.com/blogs/west-of-eden/1.555822

Shayegan, M. R. (2011). *Arsacids and Sasanians: Political Ideology in Post-Hellenistic and Late Antique Persia.* Cambridge: Cambridge University Press.

Shiraev, E. B. & Zubok, V. M. (2015). *International Relations: Brief Edition.* Oxford: Oxford University Press.

Sivers, P. V., Desnoyers, C. A., & Stow, B. G. (2012). *Patterns of World History.* Oxford: Oxford University Press.

Sluglett, P. (2013). "The Cold War In the Middle East." In L. Fawcett (Ed.), *International Relations of the Middle East* (pp. 60–76). Oxford: Oxford.

Sly, L. (2015, 4 4). "The hidden hand behind the Islamic State militants? Saddam Hussein's." Retrieved from: The Washington Post: http://www.washingtonpost.com/world/middle_east/the-hidden-hand-behind-the-islamic-state-militants-saddam-husseins/2015/04/04/aa97676c-cc32-11e4-8730-4f473416e759_story.html

Stokes, B. (2013, 05 02). "Middle Eastern and Western Publics Wary on Syrian Intervention." Retrieved from: Pew Research Center: http://www.pewresearch.org/fact-tank/2013/05/02/middle-eastern-and-western-publics-wary-on-syrian-intervention

Stiglitz, J., & Bilmes, L. (2013, 1 23). "No US peace dividend after Afghanistan." Retrieved from: Financial Times: http://www.ft.com/cms/s/0/da88f8fe-63e9-11e2-84d8-00144feab49a.html#axzz3bS8mdOJF

"Switzerland—Military expenditure." (n.d.). Retrieved from: Index Mundi: http://www.indexmundi.com/facts/switzerland/military-expenditure

"Syria: Groups Call for ICC referral." (2014, 5 15). Retrieved from: Hrw.org: http://www. hrw.org/news/2014/05/15/syria-groups-call-icc-referral

"Syria: The Story of the Conflict." (2014, 3 13). Retrieved from: BBC.com: http://www.bbc. com/news/world-middle-east-26116868

Telhami, S. (2011). PDF 2011 Annual Arab Public Opinion Poll. PDF can be found by Google search of 2011 annual Arab public opinion survey.

Telhami, S. (2011, 11 21). The 2011 Arab Public Opinion Poll. Retrieved from: Brookings: http://www.brookings.edu/research/reports/2011/11/21-arab-public-opinion-telhami

The Economist. (2013, July 27). "Syria's War: The New Normal." *The Economist*, p. 42.

The Economist. (2014, May 17–23). "Iran Nuclear Talks: Moving ahead." *The Economist*, p. 48.

The Economist. (2014, May 17–23). "Iran: The perils of yoga. Conservative clerics are wary of a popular pastime." *The Economist*, p. 48.

The Economist. (2014, May 17–23). "Women in Saudi Arabia: Unshackling Themselves." *The Economist*, pp. 45–47.

The Guardian. (2014, 11 25). "Tehran reacts to Iran nuclear deal." Retrieved from: The Guardian: http://www.theguardian.com/world/iran-blog/2014/nov/25/-sp-iranian-nuclear-talks-tehran-reactions

The Guardian. (2013, 02 01). "U.S. Military Suicides in Charts: How They Overtook Combat Deaths." Retrieved from: The Guardian: http://www.theguardian.com/news/datablog/2013/feb/01/us-military-suicides-trend-charts

"The Jefferson Monticello: Louisiana Purchase." (n.d.). Retrieved from: Monticello.org: http://www.monticello.org/site/jefferson/louisiana-purchase

"The Jefferson Monticello: The Lewis and Clark Expedition." (n.d.). Retrieved from: Monticello.org: http://www.monticello.org/site/jefferson/lewis-and-clark-expedition

"Theory Talks #22: Kevin Dunn." (2008, 10 28). Retrieved from: Theory-Talks.org: http://www.theory-talks.org/2008/10/theory-talk-22.html

Tucker, R. W. & Hendrickson , D. C. (1990). "Thomas Jefferson and American Foreign Policy." Retrieved from: Foreignaffairs.com: http://www.foreignaffairs.com/articles/45445/robert-w-tucker-and-david-c-hendrickson/thomas-jefferson-and-american-foreign-policy

"Under the Influence: AIPAC America's Pro Israeli Lobby." (n.d.). Retrieved from: USC. news21.com (University of Southern California's Annenberg School of Journalism's blog): http://usc.news21.com/madeline-story/aipac-money-0

UNDP. (2013, 10 24). "UN Development Chief Visits Iran; addresses United Nations Day Celebration in Tehran." Retrieved from: UNDP (United Nations Development Programm): http://www.undp.org/content/undp/en/home/presscenter/pressreleases/2013/10/24/un-development-chief-visits-iran-addresses-united-nations-day-celebration-in-teheran.html

United Nations. (2014). "Afghanistan: Annual Report 2013 Protection of Civilians in Armed Conflict." New York: United Nations.

United States Department Education. (n.d.). "Budget History Tables." Retrieved from: Ed.gov: https://www2.ed.gov/about/overview/budget/history/index.html?exp=6

USA Today. (2014, 5 22). "Timeline: The story behind the VA scandal." Retrieved from: USAtoday.com: http://www.usatoday.com/story/news/politics/2014/05/21/veterans-healthcare-scandal-shinseki-timeline/9373227/

USC Casden Multifamily Forecast. (2014). Retrieved from: lusk.usc.edu: http://lusk.usc.edu/casden/multifamily/forecast

Usher, B. P. & Kianpour, K. (2014, 04 25). "Iran hostage crisis wounds linger for US government." Retrieved from: bbc.com: http://www.bbc.com/news/world-us-canada-27161268

"Valerian Emperor." (n.d.). Retrieved from: Wikipedia: http://en.wikipedia.org/wiki/Valerian_(emperor)

Vandenbroucke, L. (n.d.). "Anatomy of a Failure: The Decision to Land at the Bay of Pigs." Retrieved from: Latinamericanstudies.org: http://www.latinamericanstudies.org/bay-of-pigs/failure.pdf

Waltz, K. (1979). *Theory of International Politics*. New York: McGraw-Hill.

Waltz, K. (2012, July–August). "Why Iran Should Get the Bomb." Retrieved from: Foreign Affairs: http://www.foreignaffairs.com/articles/137731/kenneth-n-waltz/why-iran-should-get-the-bomb

Washingtonblogs.com. (2013, 08 27). "The U.S., Britain and Israel Have Used Chemical Weapons Within the Last 10 Years." Retrieved from: washingtonsblog.com: http://www.washingtonsblog.com/2013/08/the-u-s-and-israel-have-used-chemical-weapons-within-the-last-8-years.html

Waterfield, R. (2006). *Xenophon's Retreat: Greece, Persia, and the End of the Golden Age*. Cambridge: The Belknap Press of Harvard University Press.

Weiss, B. (2013). "The Weekened Interview with Bernard Lewis: The Tyrannies Are Doomed." In F. Yap (Ed.), *Annual Editions: Comparative Politics* (pp. 208–210). New York: McGraw-Hill Companies.

Weiss, C. (2015, 5 19). "Al Nusrah Front and allies claim victory at Al Mastoumah, Idlib." Retrieved from: Thelongwarjournal.org: http://www.longwarjournal.org/archives/2015/05/al-nusrah-and-allies-claim-victory-at-al-mastoumah-idlib.php

Weiss, M., & Hassan, H. (2015). *ISIS: Inside the Army of Terror*. New York: Regan Arts.

"Who Is the Real Threat: Iran or Israel?" (2013, 10 22). Retrieved from: Aljazeera.com: http://www.aljazeera.com/indepth/opinion/2013/10/who-real-threat-iran-israel-2013101791830213883.html

Wike, R. (2013, 03 19). "Obama's Israel Challenge." Retrieved from: PewResearchCenter: http://www.pewglobal.org/2013/03/19/obamas-israel-challenge/

Wikipedia. (n.d.). "Erythrae." Retrieved from: Wikipedia: http://en.wikipedia.org/wiki/Erythrae

Wikipedia. (n.d.). "Halabja Poison Gas Attack." Retrieved from: Wikipedia: http://en.wikipedia.org/wiki/Halabja_poison_gas_attack

Wikipedia. (n.d.). "The Inscription of Shapur I at Naqsh-E Rustam in Fars." Retrieved from: Wikipedia: http://www.colorado.edu/classics/clas4091/Text/Shapur.htm

Wikipedia. (n.d.). "The Persians." Retrieved from: Wikipedia: http://en.wikipedia.org/wiki/The_Persians

Wikipedia. (n.d.). "Wolf Blitzer." Retrieved from: Wikipedia: http://en.wikipedia.org/wiki/Wolf_Blitzer

Williams, D. (2013, 11 15). "J Street Responds: Don't Undermine Chance for 'Good Deal' on Iran." Retrieved from: Haaretz.com: http://www.haaretz.com/opinion/.premium-1.558211

Youssef, N. A. (2014, 5 26). "Syrian Rebels Describe U.S.-Backed Training in Qatar." Retrieved from: Frontline: http://www.pbs.org/wgbh/pages/frontline/foreign-affairs-defense/syria-arming-the-rebels/syrian-rebels-describe-u-s-backed-training-in-qatar/

Zoroya, G. (2011, 12 31). "Military Divorce Rate at Highest Level Since 1999." Retrieved from: USA Today: http://usatoday30.usatoday.com/news/military/story/2011-12-13/military-divorce-rate-increases/51888872/1

Appendix A

Geneva, 24 November 2013
Joint Plan of Action

Preamble

The goal for these negotiations is to reach a mutually agreed long-term comprehensive solution that would ensure Iran's nuclear programme will be exclusively peaceful. Iran reaffirms that under no circumstances will Iran ever seek or develop any nuclear weapons. This comprehensive solution would build on these initial measures and result in a final step for a period to be agreed upon and the resolution of concerns. This comprehensive solution would enable Iran to fully enjoy its right to nuclear energy for peaceful purposes under the relevant articles of the NPT in conformity with its obligations therein. This comprehensive solution would involve a mutually defined enrichment programme with practical limits and transparency measures to ensure the peaceful nature of the programme. This comprehensive solution would constitute an integrated whole where nothing is agreed until everything is agreed. This comprehensive solution would involve a reciprocal, step-by-step process, and would produce the comprehensive lifting of all UN Security Council sanctions, as well as multilateral and national sanctions related to Iran's nuclear programme.

There would be additional steps in between the initial measures and the final step, including, among other things, addressing the UN Security Council resolutions, with a view toward bringing to a satisfactory conclusion the UN Security Council's consideration of this matter. The E3+3 and Iran will be responsible for conclusion and implementation of mutual near-term measures and the comprehensive solution in good faith. A Joint Commission of E3/EU+3 and Iran will be established to monitor the implementation of the near-term measures and address issues that may arise, with the IAEA responsible for verification of nuclear-related measures. The Joint Commission will work with the IAEA to facilitate resolution of past and present issues of concern.

Elements of a first step

The first step would be time-bound, with a duration of 6 months, and renewable by mutual consent, during which all parties will work to maintain a constructive atmosphere for negotiations in good faith. Iran would undertake the following voluntary measures:

- From the existing uranium enriched to 20%, retain half as working stock of 20% oxide for fabrication of fuel for the TRR. Dilute the remaining 20% UF6 to no more than 5%. No reconversion line.
- Iran announces that it will not enrich uranium over 5% for the duration of the 6 months.
- Iran announces that it will not enrich uranium over 5% for the duration of the 6 months.
- Iran announces that it will not make any further advances of its activities at the Natanz Fuel Enrichment Plant[1], Fordow[2], or the Arak reactor[3], designated by the IAEA as IR-40.
- Beginning when the line for conversion of UF6 enriched up to 5% to UO2 is ready, Iran has decided to convert to oxide UF6 newly enriched up to 5% during the 6 month period, as provided in the operational schedule of the conversion plant declared to the IAEA.
- No new locations for the enrichment.
- Iran will continue its safeguarded R&D practices, including its current enrichment R&D practices, which are not designed for accumulation of the enriched uranium.
- No reprocessing or construction of a facility capable of reprocessing.
- Enhanced monitoring:
  * Provision of specified information to the IAEA, including information on Iran's plans for nuclear facilities, a description of each building on each nuclear site, a description of the scale of operations for each location engaged in specified nuclear activities, information on uranium mines and mills, and information on source material. This information would be provided within three months of the adoption of these measures.
  * Submission of an updated DIQ for the reactor at Arak, designated by the IAEA as the IR-40, to the IAEA.
  * Steps to agree with the IAEA on conclusion of the Safeguards Approach for the reactor at Arak, designated by the IAEA as the IR-40.
  * Daily IAEA inspector access when inspectors are not present for the purpose of Design Information Verification, Interim Inventory Verification, Physical Inventory Verification, and unannounced inspections, for the purpose of access to offline surveillance records, at Fordow and Natanz.

* IAEA inspector managed access to: centrifuge assembly workshops[4]; centrifuge rotor production workshops and storage facilities; and, uranium mines and mills.

Footnotes

1. Namely, during the 6 months, Iran will not feed UF6 into the centrifuges installed but not enriching uranium. Not install additional centrifuges. Iran announces that during the first 6 months, it will replace existing centrifuges with centrifuges of the same type.

2. At Fordow, no further enrichment over 5% at 4 cascades now enriching uranium, and not increase enrichment capacity. Not feed UF6 into the other 12 cascades, which would remain in a non-operative state. No interconnections between cascades.

   Iran announces that during the first 6 months, it will replace existing centrifuges with centrifuges of the same type.

3. Iran announces on concerns related to the construction of the reactor at Arak that for 6 months it will not commission the reactor or transfer fuel or heavy water to the reactor site and will not test additional fuel or produce more fuel for the reactor or install remaining components.

4. Consistent with its plans, Iran's centrifuge production during the 6 months will be dedicated to replace damaged machines.

   In return, the E3/EU+3 would undertake the following voluntary measures:

   • Pause efforts to further reduce Iran's crude oil sales, enabling Iran's current customers to purchase their current average amounts of crude oil. Enable the repatriation of an agreed amount of revenue held abroad. For such oil sales, suspend the EU and U.S. sanctions on associated insurance and transportation services.

   • Suspend U.S. and EU sanctions on:

     * Iran's petrochemical exports, as well as sanctions on associated services.

     * Gold and precious metals, as well as sanctions on associated services.

   • Suspend U.S. sanctions on Iran's auto industry, as well as sanctions on associated services.

   • License the supply and installation in Iran of spare parts for safety of flight for Iranian civil aviation and associated services. License safety-related inspections and repairs in Iran as well as associated services.

   • No new nuclear-related UN Security Council sanctions.

   • No new EU nuclear-related sanctions.

- The U.S. Administration, acting consistent with the respective roles of the President and the Congress, will refrain from imposing new nuclear-related sanctions.

- Establish a financial channel to facilitate humanitarian trade for Iran's domestic needs using Iranian oil revenues held abroad. Humanitarian trade would be defined as transactions involving food and agricultural products, medicine, medical devices, and medical expenses incurred abroad. This channel would involve specified foreign banks and non-designated Iranian banks to be defined when establishing the channel.

This channel could also enable:

(a) Transactions required to pay Iran's UN obligations

(b) direct tuition payments to universities and colleges for Iranian students studying abroad, up to an agreed amount for the six-month period.

- Increase the EU authorisation thresholds for transactions for non-sanctioned trade to an agreed amount.

5. "Sanctions on associated services" means any service, such as insurance, transportation, or financial, subject to the underlying U.S. or EU sanctions applicable, insofar as each service is related to the underlying sanction and required to facilitate the desired transactions. These services could involve any non-designated Iranian entities.

6. Sanctions relief could involve any non-designated Iranian airlines as well as Iran Air.

Elements of the final step of a comprehensive solution*

The final step of a comprehensive solution, which the parties aim to conclude negotiating and commence implementing no more than one year after the adoption of this document, would:

- Have a specified long-term duration to be agreed upon.

- Reflect the rights and obligations of parties to the NPT and IAEA Safeguards Agreements.

- Comprehensively lift UN Security Council, multilateral and national nuclear-related sanctions, including steps on access in areas of trade, technology, finance, and energy, on a schedule to be agreed upon.

- Involve a mutually defined enrichment programme with mutually agreed parameters consistent with practical needs, with agreed limits on scope and level of enrichment activities, capacity, where it is carried out, and stocks of enriched uranium, for a period to be agreed upon.

- Fully resolve concerns related to the reactor at Arak, designated by the IAEA as the IR-40.

No reprocessing or construction of a facility capable of reprocessing.

- Fully implement the agreed transparency measures and enhanced monitoring. Ratify and implement the Additional Protocol, consistent with the respective roles of the President and the Majlis (Iranian parliament).

- Include international civil nuclear cooperation, including among others, on acquiring modern light water power and research reactors and associated equipment, and the supply of modern nuclear fuel as well as agreed R&D practices.

Following successful implementation of the final step of the comprehensive solution for its full duration, the Iranian nuclear programme will be treated in the same manner as that of any non-nuclear weapon state party to the NPT.

* With respect to the final step and any steps in between, the standard principle that "nothing is agreed until everything is agreed" applies.

Source: see either New York Times or Fars News Agency at http://www.nytimes. com/interactive/2013/11/25/world/middleeast/iran-nuclear-deal-document.html?hp or http://english.farsnews.com/newstext.aspx?nn=13920905001087.

The Fars News page has the following preamble:

TEHRAN (FNA) – The Iranian Foreign Ministry on Tuesday called invalid a press release by the White House alleged to be the text of the nuclear agreement struck by Iran and the Group 5+1 (the US, Russia, China, Britain and France plus Germany) in Geneva on Sunday.

"What has been released by the website of the White House as a fact sheet is a one-sided interpretation of the agreed text in Geneva and some of the explanations and words in the sheet contradict the text of the Joint Plan of Action (the title of the Iran-powers deal), and this fact sheet has unfortunately been translated and released in the name of the Geneva agreement by certain media, which is not true," Foreign Ministry Spokeswoman Marziyeh Afkham said on Tuesday.

She said that the four-page text under the name of the Joint Plan of Action (which has been released by the Iranian foreign ministry) was the result of the agreement reached during the Geneva talks and all of its sentences and words were chosen based on the considerations of all parties to the talks. In fact one of the reasons why negotiations between Iran and the G5+1 took so long pertained to the accuracy which was needed for choosing the words for the text of the agreement, Afkham said, explaining that the Iranian delegation was much rigid and laid much emphasis on the need for this accuracy.

Afkham said that the text of the Joint Plan of Action was provided to the media a few hours after the two sides agreed on it.

After the White House released a modified version of the deal struck by Iran and the six world powers in Geneva early Sunday morning, the Iranian Foreign Ministry released the text of the agreement.

Appendix B

AIPAC Contributions to Congress

Top 20 House Recipients Funded

Recipient	Amount
Eric Cantor	$228,835
Bradley Schneider	$225,757
Edward Royce	$142,700
Eliot Engel	$127,450
Ileana Ros-Lehtinen	$123,750
Nita Lowey	$117,546
Steny Hoyer	$111,250
Patrick Murphy	$108,219
Tammy Duckworth	$102,101
Theodore Deutch	$96,680
John Boehner	$89,800
Bill Foster	$88,654
Gary Peters	$81,050
Cheri Bustos	$78,575
Bill Cassidy	$77,322
Joe Garcia	$73,413
Bruce Braley	$69,550
James Lankford	$69,300
Henry Waxman	$67,750
Ann Kuster	$63,446

Top 20 Senate Recipients Funded

Recipient	Amount
Mark Kirk	$643,598
Mitch McConnell	$400,022
Robert Menéndez	$341,170
Cory Booker	$322,099
Kirsten Gillibrand	$295,637
Sherrod Brown	$272,551
Harry Reid	$267,708
Lindsey Graham	$263,050
Bill Nelson	$263,000
Timothy Kaine	$256,020
Charles Schumer	$255,499
Barbara Boxer	$245,179
Benjamin Cardin	$238,493
Ron Wyden	$235,031
Mark Udall	$224,910
JohnMcCain	$222,677
Claire McCaskill	$212,671
Mary Landrieu	$185,713
Tammy Baldwin	$180,980
Jeff Merkley	$179,830

This is a portion of the data that appears in Maplight.org for Jul. 1, 2008–Jun. 30, 2014, and is also available at http://chasvoice.blogspot.com/2012/03/aipac-campaign-contributions-to-us.htmlhttp://maplight.org/us-congress/interest/J5100/view/all?sort=asc&order=Amount.

Appendix C

The Treaty on the Non-Proliferation of Nuclear Weapons (NPT)

(Text of treaty)

The States concluding this Treaty, hereinafter referred to as the Parties to the Treaty,

Considering the devastation that would be visited upon all mankind by a nuclear war and the consequent need to make every effort to avert the danger of such a war and to take measures to safeguard the security of peoples,

Believing that the proliferation of nuclear weapons would seriously enhance the danger of nuclear war,

In conformity with resolutions of the United Nations General Assembly calling for the conclusion of an agreement on the prevention of wider dissemination of nuclear weapons,

Undertaking to co-operate in facilitating the application of International Atomic Energy Agency safeguards on peaceful nuclear activities,

Expressing their support for research, development and other efforts to further the application, within the framework of the International Atomic Energy Agency safeguards system, of the principle of safeguarding effectively the flow of source and special fissionable materials by use of instruments and other techniques at certain strategic points,

Affirming the principle that the benefits of peaceful applications of nuclear technology, including any technological by-products which may be derived by nuclear-weapon States from the development of nuclear explosive devices, should be available for peaceful purposes to all Parties to the Treaty, whether nuclear-weapon or non-nuclear-weapon States,

Convinced that, in furtherance of this principle, all Parties to the Treaty are entitled to participate in the fullest possible exchange of scientific information for, and to contribute alone or in co-operation with other States to, the further development of the applications of atomic energy for peaceful purposes,

Declaring their intention to achieve at the earliest possible date the cessation of the nuclear arms race and to undertake effective measures in the direction of nuclear disarmament,

Urging the co-operation of all States in the attainment of this objective,

Recalling the determination expressed by the Parties to the 1963 Treaty banning nuclear weapons tests in the atmosphere, in outer space and under water in its Preamble to seek to achieve the discontinuance of all test explosions of nuclear weapons for all time and to continue negotiations to this end,

Desiring to further the easing of international tension and the strengthening of trust between States in order to facilitate the cessation of the manufacture of nuclear weapons, the liquidation of all their existing stockpiles, and the elimination from national arsenals of nuclear weapons and the means of their delivery pursuant to a Treaty on general and complete disarmament under strict and effective international control,

Recalling that, in accordance with the Charter of the United Nations, States must refrain in their international relations from the threat or use of force against the territorial integrity or political independence of any State, or in any other manner inconsistent with the Purposes of the United Nations, and that the establishment and maintenance of international peace and security are to be promoted with the least diversion for armaments of the world's human and economic resources,

Have agreed as follows:

Article I

Each nuclear-weapon State Party to the Treaty undertakes not to transfer to any recipient whatsoever nuclear weapons or other nuclear explosive devices or control over such weapons or explosive devices directly, or indirectly; and not in any way to assist, encourage, or induce any non-nuclear-weapon State to manufacture or otherwise acquire nuclear weapons or other nuclear explosive devices, or control over such weapons or explosive devices.

Article II

Each non-nuclear-weapon State Party to the Treaty undertakes not to receive the transfer from any transferor whatsoever of nuclear weapons or other nuclear explosive devices or of control over such weapons or explosive devices directly, or indirectly; not to manufacture or otherwise acquire nuclear weapons or other nuclear explosive devices; and not to seek or receive any assistance in the manufacture of nuclear weapons or other nuclear explosive devices.

Article III

1. Each non-nuclear-weapon State Party to the Treaty undertakes to accept safeguards, as set forth in an agreement to be negotiated and concluded with the International Atomic Energy Agency in accordance with the Statute of the International Atomic Energy Agency and the Agency's safeguards system, for the exclusive purpose of verification of the fulfilment of its obligations assumed under this Treaty with a view to preventing diversion of nuclear energy from peaceful uses to nuclear weapons or other nuclear explosive devices. Procedures for the safeguards required by this Article shall be followed with respect to source or special fissionable material whether it is being produced, processed or used in any principal nuclear facility or is outside any such facility. The safeguards required by this Article shall be applied on all source or special fissionable material in all peaceful nuclear activities within the territory of such State, under its jurisdiction, or carried out under its control anywhere.

2. Each State Party to the Treaty undertakes not to provide: (a) source or special fissionable material, or (b) equipment or material especially designed or prepared for the processing, use or production of special fissionable material, to any non-nuclear-weapon State for peaceful purposes, unless the source or special fissionable material shall be subject to the safeguards required by this Article.

3. The safeguards required by this Article shall be implemented in a manner designed to comply with Article IV of this Treaty, and to avoid hampering the economic or technological development of the Parties or international co-operation in the field of peaceful nuclear activities, including the international exchange of nuclear material and equipment for the processing, use or production of nuclear material for peaceful purposes in accordance with the provisions of this Article and the principle of safeguarding set forth in the Preamble of the Treaty.

4. Non-nuclear-weapon States Party to the Treaty shall conclude agreements with the International Atomic Energy Agency to meet the requirements of this Article either individually or together with other States in accordance with the Statute of the International Atomic Energy Agency. Negotiation of such agreements shall commence within 180 days from the original entry into force of this Treaty. For States depositing their instruments of ratification or accession after the 180-day period, negotiation of such agreements shall commence not later than the date of such deposit. Such agreements shall enter into force not later than eighteen months after the date of initiation of negotiations.

Article IV

1. Nothing in this Treaty shall be interpreted as affecting the inalienable right of all the Parties to the Treaty to develop research, production and use of nuclear

energy for peaceful purposes without discrimination and in conformity with Articles I and II of this Treaty.

2. All the Parties to the Treaty undertake to facilitate, and have the right to participate in, the fullest possible exchange of equipment, materials and scientific and technological information for the peaceful uses of nuclear energy. Parties to the Treaty in a position to do so shall also co-operate in contributing alone or together with other States or international organizations to the further development of the applications of nuclear energy for peaceful purposes, especially in the territories of non-nuclear-weapon States Party to the Treaty, with due consideration for the needs of the developing areas of the world.

Article V

Each Party to the Treaty undertakes to take appropriate measures to ensure that, in accordance with this Treaty, under appropriate international observation and through appropriate international procedures, potential benefits from any peaceful applications of nuclear explosions will be made available to non-nuclear-weapon States Party to the Treaty on a non-discriminatory basis and that the charge to such Parties for the explosive devices used will be as low as possible and exclude any charge for research and development. Non-nuclear-weapon States Party to the Treaty shall be able to obtain such benefits, pursuant to a special international agreement or agreements, through an appropriate international body with adequate representation of non-nuclear-weapon States. Negotiations on this subject shall commence as soon as possible after the Treaty enters into force. Non-nuclear-weapon States Party to the Treaty so desiring may also obtain such benefits pursuant to bilateral agreements.

Article VI

Each of the Parties to the Treaty undertakes to pursue negotiations in good faith on effective measures relating to cessation of the nuclear arms race at an early date and to nuclear disarmament, and on a treaty on general and complete disarmament under strict and effective international control.

Article VII

Nothing in this Treaty affects the right of any group of States to conclude regional treaties in order to assure the total absence of nuclear weapons in their respective territories.

Article VIII

1. Any Party to the Treaty may propose amendments to this Treaty. The text of any proposed amendment shall be submitted to the Depositary Governments which shall circulate it to all Parties to the Treaty. Thereupon, if requested to do so by one-third or more of the Parties to the Treaty, the Depositary Governments shall convene a conference, to which they shall invite all the Parties to the Treaty, to consider such an amendment.

2. Any amendment to this Treaty must be approved by a majority of the votes of all the Parties to the Treaty, including the votes of all nuclear-weapon States Party to the Treaty and all other Parties which, on the date the amendment is circulated, are members of the Board of Governors of the International Atomic Energy Agency. The amendment shall enter into force for each Party that deposits its instrument of ratification of the amendment upon the deposit of such instruments of ratification by a majority of all the Parties, including the instruments of ratification of all nuclear-weapon States Party to the Treaty and all other Parties which, on the date the amendment is circulated, are members of the Board of Governors of the International Atomic Energy Agency. Thereafter, it shall enter into force for any other Party upon the deposit of its instrument of ratification of the amendment.

3. Five years after the entry into force of this Treaty, a conference of Parties to the Treaty shall be held in Geneva, Switzerland, in order to review the operation of this Treaty with a view to assuring that the purposes of the Preamble and the provisions of the Treaty are being realised. At intervals of five years thereafter, a majority of the Parties to the Treaty may obtain, by submitting a proposal to this effect to the Depositary Governments, the convening of further conferences with the same objective of reviewing the operation of the Treaty.

Article IX

1. This Treaty shall be open to all States for signature. Any State which does not sign the Treaty before its entry into force in accordance with paragraph 3 of this Article may accede to it at any time.

2. This Treaty shall be subject to ratification by signatory States. Instruments of ratification and instruments of accession shall be deposited with the Governments of the United Kingdom of Great Britain and Northern Ireland, the Union of Soviet Socialist Republics and the United States of America, which are hereby designated the Depositary Governments.

3. This Treaty shall enter into force after its ratification by the States, the Governments of which are designated Depositaries of the Treaty, and forty other States signatory to this Treaty and the deposit of their instruments of ratification. For the purposes of this Treaty, a nuclear-weapon State is one which has

manufactured and exploded a nuclear weapon or other nuclear explosive device prior to 1 January 1967.

4. For States whose instruments of ratification or accession are deposited subsequent to the entry into force of this Treaty, it shall enter into force on the date of the deposit of their instruments of ratification or accession.

5. The Depositary Governments shall promptly inform all signatory and acceding States of the date of each signature, the date of deposit of each instrument of ratification or of accession, the date of the entry into force of this Treaty, and the date of receipt of any requests for convening a conference or other notices.

6. This Treaty shall be registered by the Depositary Governments pursuant to Article 102 of the Charter of the United Nations.

Article X

1. Each Party shall in exercising its national sovereignty have the right to withdraw from the Treaty if it decides that extraordinary events, related to the subject matter of this Treaty, have jeopardized the supreme interests of its country. It shall give notice of such withdrawal to all other Parties to the Treaty and to the United Nations Security Council three months in advance. Such notice shall include a statement of the extraordinary events it regards as having jeopardized its supreme interests.

2. Twenty-five years after the entry into force of the Treaty, a conference shall be convened to decide whether the Treaty shall continue in force indefinitely, or shall be extended for an additional fixed period or periods. This decision shall be taken by a majority of the Parties to the Treaty.[1]

Article XI

This Treaty, the English, Russian, French, Spanish and Chinese texts of which are equally authentic, shall be deposited in the archives of the Depositary Governments. Duly certified copies of this Treaty shall be transmitted by the Depositary Governments to the Governments of the signatory and acceding States.

IN WITNESS WHEREOF the undersigned, duly authorized, have signed this Treaty.

DONE in triplicate, at the cities of London, Moscow and Washington, the first day of July, one thousand nine hundred and sixty-eight.

---

1 Source: http://www.un.org/en/conf/npt/2005/npttreaty.html

Index

List of Maps, Tables, Figures & Cartoons

Cartoons

Figures

Maps

Tables

CPSIA information can be obtained
at www.ICGtesting.com
Printed in the USA
BVHW08s2048120918
527340BV00008B/40/P